CHE GUEVARA

Recent Titles in Greenwood Biographies

Tyra Banks: A Biography
Carole Jacobs

Jean-Michel Basquiat: A Biography
Eric Fretz

Howard Stern: A Biography
Rich Mintzer

Tiger Woods: A Biography, Second Edition
Lawrence J. Londino

Justin Timberlake: A Biography
Kimberly Dillon Summers

Walt Disney: A Biography
Louise Krasniewicz

Chief Joseph: A Biography
Vanessa Gunther

John Lennon: A Biography
Jacqueline Edmondson

Carrie Underwood: A Biography
Vernell Hackett

Christina Aguilera: A Biography
Mary Anne Donovan

Paul Newman: A Biography
Marian Edelman Borden

George W. Bush: A Biography
Clarke Rountree

CHE GUEVARA
A Biography

Richard L. Harris

GREENWOOD BIOGRAPHIES

GREENWOOD
AN IMPRINT OF ABC-CLIO, LLC
Santa Barbara, California • Denver, Colorado • Oxford, England

Copyright 2011 by Richard L. Harris

All rights reserved. No part of this publication may be reproduced, stored in a retrieval system, or transmitted, in any form or by any means, electronic, mechanical, photocopying, recording, or otherwise, except for the inclusion of brief quotations in a review, without prior permission in writing from the publisher.

Library of Congress Cataloging-in-Publication Data

Harris, Richard L. (Richard Legé), 1939–
  Che Guevara : a biography / Richard L. Harris.
    p. cm. — (Greenwood biographies)
  Includes bibliographical references and index.
  ISBN 978-0-313-35916-3 (alk. paper) — ISBN 978-0-313-35917-0 (ebook)
1. Guevara, Ernesto, 1928–1967. 2. Revolutionaries—Argentina—Biography.
3. Revolutionaries—Bolivia—Biography. 4. Revolutionaries—Latin America—Biography. 5. Guerrillas—Latin America—Biography. 6. Latin America—History—1948–1980. 7. Cuba—History—Revolution, 1959–
8. Argentina—Biography. 9. Bolivia—History—1938–1982—Biography.
I. Title.
  F2849.22.G85H29 2010
  972.9106'4092—dc22
  [B]   2010031790

ISBN: 978-0-313-35916-3
EISBN: 978-0-313-35917-0

15 14 13 12 11   1 2 3 4 5

This book is also available on the World Wide Web as an eBook.
Visit www.abc-clio.com for details.

Greenwood
An Imprint of ABC-CLIO, LLC

ABC-CLIO, LLC
130 Cremona Drive, P.O. Box 1911
Santa Barbara, California 93116-1911

This book is printed on acid-free paper ∞

Manufactured in the United States of America

For Melinda
Aloha ʻoe, *until we meet again*.

CONTENTS

Series Foreword		ix
Introduction: The History of a Legendary Revolutionary		xi
Timeline: Events in the Life of Che Guevara		xxiii
Chapter 1	Guevara's Early Life in Argentina	1
Chapter 2	The Motorcycle Diaries: Guevara's South American Odyssey	19
Chapter 3	A Call to Arms in Guatemala and Mexico	37
Chapter 4	El Che: The Heroic Guerrilla Warrior	69
Chapter 5	Che's Role in Cuba's Revolutionary Government	91
Chapter 6	Che's Contribution to Revolutionary Guerrilla Warfare	105
Chapter 7	Che's Ideas about Imperialism and Socialism	119
Chapter 8	The Secret Mission in Africa	131
Chapter 9	Che's Final Mission in Bolivia	145

Chapter 10	The Tragic Death of a Revolutionary	161
Chapter 11	Che's Diary and Hidden Remains	179
Chapter 12	Che's Enduring Legacy	193
Chapter 13	¡Che Vive!—Che's Continuing Influence in Latin America	205

Bibliography — 217

Further Reading: Print and Electronic Sources — 223

Index — 229

SERIES FOREWORD

In response to high school and public library needs, Greenwood developed this distinguished series of full-length biographies specifically for student use. Prepared by field experts and professionals, these engaging biographies are tailored for high school students who need challenging yet accessible biographies. Ideal for secondary school assignments, the length, format and subject areas are designed to meet educators' requirements and students' interests.

Greenwood offers an extensive selection of biographies spanning all curriculum related subject areas including social studies, the sciences, literature and the arts, history and politics, as well as popular culture, covering public figures and famous personalities from all time periods and backgrounds, both historic and contemporary, who have made an impact on American and/or world culture. Greenwood biographies were chosen based on comprehensive feedback from librarians and educators. Consideration was given to both curriculum relevance and inherent interest. The result is an intriguing mix of the well known and the unexpected, the saints and sinners from long-ago history and contemporary pop culture. Readers will find a wide array of subject choices from fascinating crime figures like Al Capone to inspiring pioneers like Margaret

Mead, from the greatest minds of our time like Stephen Hawking to the most amazing success stories of our day like J. K. Rowling.

While the emphasis is on fact, not glorification, the books are meant to be fun to read. Each volume provides in-depth information about the subject's life from birth through childhood, the teen years, and adulthood. A thorough account relates family background and education, traces personal and professional influences, and explores struggles, accomplishments, and contributions. A timeline highlights the most significant life events against a historical perspective. Bibliographies supplement the reference value of each volume.

INTRODUCTION: THE HISTORY OF A LEGENDARY REVOLUTIONARY

Ernesto Guevara de la Serna, commonly known as "Che Guevara," "El Che," or just "Che," is arguably one of the most famous revolutionaries in world history, certainly in the history of the last century or more. In January 2000, *Time* magazine named him one of the 100 most influential people of the 20th century, and the famous photograph that Alberto Korda took of Che, entitled "Guerrillero Heroico" (Heroic Guerrilla Fighter) has been called "the most famous photograph in the world and a symbol of the 20th century" (BBC News 2001). His name, his ideals, and his romantic image have become part of the spirit and symbolism of those who believe that the social injustices and worst forms of human exploitation in this world can be erased only by revolutionary means. Rarely in history has a single figure been so passionately and universally accepted as the personification of revolutionary idealism and practice. Moreover, even those who feel no sympathy for the ideals he upheld continue to be affected by the charisma of his historical persona and the enduring legacy of his revolutionary life.

He personified the revolutionary ferment that swept the world during the momentous decades of tumultuous change that shook the world during the 1960s and 1970s. Thus, a prominent Mexican political writer

Famous "Heroic Guerrilla" photo, 1960. Museo Che Guevara, Havana, Cuba.

(who was the foreign minister of Mexico from 2000 to 2003) has written the following about Che: "Many of us today owe the few attractive and redeeming features of our existence to the sixties, and Che Guevara personifies that era . . . better than anyone" (Castañeda 1997:410). More important, however, is since his death in 1967, Che's defiant and charismatic image in the 1960s' photographs of him has become an almost universal symbol of revolution and resistance to social injustice around the globe (Anderson 1998:xiv). Che's iconic face appears on posters, banners, billboards, flags, books, periodicals, murals, Web sites, T-shirts, and walls in every region of the world. Indeed, his face and to a lesser extent his name are known to people of all ages everywhere.

Che Guevara continues to be regarded by millions of people as a heroic figure because of his legendary revolutionary life and his self-sacrifice for his revolutionary beliefs. He was a man who not only lived by his principles but died fighting for them. Four decades after his death, he remains a figure of veneration among the oppressed, young rebels, radical intellectuals, social activists, revolutionaries, guerrilla fighters of all kinds, and the international global justice movement (often referred to by the mainstream media as the anti-globalization movement). He is also hated and vilified by many people in high places and in Cuban-exile communities throughout the Americas which remain vehemently opposed to the socialist government of Cuba and to the role played by Che in this government: first as one of the most outstanding leaders of the revolutionary guerrilla war that brought this government to power and subsequently as one of the most internationally famous leaders of Cuba's new socialist government and champion of expanding Cuban-style socialist revolutions throughout the rest of Latin America and the world.

Today, he is widely perceived in Latin America as "the herald" of a region-wide social revolution (Taibo 1997:10), which many Latin Americans believe is as urgently needed today as it was in the 1960s when Che gave his life fighting for this cause. In fact, the idealistic origins of this cause can be traced back to the 1800s, when many of the inhabitants of the region rose up in rebellions and revolutions against foreign domination, colonialism, slavery, and ethnic discrimination (particularly the extreme forms of discrimination suffered by the Afro-Latino and indigenous peoples of the Americas).

There is increasing interest throughout Latin America in his revolutionary example and ideals due to the continuing social injustices, extreme social inequality, chronic poverty, and political corruption in the region as well as the rise of new leftist political movements and the election of popular leftist governments throughout Latin America. In response to this growing resurgence of interest in Che's revolutionary life and the 40th anniversary of his death (October 9, 2007), a two-part biographical feature film directed by the well-known Hollywood director, screenwriter, and cinematographer Steven Soderbergh was released in 2008 at the Cannes Film Festival in France. Moreover, to memorialize in 2007 the 40th anniversary of his death and in 2008 the 80th anniversary of his birth, many international conferences and public events were held around the world, especially in Latin America and Europe.

The extensive body of recent literature (hundreds of books and thousands of articles), video documentaries, Hollywood films, Web sites, songs, poems, and works of popular art on Che Guevara have ensured that his legend lives on and that he is known to people all over the world. Many of his own writings have been published, translated into many languages, and read by people of all ages. In fact, Che's revolutionary legend has grown as the years have passed since his death in 1967, and many of the revolutionary ideals that he lived and died for now appeal to a new generation of 21st-century men and women around the world, particularly in Latin America.

The continued political importance of his revolutionary example and ideals can be found nearly everywhere in contemporary Latin America, especially in socialist Cuba but also in Central and South America. His revolutionary image and many of his ideals have been adopted by the Zapatista liberation movement in Mexico; the newly elected leftist leaders and governments in Bolivia, Ecuador, Nicaragua, and Venezuela; and the international global justice movement, which is composed of hundreds of environmental, women's, indigenous peoples, fair trade, radical labor, and peace and social justice organizations around the world. Indeed, the familiar revolutionary political slogan "¡Che vive!" (Che lives!), which was shouted in the 1960s and early 1970s at antiwar protests and political demonstrations and painted as political graffiti on walls and buildings around the world, has as much political significance today in Latin America and the Caribbean as it did in the past.

This book provides a comprehensive account of all aspects and periods of Che Guevara's life. It is for readers who know very little about him as well as those who know something about him and want to know more. It provides a chronological account of his life, starting with his early life in Argentina during the 1930s, 1940s, and early 1950s; his travels throughout Latin America during the early 1950s; the important role he played in the Cuban Revolution during the late 1950s and early 1960s; his unsuccessful revolutionary mission to Africa in 1965; his last revolutionary mission, in Bolivia, during 1966–1967; and the circumstances surrounding his death on October 9, 1967. It also discusses Che's contributions to the theory and tactics of revolutionary warfare and socialist theory and practice.

Among other things, this book reveals that in addition to being a famous revolutionary and international political figure, over the course of his life Che was a road and materials analyst, medical research assistant, ship's nurse, traveling salesman, street photographer, doctor, author, head of the Central Bank of Cuba, military commander, director of Cuba's Central Planning Board, minister of industry, and an important foreign statesman. This book also reveals a great deal about his family life, his likes and dislikes, personality traits, and the most important people in his life. Moreover, it provides a great deal of information about the geography, history, politics, economics, and social problems of Latin America that were the context for his life and his contemporary legacy.

This book does not focus exclusively on the life and the death of Che Guevara. It also includes an account of the fascinating story behind the publication of his Bolivian campaign diary, which was taken from him when he was captured and killed by elements of the Bolivian army. Moreover, this account of the posthumous publication of his diary is followed by the equally fascinating story of how his body, which was secretly buried after he was killed, was discovered in Bolivia and transferred to Cuba in 1997—30 years after his death.

The last chapters of this book examine how Che has been celebrated and held up as a revolutionary hero by the government leaders and people of socialist Cuba and by the new leftist political leaders, movements, and governments that have emerged in Latin America in recent years. Thus, the last two chapters of the book focus on Che's enduring political legacy and the important contemporary political influence of his revolutionary example and ideals throughout Latin America and the Caribbean.

Readers of this book are encouraged to approach the subjects discussed in the following pages with compassionate objectivity. Adopting this perspective is especially advisable for those readers who have had the good fortune to be raised in relatively affluent and secure living conditions and who now are fortunate enough to find themselves living in comparatively stable and nonthreatening political, economic, and social circumstances. Unlike these readers, the majority of humanity has been raised in poverty, and they are now living in relatively unstable, impoverished, and threatening political, economic, and social circumstances. Consequently, their views of the world around them and their aspirations and frustrations are quite different from the views and aspirations of the minority of humanity who live in affluence and relative security. For this reason, they are more willing to support revolutionary leaders and movements that promise to improve their living conditions and circumstances through the violent overthrow of the existing social order.

Che's life provides an excellent case study of how individuals become revolutionaries—how the conditions and circumstances in which they live can lead them to follow this path. Che Guevara the revolutionary was molded by specific historical circumstances, societal conditions, and sociopsychological factors. The term "revolutionary" conjures up in the minds of many people a stereotype of a wild-eyed, bearded extremist who is driven by some fanatical urge to destroy the existing order of things, no matter what the cost in human life and property. Che Guevara does not fit this stereotype. In order to understand why Che became a revolutionary and why he died as one, it is necessary to put aside any preconceptions one has about revolutionaries and examine carefully his life and circumstances. Only by examining carefully the life of this remarkable man is it possible to gain insight into why he became a famous revolutionary and why he died a tragic death as a revolutionary guerrilla fighter in Bolivia at the age of 39.

To understand why men and women like Che Guevara choose to live and die as revolutionaries, it is also necessary to recognize that the mainstream media's coverage of subjects such as revolutions, revolutionaries, socialism, communism, democracy, poverty, guerrilla fighters, terrorism, Latin America, imperialism, the role of the U.S. government in international affairs, and many of the other subjects discussed in this book often provides a quite biased and misleading perspective on these subjects (see NACLA). One of the main reasons their coverage is biased and misleading is because they tend to frame, or explain, these subjects using a culturally and politically ethnocentric perspective.

That is to say, they present the world from a middle-class (and above) North American or European cultural and political perspective, and they rarely present alternative views of the world from other social-class, cultural, or political perspectives. Moreover, they often do not provide adequate or accurate information on the political, economic, social, and cultural circumstances in which the majority of the people in Latin America (and Africa, the Middle East, and Asia) live. Apart from inaccurate reporting, they often misrepresent historical processes and report on political leaders, social movements, and political events using a narrative that reflects the fear of change and perceptions held by those who hold power and enjoy many privileges rather than the views and interests of those who have little power and few or no privileges (see

NACLA). Consequently, they do not do a good job of presenting the often radically different and opposing views people in this important region hold on subjects such as the ruling political and economic elites, social inequality and social justice, revolution and revolutionaries, socialism and capitalism, democracy and oligarchy, the military and police, poverty and human insecurity, and the role of the U.S. government and large transnational corporations in the affairs of their countries and the region.

In order to understand the conditions, circumstances, people, and events that shaped Che's life, it is important to have at least a basic understanding of Latin America's history, politics, economies, cultures, and social problems. In this regard, it is important to understand first of all that there is no single, uniform pattern of characteristics that fits all the countries of Latin America (Harris 2008). In fact, there are considerable differences between the 20 countries usually considered to make up this region. There are differences in terms of the size of these countries. The biggest by population and territory are Brazil, Mexico, and Argentina, which are some of the largest countries in the world, while the smallest are countries such as Panama, Costa Rica, and Uruguay, which are some of the smallest in the world. They are all multicultural societies, but they differ in terms of the ethnic and cultural composition of their populations—some Latin American countries such as Bolivia, Mexico, and Ecuador have large indigenous (Indian) populations while others, such as Haiti, Cuba, and Brazil, have a large number of people of African descent. They also differ greatly in terms of their geography. For example, Bolivia and Paraguay are landlocked countries in the center of the South American continent, while Cuba, Haiti, and the Dominican Republic are located on tropical islands in the Caribbean; and some countries like Brazil and Mexico have lots of natural resources, while others such as Uruguay and Haiti have very few natural resources.

They differ greatly in terms of their extent of industrialization (e.g., Argentina, Brazil, and Mexico are the most industrialized, while Bolivia, Haiti, and Nicaragua are some of the least industrialized in the Americas, and in terms of their main exports (for example, Venezuela's main exports are oil and bauxite, while Chile's main exports are copper and fruit, and Guatemala's main exports are coffee, sugar, and bananas). Moreover, they differ in terms of their relations with the United States and each other. Thus, the governments of Cuba and Venezuela, which consider Che to be a revolutionary hero, have relatively close relations with each other but relatively hostile relations with the government of the United States, while the government of Mexico has more or less friendly relations with the government of the United States but strained relations with the governments of Venezuela and Cuba.

The Latin American countries also differ considerably in terms of how unequal the distribution of their total national income is among the population (Harris 2008:52). The income of the richest 20 percent of the population is 40 times the income of the poorest 20 percent of the population in Bolivia, whereas in Uruguay and Venezuela the income of the richest 20 percent is approximately 11 times the income of the poorest 20 percent. For Latin America as a whole, the income of the richest 20 percent of the population is 19 times the income of the poorest 20 percent. By world standards, this 19-to-1 ratio of unequal distribution is quite high and is one of the reasons why Latin America is considered the region with the greatest social inequality and why Che Guevara believed a socialist revolution was needed in Latin America. In contrast, in the United States the income of the richest 20 percent of the population is about 8 times the income of the poorest 20 percent, which is considered relatively high for an advanced industrial country; for example, the ratio in Canada is only 5.5 to 1.

Despite their differences, however, the Latin American countries do share many characteristics and conditions. In fact, the differences that exist between the Latin American countries do not detract from the importance of their commonalities. With the exception of socialist Cuba (where most sectors of the economy were placed under state control in the early 1960s), all the Latin American countries have capitalist economies, and these economies all hold a subordinate status in the global economic order (Harris 2008). This subordinate status has to do with their historical development—they have all been shaped by the same international economic and political forces over the last 500 years. That is to say, they all have a history of European colonial conquest and domination, slavery, and other extreme forms of labor exploitation. Their economies were established under European colonial rule, primarily to produce and send agricultural products or mineral resources to the European markets of their colonial masters. In addition, their political systems were created to serve the interests of their colonial rulers and then, after colonial rule came to an end, to serve the interests of their wealthy landowning elites (called "oligarchies") rather than the general population. As a result they have inherited government institutions such as the military and police that have strong authoritarian and repressive tendencies. This is one of the main reasons Che Guevara thought that an armed revolution was needed to bring about progressive change in Latin America.

The economies of the region have all undergone a similar process of highly uneven, inequitable, and foreign-dominated economic development over the last 500 years (Harris 2008). And over the last 100 years, this form of distorted economic development, which has been variously labeled with terms such as "underdevelopment" or "dependent development," has produced an unstable and slower rate of economic growth and more frequent and more severe economic crises than has been the case in the advanced industrial countries of the United States of America, western Europe, and Japan. In this regard, many critical thinkers in Latin America and elsewhere, Che Guevara included, have argued that these countries were able to develop faster and create more advanced industrial economies because they have done so at the expense of the Latin American (and African, Middle Eastern, and Asian) countries, which have supplied them with cheap natural resources, cheap agricultural goods, and cheap labor as a result of the unfair prices and unfair trade relations imposed on them by the now advanced countries (Chilcote 2003).

Since the end of World War II (and even before this in many countries of the region), the most important sectors of the Latin American economies have been dominated by transnational corporations and foreign investors with home bases in North America, western Europe, or Japan. In addition, most of the Latin American countries are burdened by large foreign debt owed to large international private banks and the three powerful intergovernmental financial institutions that operate in the region—the International Monetary Fund, the World Bank, and the Inter-American Development Bank. These three intergovernmental financial institutions are heavily influenced by the U.S. government and together they tend to promote the interests of the large transnational corporations and foreign investors that are involved in the economies of the Latin American region. And, again, all the Latin American countries have been historically handicapped by unfavorable terms of trade that give unfair advantages to the more advanced industrial countries that dominate the global economic system. This situation was criticized by Che Guevara in his writings, speeches, and relations with government officials and leaders of countries around the world.

After World War II, the increasingly powerful transnational corporations based in the United States and in some of the other advanced industrial countries invested heavily in Latin American economies to take advantage of their abundant supply of natural resources, cheap labor, lax environmental regulations, and captive consumer markets (Harris 2008). Over the last several decades, these powerful corporations and the international financial institutions mentioned above have promoted what they call the increasing integration of the Latin American economies into the global economic system, which is dominated by these very same corporations and financial institutions. Consequently, the most profitable sectors of the Latin American economies generally are dominated by these transnational corporations and foreign investors. These economies are also excessively dependent on the limited number of products they export to the advanced industrial countries, rather than producing products for their domestic markets, and as a result most of the Latin American countries trade more with the United States and other advanced industrial economies than with each other.

Along with these common economic traits these countries have other, more distressing similarities. In most of these countries, a large percentage of the population lives in poverty, there is widespread unemployment, and a large sector of the population is forced into the so-called informal economy in which they are precariously employed as street peddlers, small vendors, domestic workers, and day laborers or engaged in illegal commercial activity such as prostitution or drug trafficking (Harris and Nef 2008). The majority of the workers in the so-called formal sector of these economies are low-skilled and semiskilled workers, who receive much lower wages and many fewer benefits (if any) than comparable workers in the advanced industrial economies.

Moreover, because a large percentage of the population is either unemployed, underemployed in temporary and part-time jobs, precariously employed in the informal sector, or engaged in subsistence or semi-subsistence agriculture, these economies are also characterized by the kind of unequal distribution of income mentioned above. That is to say, the majority of the population receives a small fraction of the total income of these societies, while the wealthy elites receive a major proportion of the total income and own most of the land. This unequal distribution of income and land is coupled with the increasing concentration of other forms of wealth (personal property, stock ownership, etc.) in the hands of the relatively small elite, who form the top layer of the steep pyramidal class structures that exist throughout Latin America. Indeed, there is a growing polarization and income gap between the extremely wealthy upper classes at the top of these class structures and the middle and lower classes below them. As a result of this unequal distribution of income and wealth, there is extensive poverty, social exclusion, and political inequality throughout Latin America.

These distressing characteristics of Latin American countries have been criticized for a long time as immoral and unjust by progressive thinkers, social activists, and critical intellectuals—particularly from the middle and working classes. Che Guevara was a progressive thinker who became personally outraged by the social inequality, political oppression, social injustice, class discrimination, political corruption, and forms of foreign domination he saw in his travels around Latin America. Trained as medical doctor in his native Argentina to heal the sick and do no harm, Che's social consciousness and humanitarianism were challenged by his experiences on the road, where he encountered widespread poverty, social inequality, exploitation, discrimination, political repression, and the diseases and ill health caused by these unjust conditions.

He was greatly influenced by these experiences as well as the political events, leaders, and situations he witnessed firsthand in Latin America and the practical political education he received as a result of his participation in many of these events and situations. In the following pages, Che's observations and insights, convictions, opinions, and actions will be examined in relation to the circumstances, events, ideas, prominent intellectuals, and political leaders he encountered over the course of his adult life in Latin America and around the world.

TIMELINE: EVENTS IN THE LIFE OF CHE GUEVARA

May 14, 1928	Ernesto Guevara de la Serna is born in Rosario, Argentina, but his parents, Ernesto Guevara Lynch and Celia de la Serna, register his official date of birth as June 14, 1928.
1932	Because of young Ernesto's asthma the Guevara family moves to Alta Gracia, Argentina.
1934	His mother begins schooling young Ernesto at home in Alta Gracia.
1937	Ernesto attends primary school in Alta Gracia at the Colegío San Martín and later attends the Santiago de Liniers School and the Victor Mercante School.
1942	Ernesto travels daily by bus to attend secondary school at the Colegío Nacional Deán Funes in Córdoba, Argentina.
1943	Guevara family moves to Córdoba.
1946	Ernesto graduates from secondary school.
April 22, 1947	Ernesto receives his Certificado de Bachiller from the Colegío Nacional Deán Funes in Córdoba.

TIMELINE

1947	Guevara family moves to Buenos Aires. Ernesto begins medical school at the University of Buenos Aires.
1950	Ernesto travels by motorbike throughout northern Argentina.
1951	Ernesto works for six months at sea as a nurse on oil tankers.
1952	With his friend Alberto Granado, Ernesto travels through Latin America (recorded in his famous *Motorcycle Diaries*, first published in 1993 and popularized in a film version in 2004).
1953	Ernesto graduates from medical school at the University of Buenos Aires; travels to Bolivia, Peru, Ecuador, Panama, Costa Rica, and Guatemala, where he decides to stay.
1954	Árbenz government in Guatemala is overthrown by CIA mercenary force; Ernesto flees to Mexico.
1955	Ernesto meets Raúl and Fidel Castro in Mexico City and joins the Cuban revolutionary 26th of July Movement.
August 18, 1955	Ernesto marries Hilda Gadea Acosta, whom he met in Guatemala.
December 1956	Ernesto, now known as "Che," arrives in Cuba with Castro brothers to launch revolutionary armed struggle from the Sierra Maestra mountains against the Batista dictatorship.
1957	Che becomes outstanding guerrilla fighter and is promoted to top rank of comandante by Fidel Castro.
1958	Che leads a column of guerrilla fighters who capture the critical provincial capital city of Santa Clara; sensing the end is near, the dictator Batista flees Cuba.
1959	Che is appointed commander of the La Cabaña fortress in Havana and president of the Central Bank of Cuba; also undertakes a two-month diplomatic mission to Europe, Africa, and Asia.

June 2, 1959	Che marries Aleida March Torres in Havana after divorcing his first wife, Hilda Gadea Acosta, who decides to reside in Havana with their daughter Hildita.
1960	Che publishes his first book *La Guerra de Guerrillas* (*Guerrilla Warfare*); heads several Cuban diplomatic missions—to the Soviet Union, Europe, and Asia.
1961	Che appointed Minister of Industry, heads Cuban mission to the Soviet Union and other socialist countries in Europe, China, and North Korea; also visits Uruguay, Argentina, and Brazil, where he receives the distinguished National Order of the Southern Cross from President Janiro Cuadros.
1962	Che heads important Cuban mission to the Soviet Union that finalizes secret negotiations that lead to placement of Soviet missiles in Cuba; this provokes the infamous Cuban Missile Crisis and U.S. naval blockade of Cuba.
1964	Che speaks at United Nations General Assembly on the international crisis in the Congo, and at the end of the year undertakes an extended trip to Africa and China.
1965	Che returns to Cuba in March and drops out of sight; between April and November he heads a secret Cuban military mission that unsuccessfully attempts to establish a training base in the Congo for revolutionary guerrilla movements in Africa.
1966	Following the failure of his Congo mission and a short stay in Tanzania, Che returns secretly to Cuba and prepares for a clandestine mission in Bolivia; he enters the country disguised as an Uruguayan economist in early November.
1967	Che attempts to establish in Bolivia a continental base for revolutionary guerrilla operations in Latin America.
October 9, 1967	Che is captured and executed.

TIMELINE

1979–1989 The Sandinista revolutionary movement overthrows the Somoza dictatorship in Nicaragua and over the next 10 years the country's revolutionary leaders honor Che as one of the major sources of inspiration for their revolution.

1994 The Zapatista revolutionary movement in southern Mexico begins to gain international attention and its leaders publicly pay homage to Che; their primary spokesperson, Subcomandante Marcos, is even described by the media as the new Che Guevara.

1997 A team of Cuban geologists and Argentine forensic anthropologists discover the remains of Che's body in an unmarked grave in Vallegrande, Bolivia; in October his remains are returned to Cuba and placed in a special mausoleum in Santa Clara.

1999 Che is included as one of the 20th century's 100 most influential people in a special issue of *Time* magazine.

2006 Bolivia's newly elected, socialist president Juan "Evo" Morales pays homage to Che in his inauguration speech and prominently displays his photo in his presidential office.

2009 *Che*, a two-part biographical film on Guevara directed by Steven Soderbergh and starring Benicio del Toro, is released internationally; by October 2009, this film grossed over $40 million worldwide.

Chapter 1
GUEVARA'S EARLY LIFE IN ARGENTINA

Che Guevara was born on May 14, 1928 (although his birth certificate indicates he was born a month later, on June 14, 1928), in the Argentine city of Rosario, which is located in northern Argentina on the famous Paraná River. His parents named him Ernesto (his father's first name) and as is the custom throughout most of Latin America, his full name consisted of both his father's family name and his mother's family name. Thus, as a boy and young man he was known as Ernesto Guevara de la Serna—Guevara being his father's family name and de la Serna being his mother's family name. Since he did not assume the first name of Che until much later in his life, in this chapter and the following two chapters, he will be referred to as Ernesto Guevara.

His parents were of upper-class origin. His father, Ernesto Guevara Lynch, was an entrepreneur and a builder-architect who studied architecture but never received his degree. During the more entrepreneurial phase of his career, he tried his hand at ranching, yacht building, and the cultivation of maté (the herbal tea that is the national drink in Argentina). However, he ended up as a builder-architect. His ancestry was both Spanish (Guevara) and Irish (Lynch) and one of his great-grandfathers was one of the wealthiest men in South America

(Anderson 1997:4), but over the years the Guevara family lost most of their wealth. Ernesto's (Che's) great-grandfather Juan Antonio Guevara left Argentina for the gold rush in California, where he married a beautiful Mexican woman named Concepción Castro. Their son, Roberto Guevara Castro, was born in California but returned with his parents to Argentina, where he married Ana Isabel Lynch, who was also born in California. She was the daughter of an Argentine family of Irish ancestry that like the Guevaras went to California during the gold rush but returned later to Argentina. Their son, Ernesto Guevara Lynch, was Ernesto's (Che's) father. During Ernesto's (Che's) childhood, he loved listening to his grandmother Ana Isabel's tales of frontier life in California.

His mother, Celia de la Serna y Llosa, came from a wealthy landowning family of Spanish ancestry. Her parents died when she was quite young, and as a result she received a sizable inheritance at the age of 21, which was the same year Ernesto was born. She graduated from an exclusive Catholic girls' school in Buenos Aires. She was an intelligent, quite literate, unconventional, and generous person who remained devoted to Ernesto, her firstborn, until her death just a few years before his own.

Soon after Ernesto's birth, his parents moved to San Isidro, Argentina, where Ernesto's father was a partner in a yacht-building business. It was while they were living in this city along the banks of the La Plata River that his parents discovered the young Ernesto had asthma (which he suffered from the rest of his life). His mother was an avid swimmer and used to take him with her to the yacht club in San Isidro when she went swimming. On one particularly chilly day, by the time she was ready to leave the club she discovered he was very ill. She and her husband took him immediately to a local doctor, who informed them that their son had a severe asthmatic condition. For the next two years, Che's parents tried every possible cure, but in the end they were advised that they would have to move to a much drier climate if they wanted their son's health to improve. As a result, they moved to the little town of Alta Gracia on the gentle western slopes of the Sierra Chica in the central Argentine province of Córdoba.

Ernesto grew up in Alta Gracia and later in the provincial capital city of Córdoba, along with his two brothers and two sisters, who were born there. The dry climate of the region greatly benefited his health, although he continued to suffer periodic asthma attacks, which at times forced him to stay in bed for days. Nevertheless, as he grew older, Ernesto spent as much time outdoors as possible. His childhood friends recall that he was always organizing hikes to the hills and playing games requiring physical skill and endurance (Caligiuri and Piccon 2007). He learned to swim at an early age, and this sport became one of his passions. His parents, especially his mother, encouraged him to swim, since they believed this sport would improve his health and particularly his breathing problems. As he grew older, he also became an avid golfer and loved to ride horses.

His friends remember him as a decisive and bold youth who was very sure of himself (Caligiuri and Piccon 2007). He had several nicknames during his childhood. His family members often called him "Tete," while his friends called him "Ernestito," "Fuser," and "Chancho." His childhood and school friends remember him for his enthusiasm, mischievous and courageous nature, and adventurousness. Evidently, he was a real daredevil, willing to do almost anything, perhaps to prove to himself that in spite of his chronic illness he was just as good or better at doing things as his friends. Enrique Martin, one of his childhood friends, remembers him as a "real friend when somebody needed him" and as "a charismatic person" who "never got angry more than two minutes." According to Martin: "We all respected and admired him for his kindness" (Caligiuri and Piccon 2007:52).

The family rented various houses in Alta Gracia, but the house where they spent the most time was Villa Nydia, which is today the Museo Casa del Che Guevara (Museum of Che Guevara's House). The family lived in Villa Nydia from 1935 to 1937 and again from 1939 to 1943 (Caligiuri and Piccon 2007:41). It is the house that was most thought of by the Guevara family as their home in Alta Gracia.

Ernesto's family life was relatively happy, although his parents separated when he was a young adult. His father gave him considerable freedom and moral support. His mother gave him a great deal of love and attention; they had a special bond between them. Ernesto always confided in her, even years later when he became an important leader in the Cuban Revolution. Because of his asthma, he was unable to attend school during the first years of his primary education (Caligiuri and

Piccon 2007:72). During this period, his mother tutored him at home, and Ernesto spent hours reading alone or playing chess with his father. Later on, when he was enrolled in school, his mother taught him to speak and read French, in which he was fluent. By this time the frequency of his asthmatic attacks had decreased considerably, and his attendance in secondary school was quite regular.

Despite his asthma, as he grew older Ernesto became involved in a wide variety of outdoor activities and sports. He swam, played soccer and golf, rode horses, took up target shooting, and loved biking and hiking (Anderson 1997:18). Although he sometimes had to be carried home by his friends because of an asthma attack, he was determined to do everything his friends could do and refused to let his asthma limit him. The administrator of his primary school, Elba Rossi de Oviedo, remembered him as a "mischievous boy" who exhibited leadership qualities on the playground (Anderson 1997:19). She said: "Many children followed him during recess. He was a leader, but not an arrogant person. Sometimes he climbed up trees in the schoolyard." She also said he was "an intelligent and independent person," who "had the qualities necessary to lead a group," and "he never sat at the same desk in the classroom, he needed all of them" (Caligiuri and Piccon 2007:72).

Ernesto's parents wanted their children to be freethinkers. At home, the parents never spoke of religion except to occasionally criticize the conservative hierarchy of the Catholic Church, and the children were given considerable freedom to think and talk about all kinds of subjects as well as indiscriminately associate with people from all classes (Caligiuri and Piccon 2007). They were given no religious instruction, and his parents asked that their children be excused from religion classes in school. Although he was baptized as a Roman Catholic when he was an infant to please his grandparents, Ernesto was never confirmed as a member of the church. His parents, especially his father, were critical of the hypocritical role played by the conservative Catholic clergy in Latin American society. They felt strongly that their children should not be overprotected and that they should learn about life's secrets and dangers at an early age.

Their home life was somewhat Bohemian, and they followed few social conventions (Anderson 1997:20). Ernesto's mother, Celia, challenged the prevailing gender norms for women in Alta Gracia and was a liberated woman for her time. She was the first woman in town to drive a car, wear trousers, and smoke cigarettes in public. She was able to get away with breaking many of the social norms in the socially conservative community because of her social standing and generosity. She regularly transported her children and their friends to school in the family car and started a daily free-milk program in the school for the poorer children, which she paid for herself.

Ernesto's father considered Celia to be "imprudent from birth" and "attracted to danger" and chided her for passing these character traits on to her son (Anderson:21). Ernesto's father in turn was known to have an Irish temper, and it appears he passed this trait on to Ernesto, who as a child could become "uncontrollable with rage" if he felt he was treated unjustly. In temperament, however, Ernesto was more like his mother, who was his confidant and at times his co-conspirator in criticizing what they considered to be the hypocritical and outmoded social norms of their provincial community.

Ernesto enjoyed playing soccer (or football as it is called in Latin America and most of the world) and rugby. In the former sport, he usually played the position of goalkeeper, always with an inhaler for his

Author at entrance to Che Guevara House Museum in Alta Gracia, Argentina. Richard L. Harris.

asthma in his pocket. However, it was at rugby that he really excelled. Hugo Gambini, in his biography of Che, claims that the position he played as a youth in this game helped to define his personality (Gambini 1968:18). It seems he played the position of forward, which is generally the key position in rugby since the majority of advances depend on it. Ernesto played this position fearlessly, as though both his personality and his physical attributes had been made to order for it. Perhaps, as Gambini suggests, this game was instrumental in shaping Ernesto's personality as a daring leader.

All those who knew Ernesto Guevara as a youth were impressed by his intelligence and the ease with which he learned new things. However, he was not an exceptional student and he was not interested in getting high grades in school, since his interests lay outside of school. He was preoccupied with hiking, football, rugby, and chess. In the case of chess, he was an excellent player and it became his main hobby. Ernesto also was an avid reader. From his father he developed a love for books on adventure and history, especially the works of Jules Verne (Taibo 1996:24), and from his mother he gained a love for fiction literature, philosophy, and poetry. He had read nearly every book in his parents' relatively large home library by the time he was in his early adolescence.

Ernesto grew up in a highly politicized environment. Both his mother and father identified with the leftist Republican cause during the Spanish Civil War, and after the war they became close friends with two Spanish Republican families who had been forced to flee Spain and seek exile in Argentina after the fall of the republic when the dictatorship of General Francisco Franco was established. The Guevara family was also fiercely anti-Nazi. His father belonged to an anti-Nazi and pro-Allies organization called Acción Argentina, and Ernesto joined the youth wing of this organization when he was 11 (Anderson 1997:23). His mother formed a committee to send clothes and food to Charles de Gaulle's Free French forces during World War II. She was leftist in her political orientation and far more progressive minded in her political views than his father, who was more of a libertarian conservative. However, both of Che's parents strongly opposed the spread of fascism in Europe (and Argentina) and opposed the popular military strongman Juan Perón as he rose to political power in Argentina. During the presidency of Perón, Ernesto's mother was an outspoken critic of this famous Argentine political leader and the mass political movement called Peronism that he created in Argentina.

Because of his parents' active support for the Republican cause in Spain and the Allied countries fighting against fascism in Europe during World War II, and their opposition to Peronism in Argentina after the war, Ernesto was caught up in his parents' political activities at a crucial time in the early formation of his political consciousness (Anderson:23–25). His family's involvement in anti-fascist and anti-Peronist politics helped shape his view of the world as well as his political ideals and views.

According to those who knew him as a youth, many of the character traits for which he became famous as an adult were already present when he was a boy: "physical fearlessness, inclination to lead others, stubbornness, competitive spirit, and self-discipline" (Anderson 1997:21). However, at this stage in his life, his interest in politics was secondary to his other interests.

In the summer of 1943, Ernesto and his family moved from Alta Gracia to the nearby city of Córdoba, to which he was already commuting daily by bus to attend a secondary school more liberal than the one in Alta Gracia. Largely because of his mother's wishes, their home in Córdoba had the same casual open-door policy as their home in Alta Gracia. All the friends and acquaintances of the Guevara children were always welcome, there was no regular schedule for meals and they ate when they were hungry, and there was nearly always a wide assortment of interesting guests (Anderson:27). Although the Guevaras welcomed everyone into their home, Ernesto and his mother would tease mercilessly any visitor who showed any pretentiousness, snobbery, or pompous behavior.

Among the new friends Ernesto made in Córdoba were two brothers, Tomás and Alberto Granado (Taibo:25). Tomás was Ernesto's schoolmate, and Alberto was Tomás's older brother. Alberto was a first-year student in biochemistry and pharmacology at the University of Córdoba when they first met. He was also the coach of a local rugby team. Even though Ernesto was relatively inexperienced and his father was afraid he would suffer a heart attack from playing such a strenuous sport, Ernesto convinced Alberto to let him join the team; he soon earned a reputation for being a fearless rugby player despite his frequent asthma attacks. Alberto was impressed by his fearlessness and his determination to excel at the sport. He was also pleasantly surprised to discover Ernesto was an avid reader like himself. In fact, Alberto and Tomás found it difficult to believe that the young teenager Ernesto had already read so many books. Moreover, his reading list included the works of preeminent authors such as Sigmund Freud, Charles-Pierre Baudelaire, Émile Zola, Jack London, Pablo Neruda, Anatole France, William Faulkner, John Steinbeck, and Karl Marx. He especially liked the poetry of Chile's famous poet Pablo Neruda, and his personal hero was Mahatma Gandhi, whom he deeply admired (Taibo:26).

Hilda Gadea (his first wife) remembers that Ernesto told her he read everything in his father's library when he was teenager:

> Ernesto told me how when he was still in high school he decided to start reading seriously and began by swallowing his father's library, choosing volumes at random. The books were not classified and next to an adventure book he would find a Greek tragedy and then a book on Marxism. (Gadea 2008:40)

His interests were eclectic, but he took a special interest in poetry and could recite many of his favorite poems from memory. Although he read books on political topics and enjoyed discussing politics with his family and friends, most of his schoolmates remember him as being for the most part "politically disinterested" during his secondary school years (Anderson:33).

As for sex, he was definitely interested. In the mid-1940s in Argentina, good girls were expected to remain a virgin until they married and boys from the upper classes were expected by their families and the social norms of their class to respect the virginity of the girls they dated, especially if they were from their same social circles. For their first sexual experiences, therefore, boys from Ernesto's class went to brothels or had sexual relations with girls from the lower classes—often the young maids who worked in their homes or the homes of their friends. In Ernesto's case, his first sexual experience appears to have occurred with a young maid when he was 15.

A friend from Alta Gracia, Carlos "Calica" Ferrer, arranged a sexual liaison for him with a Ferrer family maid, a young woman called "La Negra" Cabrera. Unknown to Ernesto at the time, Calica and a few of his friends spied on him while he had sex with the young woman. The following is a brief account of Ernesto's sexual initiation with La Negra:

> They observed that, while he conducted himself admirably on top of the pliant maid, he periodically interrupted his lovemaking to suck on his asthma inhaler. The spectacle soon had them in stitches and remained a source of amusement for years afterward. (Anderson:35)

According to his friends, Ernesto was not perturbed by their jokes about his first experience in lovemaking and continued for some time thereafter to have sexual relations with La Negra.

By the time he graduated from secondary school, Ernesto had "developed into an extremely attractive young man: slim and wide-shouldered, with dark-brown hair, intense brown eyes, clear white skin, and a self-contained, easy confidence that made him alluring to girls" (Anderson:36). By the time he was 17, he had developed a devil-may-care and eccentric attitude that was characterized by his contempt for formality and social decorum and a penchant for shocking his teachers and classmates with his unconventional comments and behavior. He also bragged about how infrequently he took a bath or changed his clothes, and as a result he earned the nickname among his friends of "El Chancho" (the Pig) for his unkempt appearance and reluctance to bathe. What most of his friends did not realize was that he often had asthma attacks when he took a bath or shower, especially if the water was cold (Taibo:27).

In general, his grades in secondary school reflected his interests. He did best in the subjects that most interested him: literature, history, and philosophy; his grades were weak in mathematics and natural history because they didn't interest him; and they were poor in English and music (Taibo 1996:28). He had no ear for music, and he was a poor dancer because he couldn't follow the music. In 1945 he took a serious interest in philosophy and compiled a 165-page notebook that he called his philosophical dictionary (the first of seven such notebooks that he produced over the next 10 years). It contained in alphabetical order his notes on the main ideas and biographies of the important thinkers he had read and quotations of their definitions of key concepts such as love, immortality, sexual morality, justice, faith, God, death, reason, neurosis, and paranoia (Taibo:28). It also contained his commentaries on these notes, which he often wrote in the margins.

Thanks largely to his mother Celia's "egalitarian informality," his home was "a fascinating human zoo" that was frequented by a diverse range of colorful people of all social classes, occupations, levels of education, and ages, who often ate there and sometimes stayed a week or a month at a time (Anderson:39). His mother presided over this mélange of adults, teenagers, and children while Ernesto's father came and went on his old motorbike named "La Pedorra" (the Farter). Ernesto

Ernesto Che Guevara, here as a child in Argentina, c. 1940. Photo by Apic/Getty Images.

found it difficult to study or read in such a chaotic and distracting environment, so he got into the habit of closing himself in the bathroom where he would read for hours. During this period, his parents became estranged but continued to live under the same roof.

In 1946, Ernesto graduated from secondary school. He and his friend Tomás Granado (Alberto's younger brother) made plans to study engineering the following year at the University of Buenos Aires, and in the meantime they obtained jobs working for the provincial public highways department after taking a special course for field analysts. Ernesto was hired as a materials analyst and sent to the north to inspect the materials being used on the roads around Villa María, where he was given free lodging and the use of a vehicle (Anderson:40). While he was there he was confronted with the news of two tragedies: he learned his hero from boyhood, Mahatma Gandhi (the famous leader of India's national independence movement against British colonial rule), had been assassinated and his beloved grandmother Ana Isabel Guevara was terminally ill (Taibo 1996:29).

Before he left Villa María, he wrote a prophetic poem about his own death and his personal struggle to overcome his frequent asthma attacks. The following is an extract from this free-verse poem:

> The bullets, what can the bullets do to me if my destiny is to die by drowning.
> But I am going to overcome destiny.
> Destiny can be overcome by willpower.
> Die yes, but riddled with bullets, destroyed by bayonets, if not, no.
> Drowned, no . . . a memory more lasting than my name is to fight, to die fighting. (quoted in Anderson:44)

As this extract from a poem he wrote in January 1947 reveals, Ernesto had a premonition that he would die fighting—"riddled with bullets"—rather than drowning (from his asthma). This poem was written 20 years before he died—riddled with bullets—in 1967.

During his absence from Córdoba, his family moved to Buenos Aires. His father's business was doing poorly and the family was forced to sell their house in Córdoba and move into the apartment his grandmother

Ana Isabel Guevara owned and lived in. By May 1947 his grandmother was on her deathbed, and Ernesto gave up his job in Villa María to be at her bedside. According to his father:

> Ernesto [was] desperate at seeing that his grandmother didn't eat [so] he tried with incredible patience to get her to eat food, entertaining her, and without leaving her side. And he remained there until [she] left this world. (quoted in Anderson:41)

He was greatly affected by the death of his grandmother, with whom he had a special emotional attachment; his sister Celia had never seen her older brother so upset and grief-stricken. Many years later she observed that "it must have been one of the greatest sadnesses of his life" (Anderson:41).

Apparently, the painful death of his beloved grandmother and his personal interest in finding a cure for asthma led him to change his mind about pursuing a degree in engineering and to study medicine instead (Anderson:42; Taibo:29). Within a month of arriving in Buenos Aires, he enrolled in the Faculty of Medicine at the University of Buenos Aires. His family believed he made this decision to change careers because of the shock of his grandmother's painful death and his desire to pursue a career that would alleviate human suffering. But his choice of specialties and research interests in medicine suggested he was also motivated by a desire to find a cure for asthma. Years later, he said he chose a career in medicine because "I dreamed of becoming a famous investigator . . . of working indefatigably to find something that could be definitively placed at the disposition of humanity" (quoted in Anderson:42).

In addition to his studies at the university, he held a number of part-time jobs. The one he held the longest was in the clinic of Dr. Salvador Pisani, where he also received treatment for his asthma (Anderson:43). Dr. Pisani gave him the opportunity to work as a research assistant in the laboratory of his clinic, specifically on the pioneering use of vaccinations and other innovative types of treatment for the allergies associated with asthma. Ernesto became so enthralled in this research that he decided to specialize in the treatment of allergies for his medical career. He became a fixture of Dr. Pisani's clinic and his home, where the doctor's mother and sister prepared a special antiasthma diet for Ernesto and took care of him when he suffered severe asthma attacks.

What little spare time he had he devoted to rugby, chess, and travel. He registered for military service as required when he was 18, but he was given a medical deferment from military service because of his asthma. As for his political orientation at this stage of his life, he was a "progressive liberal" who avoided affiliation with any political organization (Anderson:50). His political views were nationalist, anti-imperialist, and anti-American, but he was quite critical of the Argentine Communist Party and its youth organization at the university for their sectarianism (intolerance of other political organizations and ideologies). While he was not a Marxist, he did already have a special interest in Marx's writings and in socialist thought. At this stage of his life he was an engaging and intelligent nonconformist—an oddball who most of his friends and acquaintances found difficult to categorize.

Since he was not quite 18 when the national election was held that elected Juan Perón to the presidency of Argentina in 1946, he was not able to vote in this historic election, but like most other students of his generation, he did not support Perón. His views regarding Perón have been characterized as "a-Peronism" (Castañeda:30–35), meaning he did not care much one way or the other about Perón and his policies. However, he reportedly told the maids who worked for his family that they should vote for Perón since his policies would help their class. It is not clear what he thought of Argentina's popular female political figure during this period—the beautiful blond radio actress Evita who was Perón's controversial mistress until he married her a few months before his election to the presidency in 1946.

During the years Ernesto was a university student, Eva "Evita" Duarte Perón became the darling of Argentina's popular classes because of her charismatic populist speeches and her highly publicized personal crusade for labor and women's rights (EPHRF 1997). While her husband was president, she ran the Argentine federal government's ministries of labor and health; founded and led the Eva Perón Foundation, which provided charitable services to the poor (especially to the elderly, women, and children); and created and served as the president of the nation's first mass women's organization, called the Peronist Women's Party. After her death from cancer in 1952, Evita—like Che Guevara later—became a powerful icon in the political culture of Argentina and Latin America. However, there is no evidence there was ever any personal or political connection between these two historic figures.

After living in his deceased mother's apartment for a year, Ernesto's father sold his maté plantation and gave the money to Celia to buy a modest home in Buenos Aires at the edge of the desirable Palermo district (Anderson:44–45). However, to make ends meet, the older children had to find jobs. Despite the now obvious separation between his parents—his father slept on the sofa in the living room of the new house—Ernesto maintained his close and open relationship with both parents, his father fondly describing their relationship during this period as follows:

> We joked with one another as if we were the same age. He teased me continuously. As soon as we found ourselves at the table in our house, he would goad me with arguments of a political character. . . . Ernesto, who at that time was twenty years old, surpassed me in this area, and we argued constantly. Those who overheard us might have thought we were fighting. Not at all. Deep down there existed a true camaraderie between us. (quoted in Anderson:45)

Although his relationship was one of camaraderie with his father, with his mother it was more attentive and considerate, especially after she was diagnosed with breast cancer and had a mastectomy in 1946 (Anderson:56–57). She presided over the household in Buenos Aires in much the same way she did in Córdoba and Alta Gracia—she showed a complete disregard for social decorum and housekeeping but generously offered informal hospitality to all manner of guests. There was very little furniture and few decorations in the house, books were everywhere, and the walls in the kitchen gave electrical shocks because of a chronic short circuit in the electrical wiring.

Ernesto often went to his Aunt Beatriz's (and deceased grandmother's) apartment to study, and his father went there often to sleep, because of the noise and people coming and going in the family's house. Ernesto had a special relationship with his spinster aunt, who loved to mother him. She would prepare meals for him and, according to his father, his Aunt Beatriz "didn't sleep while Ernesto studied; she always had his maté ready to prepare for him and accompanied him when he took a break, and she did this all with the greatest of affection" (quoted in Anderson:46). She was quite conservative and proper, so Ernesto loved to scandalize her with his ideas and stories but always in an affectionate and respectful manner. According to a cousin who accompanied him frequently to his aunt's apartment, Ernesto secretly seduced her maid without their aunt knowing anything about it (Anderson:47).

From this period of his life, there is a photograph of Ernesto with his classmates in one of the classrooms of the Faculty of Medicine at the University of Buenos Aires. A careful examination of this photograph provides some clues to Ernesto's character, state of mind, and his relationships at the time. In the photograph 28 white-coated students stand in three rows on different levels behind a naked cadaver with an open chest cavity on a metal table in the foreground. A few of the students are smiling at the camera and the rest have assumed a serious professional look, but in the third row is one student who is looking open-eyed at the camera with a broad joking smile—it is Ernesto. All the men are wearing ties, except for Ernesto, who is wearing a white shirt—probably the one white nylon shirt he owned and which he called "La Semanera" (the Weekly One) because he wore it all the time and washed it once a week. There are only three women in the group photograph, one of whom is Berta "Tita" Infante, with whom Ernesto had a deep but platonic relationship. She is looking at the camera with an intense gaze.

Tita and Ernesto met in an anatomy course and became very close friends and confidants. It appears she wanted more from the relationship than he did or at least more than he was willing to give at the time. What follows is her description of Ernesto:

> By his accent he was a provincial, by his appearance he was a beautiful and uninhibited young man. . . . A mixture of shyness and arrogance, maybe the audacity hid his profound intelligence

Ernesto Che Guevara, c. 1950, when he was a medical student. Photo by Apic/Getty Images.

and insatiable desire to understand things and there at the bottom [of his heart], an infinite capacity to love. (quoted in Taibo:32)

They met often, studied together, and discussed their personal problems. Their friendship lasted beyond medical school, and he corresponded almost as frequently with her after he left Argentina as he did with his mother and Aunt Beatriz.

As for Ernesto's own reflection on this period of his life, years later he said the following:

When I began to study medicine, the majority of the concepts that I have as a revolutionary were absent from the storehouse of my ideas. I wanted to succeed, like everyone; I dreamed of being a famous researcher, dreamed of working untiringly to succeed at doing something that could be definitively placed at the disposal of humanity, but in that moment it was a personal achievement [that I wanted]. I was, as we all are, a child of my environment. (quoted in Taibo:32)

Thus, Che (the revolutionary), looking back on his student years, saw himself as a product of his own environment—someone who was primarily concerned with his own individual success and not yet someone who was prepared unselfishly to place himself at the service of humanity.

Chapter 2

THE MOTORCYCLE DIARIES: GUEVARA'S SOUTH AMERICAN ODYSSEY

Ernesto loved to travel. His father wrote that with time he came to understand "his obsession with travelling was just another part of his zeal for learning" (Guevara 1995:2). However, Ernesto disguised this motivation for his early trips by talking casually about his travel plans and by at least pretending to be motivated primarily by the desire for adventure. His diary of his now famous 1951–1952 trip (Guevara 1995) throughout South America is written primarily in this vein. However, his subsequent 1953–1954 trip throughout South and Central America was clearly motivated by more serious intentions, especially after he reached Central America (see chapter 3).

Ernesto's first noteworthy journey on his own took place in 1950, when he toured all of central and northern Argentina by motorbike—a trip of some 4,000 miles (Gambini 1968:22). He was 21 and a medical student at the University of Buenos Aires at the time. On his journey he stopped off in Córdoba to visit his friends Tomás and Alberto Granado. Alberto was conducting research on lepers at a leprosarium near San Francisco del Chañar, and because Ernesto was intrigued by Alberto's research he spent several days with Alberto at the leprosarium.

From there he headed north and met an interesting assortment of hobos, vagabonds, seasonal workers, poor indigenous inhabitants, and other socially marginalized people along the way. He often stayed overnight in police stations and provincial hospitals where he asked if he could sleep in vacant jail cells or empty hospital beds. As a result, "for the first time in his adult life, Ernesto . . . witnessed the harsh duality of his country by crossing the divide from its transported European culture, which was also *his* [culture], and . . . its ignored, backward, *indigenous* heartland" (Anderson 1997:63).

What he learned from this trip to the poorer northern region of his country was that Argentina's more modern and superficial European culture was "a luxurious façade under which the country's true soul lay; and that soul was rotten and diseased." It was from this region of the country that "the Argentine Indians, commonly referred to as *coyas*, and the mixed-blood *cabezitas negras* (little black heads) fled in steadily increasing numbers, pouring into the cities in search of work and setting up shantytowns like the one in front of the Guevaras' home in Córdoba" (Anderson 1997:64). They were the social class of domestic servants and day laborers called *descamisados* (shirtless ones) whom Péron and his wife Evita promised to incorporate into the nation and whom Argentina's white elite still exploit and despise.

When Ernesto returned to Buenos Aires from this trip he took the motorbike back to the store where he bought it in order to have it reconditioned. When the store owner discovered the details of the trip, he was astounded and asked Ernesto to give him a letter attesting to his having made such a fantastic trip using the particular brand of motorbike that he used. This letter, along with a picture of Ernesto sitting on his motorbike, was published in a local sports magazine as an advertisement for this type of motorbike (Taibo 1996:35).

Ernesto returned to his studies in medical school, resumed playing rugby, and continued working in Dr. Pisani's clinic. He also fell in love for the first time. The object of his affection was the 16-year-old daughter of one of Córdoba's wealthiest families. Her name was María del Carmen "Chichina" Ferreyra, and they met in October 1950 at a wedding in Córdoba attended by Ernesto and his family. By all accounts, she was a strikingly beautiful, intelligent, and charming young woman, who was as infatuated with him as he was with her (Taibo:37). However, this romance was doomed from the start since Chichina was a pampered young princess from the "blue-blooded Argentina gentry, heiress to the Ferreyra family empire," while Ernesto was the Bohemian prodigal son of "a family of pauperized aristocrats" who after generations of decline were at best precarious members of Argentina's upper middle class (Anderson 1997:65).

Chichina's family lived in an imposing French-style chateau with parklike gardens in Córdoba and on a large estate called La Malagueño outside of the city. According to her cousin, Dolores Moyano:

> [This estate] included two polo fields, Arabian stallions, and a feudal village of workers for the family's limestone quarries. The family visited the village church every Sunday for Mass, worshipping in a separate alcove to the right of the altar with its own separate entrance and private communion rail, away from the mass of workers. In many ways, La Malagueño exemplified everything that Ernesto despised. Yet, unpredictable as always, Ernesto had fallen madly in love with the princess of this little empire, my cousin Chichina Ferreyra, an extraordinarily beautiful and charming girl, who, to the dismay of her parents, was equally fascinated by Ernesto. (quoted in Anderson:65)

Ernesto became a frequent, if not always welcome, visitor at the Ferreyras' homes in Córdoba and at La Malagueño.

Ernesto was madly in love with Chichina and wanted to marry her. But the differences in their age and social class, her parents' disapproval of him, and the distance between them began to strain their relationship. At the beginning of 1951, Ernesto needed to earn some money, so he signed up to serve as a ship's nurse on Argentina's merchant marine freighters and oil tankers (Taibo:38). Between February and June 1951, he made various trips back and forth between Argentina and Brazil, Venezuela, and the Caribbean islands. These trips gave him plenty of time to study for his medical exams and exposed him to life at sea as well as most of the ports of call on the Atlantic Coast of South America and in the Caribbean. At the end of June 1951, he went back to medical school.

On one of his visits to Córdoba to see Chichina he also visited his friends the Granado brothers. In the course of a conversation with Alberto

Granado while working on his motorcycle, nicknamed La Poderosa (the Powerful One), the idea of making a yearlong trip together took shape. Ernesto's account of this momentous occasion is as follows:

> Our fantasizing took us to far away places, sailing tropical seas, travelling through Asia. And suddenly, slipping in as if part of our fantasy, came the question: "Why don't we go to North America?" "North America? How?" "On La Poderosa, man." That's how the trip came about, and it never deviated from the general principle laid down then: improvisation. . . . My task before leaving was to take as many exams in as many subjects as possible; Alberto's to get the bike ready for the long journey. . . . At that stage the momentousness of our endeavor hadn't dawned on us, all we could see was the dusty road ahead and us on our bike devouring kilometers in the flight northward. (Guevara 1995:13)

They were both restless and anxious to set out on an adventure. Alberto had quit his job, and Ernesto was tired of medical school, hospitals, and studying for exams. He was also frustrated by the opposition of Chichina's parents to their relationship. For these reasons, they both wanted to take a break from their existing circumstances.

Thus, in December 1951, when he lacked only one year of receiving his medical degree, Ernesto and his friend Alberto Granados decided to set out to explore all of Latin America by motorcycle. Ernesto's *Motorcycle Diaries* (Guevara 1995), which were published many years after his death, provide a valuable personal narrative of this journey. They shed light on a little known period in his young adulthood and provide important insights into his personality and the development of his views about the world. Written while he was traveling around South America in his early 20s, they allow the reader to gain an intimate portrait of him at an important and formative period in his life. Ironically, most of this trip was not made on a motorcycle. In fact, Ernesto and Alberto traveled on just about every mode of transportation available at the time—horses, railroads, buses, trucks, cars, ships, ferries, boats, rafts, and airplanes—and of course on their feet. After their motorcycle died in Chile, they were forced to walk, hitchhike, and use whatever means was available to make their way from one end of the South American continent to the other.

Ernesto's lucid and brief accounts in his diary enable the reader to almost hear his thoughts, view the world through his eyes, and sense his spirit. In a certain sense they allow the reader to travel back in time to meet the man before he made his grand entrance on the stage of world history as one of the most charismatic and emblematic revolutionaries of all time.

From Buenos Aires, Ernesto and Alberto traveled to the Atlantic Coast of Argentina and across the pampa to the south of Argentina, where they crossed the Andes Mountains into Chile. They had increasing problems with the motorcycle as they traveled over the Andes and through southern Chile. As they neared the Chilean capital of Santiago, the motorcycle finally gave out and they had to continue the rest of their trip on foot. They also quickly ran out of money. They were forced to panhandle, freeload, and work at numerous odd jobs in order to continue their journey northward through Chile to Peru, through Peru to Colombia, and finally to Venezuela. Along the way, Ernesto developed a critical social consciousness based on the many instances of social injustice, human exploitation, and racial and ethnic discrimination he witnessed in all the countries he visited. He also developed a Latin American identity as he discovered that the people in these countries shared common values, aspirations, and sociohistorical conditions.

When Ernesto announced his travel plans to his family they were surprised to learn he planned to be away for a whole year, particularly because of his love affair with Chichina (Guevara 1995:1). When his father asked him about her, Ernesto said: "If she loves me, she'll wait." Years later, his father reflected on Ernesto's motivations for this trip in the prologue he wrote for the so-called *Motorcycle Diaries*. He said he really did not understand his son's motivations at the time and it was only many years later that he realized what truly motivated him. He wrote:

> I was puzzled. I didn't understand Ernesto. There were things about him I couldn't quite fathom. They only became clear with time. I didn't realize then that his obsession with travelling was just another part of his zeal for learning. He knew that really to understand the needs of the poor he had to travel the world, not as a tourist stopping to take pretty pictures and enjoy the scenery, but . . . by sharing the human suffering found at every bend in the road. . . . Years later, thinking back over his continuous

travelling, I realized that it had convinced him of his true destiny. (Guevara 1995:2)

His father also noted that he was fooled by the very casual manner in which his son talked about his trips, mistakenly assuming he was primarily motivated by curiosity and adventure. However, through reading his letters and later his diaries, his father realized his son "was following a true missionary impulse which never left him" and possessed a "mystical and certain knowledge of his own destiny" (Guevara 1995:3–4). The choice of the term "missionary" is somewhat misleading, since Ernesto at this stage was certainly not concerned with propagating a specific ideology or doctrine. He was very open-minded, quite secular in his thinking, and generally respectful of the cultural differences he encountered in his travels. In fact, there is very little evidence of the kind of dogmatism and ethnocentrism in his thinking that one associates with the thinking of most missionaries.

His father had to suffer in silence the fears he had for his son when he learned he was planning to take a year away from his studies to go on the incredible transcontinental odyssey he and his friend Alberto Granado had planned. According to his father:

When he told me of the journey he planned with Granado, I took him aside and said: "You've some hard times ahead. How can I advise against it when it's something I've always dreamed of myself? But remember, if you get lost in those jungles and I don't hear from you at reasonable intervals, I'll come looking for you, trace your steps, and won't come back until I find you." (Guevara 1995:3)

In response, Ernesto promised his father he would write frequently and keep him informed of his route of travel, which he faithfully did.

He and Alberto started out on their journey on January 4, 1952—midsummer in the Southern Hemisphere. They went first to the Atlantic Coast of Argentina to visit one of Ernesto's uncles in Villa Gisell and then to the beach resort city of Miramar to say good-bye to Chichina, who was vacationing there with one of her aunts. Ernesto brought with him a puppy for Chichina whom he significantly named "Come Back." He ended up staying eight days in Miramar, and Alberto was worried he was going to change his mind about going ahead with their trip.

Ernesto wrote the following in his diary about this romantic interlude at the outset of their long journey:

> The trip hung in the balance, in a cocoon, subordinate to the word which consents and ties. Alberto saw the danger and was already imagining himself alone on the highways and byways of America, but he said nothing. The tug of war was between her and me.... The two days I'd planned stretched like elastic into eight and with the bittersweet taste of goodbye mingling with my inveterate halitosis I finally felt myself wafted away on the winds of adventure. (Guevara 1995:17)

In Miramar, he tried to obtain both Chichina's promise to wait for him and her gold bracelet as a keepsake to take with him on the trip. She didn't give him either, but she did give him $15 to purchase a scarf for her in the United States (the planned end point of their journey).

Several weeks later in the Andean mountain resort of Bariloche, Ernesto found a letter from Chichina waiting for him at the local post office, where they had previously arranged he would pick up his mail. In this letter, she informed him she had decided not to wait for him. In his diary, he wrote the following about his reactions: "I read and re-read the incredible letter. Suddenly all my dreams of home, bound up with the eyes which saw me off in Miramar, were shattered, apparently for no good reason" (page 35). Although he was clearly hurt and wanted at first to write "a weepy letter," he realized it was hopeless to convince her to change her mind. He also wrote: "I thought I loved her until this moment when I realized I couldn't feel, I had to think her back again."

The next day Ernesto and Alberto crossed a mountain lake into Chile on a leaking ferry boat that they kept afloat by pumping out the bilge water in return for their free passage. On this boat they met some Chilean doctors who told them there was a leper colony on Easter Island (Rapa Nui, or Isla de Pascua), some 2,000 miles from mainland Chile in the southeastern Pacific. As Ernesto wrote in his diary: "It was a wonderful island, they said, and our scientific appetites were whetted" (page 37). They resolved to travel to the island and asked one of the doctors to give them a letter of introduction to the president of the Friends of Easter Island in Valparaíso, where they hoped they could secure passage on a ship going to the island.

With their money running low, they were forced to freeload their way through southern Chile. In the southern port city of Valdivia they dropped in on the local newspaper, which interviewed them for an article about their journey. As a result, they decided in a gesture of great magnanimity to dedicate their trip to the city since it was celebrating the 400th anniversary of its founding. At their next stop, in the picturesque central Chilean town of Temuco, they were interviewed again by the local newspaper, which was printed under the title: "Two Argentine Leprology Experts Tour South America by Motorbike" (page 40).

Ernesto's account in his diary of this article and their short stay in Temuco reveals some of the flavor of their trip at this point as well as his tongue-in-cheek view of their freeloading style of travel. He wrote:

> We had asked permission to leave the bike in the garage of a man who lived on the outskirts and we now made our way there, no longer just a pair of reasonably likeable bums with a bike in tow. No, we were now "the experts," and that's how we were treated. We spent the day fixing the bike and a little dark maid kept coming up with edible treats. At five o'clock, after a sumptuous "snack" laid on by our host, we said goodbye to Temuco and headed north. (page 40)

They didn't get very far before they noticed their back tire had a puncture that they couldn't fix. They were worried they would have to spend the night in the open, but as Ernesto recounts in his diary: "We weren't just anybody now, we were the experts; we soon found a railway worker who took us to his house where we were treated like kings" (page 41).

They fixed the tire at a garage the next day and resumed their trip, but they soon encountered more trouble. Without any warning, their motorcycle veered sideways and threw them off. The crash broke the bike's steering column and smashed its gearbox. This was the beginning of the end of La Poderosa. Although they managed to weld the steering column and fix the gearbox at a local garage, the bike was never the same again.

While they were working on the bike at this garage they bummed something to eat and drink at the homes of the curiosity seekers who dropped by to see the two famous travelers working on their motorcycle.

Their last night in Temuco they were invited by the mechanics at the garage to have drinks with them and go to a village dance, where Ernesto got drunk and caused an altercation on the dance floor. He wrote the following account of this incident in his diary:

> Chilean wine is very good and I was downing it at an amazing rate, so by the time we went on to the village dance I felt ready for anything. . . . One of the mechanics from the garage, a particularly nice guy, asked me to dance with his wife because he'd been mixing his drinks and was the worse for wear. His wife was pretty randy [feeling horny] and obviously in the mood, and I, full of Chilean wine, took her by the hand to lead her outside. She followed me docilely but then realized her husband was watching and changed her mind. I was in no state to listen to reason and we had a bit of a barney [quarrel] in the middle of the dance floor, resulting in me pulling her toward one of the doors with everybody watching. She tried to kick me and as I was pulling her she lost her balance and went crashing to the floor. (page 42)

He and Alberto had to quickly leave the scene, "pursued by a swarm of enraged dancers." Since they had now worn out the hospitality of their local hosts, they left the next day, but only after having lunch at the house of the family that lived next to the garage.

On the road north to Santiago, they had another bad spill on the motorcycle and they had to repair it once again. Shortly thereafter, the bike finally gave its last gasp going up a steep hill, and they had to hitch a lift on a truck going to the town of Los Angeles. They arranged to stay in a volunteer fire station in Los Angeles and in a few days found a truck to take them and the bike to Santiago, where they left the corpse of La Poderosa at a garage. At this point in their journey Ernesto noted they ceased being "motorized bums" and became "non-motorized bums" (page 44).

From this point forward they had to rely on their freeloading skills to hitch rides, bum meals and lodgings, work at odd jobs when they could, and panhandle their way northward to Peru. Ernesto noted in his diary their transition to this new stage in their journey:

> We were used to attracting idle attention with our strange garb and the prosaic figure of La Poderosa II, whose asthmatic wheezing aroused pity in our hosts. All the same, we had been, so to speak, gentlemen of the road. We'd belonged to a time-honored aristocracy of wayfarers, bearing our degrees as visiting cards to impress people. Not any more. Now we were just two tramps with packs on our backs, and the grime of the road encrusted in our overalls, shadows of our former aristocratic selves. (page 49)

They went from Santiago to Valparaíso only to discover there were no ships leaving from this port city to go to Easter Island for another six months.

While they were in Valparaíso they made friends with the owner of a bar named La Gioconda (the name of a famous Italian opera and another name for the Mona Lisa painting). The bar owner would not let them pay for their food or drink and even let them sleep in the kitchen. He was found of saying: "Today it's your turn, tomorrow it'll be mine" (page 51). While they were there, he asked Ernesto to visit one of his elderly customers who was suffering from asthma and a bad heart.

Ernesto's comments in his diary about this old woman reveal a great deal about his social views at this stage in his life. He observed that "the poor thing was in an awful state, breathing the smell of stale sweat and dirty feet that filled her room, mixed with the dust from a couple of armchairs," which were "the only luxuries in her house" (page 52). Such circumstances, he said, made a doctor feel powerless and long for change that would end the social injustices of the present order. He noted that in such cases "we see the profound tragedy which circumscribes the life of the proletariat [working class] the world over," since the poverty of their existence makes them at the end of their lives a bitter burden for the poor family members who have to take care of them. His concluding comments were these: "How long this present order, based on an absurd idea of caste, will last I can't say," but he added it was time for governments to spend "more money, much more money, funding socially useful projects."

From Valparaíso, Ernesto and Alberto stowed away on a boat that was headed for the northern port of Antofagasta. They were discovered after the boat was at sea and forced to do menial chores such as cleaning the latrines and the decks. However, at night the captain invited them to drink and play cards with him. When they arrived in Antofagasta they tried to stow away on another boat headed farther north, but they were caught before it sailed and put onshore. Instead, they traveled north overland through the desert by hitching rides on trucks. So it was that they ended up visiting Chile's largest copper mine at Chuquicamata.

On the way they made friends with a married couple who were mine workers and members of the Chilean Communist Party. The husband told them about his three months in prison as a result of the Chilean government's proscription of the party and persecution of its members, and about "his starving wife who followed him with exemplary loyalty, his children left in the care of a kindly neighbor, his fruitless pilgrimage in search of work and his comrades who had mysteriously disappeared and were said to be somewhere at the bottom of the sea" (page 59). According to his diary, when Ernesto and Alberto encountered the couple, they were "numb with cold, huddling together in the desert night" without "a single miserable blanket to sleep under, so we gave them one of ours and Alberto and I wrapped the other around us as best we could."

Ernesto saw them as "a living symbol of the proletariat the world over" and wrote that "it's really upsetting to think they use repressive measures against people like these," since what motivated them to join the Communist Party was "nothing more than the natural desire for a better life" and their "protest against persistent hunger." He observed that this motivation had led them to adopt Communist ideology, whose real meaning he felt they could never grasp, but when it was translated into "bread for the poor" was something that they could understand and that gave them hope for the future (page 60).

When he and Alberto visited the huge U.S.-owned, open-pit copper mine at Chuquicamata, they were offended by the condescending manner of the U.S. managers and the hazardous working conditions and poor pay of the Chilean mine workers. In his diary, he wrote: "The bosses, the blond, efficient, arrogant managers, told us in primitive Spanish: 'this isn't a tourist town. I'll get a guide to give you a half-hour tour around the mine and then please be good enough to leave, we have a lot of work to do'" (page 60). He also noted that a strike was being planned at the mine and wrote in his diary that their guide, who he called "the Yankee bosses' faithful lapdog, told us: 'Stupid gringos, they lose thousands of pesos every day in a strike so as not to give a poor worker a couple of extra centavos.'"

Ernesto noted in his diary that "Chile offers economic possibilities to anyone willing to work as long as he's not from the proletariat," since the country had enough mineral resources (copper, iron, coal, tin, gold, silver, manganese, nitrates, etc.) to make it an industrial power. However, he observed that "the main thing Chile has to do is to get its tiresome Yankee friend off its back, a Herculean task, at least for the time being, given the huge US investment and the ease with which it can bring economic pressure to bear whenever its interests are threatened" (page 71).

From Chuquicamata, Ernesto and Alberto hitchhiked to the Peruvian border. In Peru, they adopted a pattern of hitching rides on the trucks carrying people and freight between the main towns and asking if they could stay overnight in the guard stations of the Peruvian Civil Guard (the country's paramilitary national police force) or the hospitals in the towns where they stopped. As they traveled, they came in close contact with Peru's exploited and suffering Indian masses, who represent a majority of the population. They saw how the Indians of the Peruvian altiplano (high plateau) were (and still are) exploited and oppressed.

In Tarata, Peru, Ernesto wrote in his diary about how the local Peruvian Indians (the Aymarás) "are not the same proud race that time after time rose up against Inca rule and forced them to maintain a permanent army on their borders"; rather, they had become "a defeated race" since the Spanish Conquest and centuries of colonial domination. He noted that "they look at us meekly, almost fearfully, completely indifferent to the outside world," and "some give the impression that they go on living simply because it's a habit they can't give up" (page 77).

After they left Tarata, they traveled on the same truck with a schoolteacher who had been fired by the government because he was a member of the leftist APRA party (American Popular Revolutionary Alliance). He was part Indian and seemed to know a great deal about Peru's indigenous cultures and customs. He told Ernesto and Alberto about the animosity that exists between the Indians, whom he admired, and the mestizos (half-bloods), whom he considered "wily and cowardly," even though he was technically one himself. According to Ernesto: "The teacher's voice took on a strange inspired resonance whenever he spoke about his Indians . . . and it switched to deep despondency when he spoke of the Indians' present conditions, brutalized by modern civilization and the impure mestizos" (page 81).

The teacher told Ernesto and Alberto about the need to establish schools for the Indians that would teach them to "value their own world" and that would "enable them to play a useful role within it." He also spoke about "the need to change completely the present system of education," which he said "on the rare occasions it does offer Indians an education (education, that is, according to the white man's criteria), only fills them with shame and resentment, leaving them unable to help their fellow Indians and at a tremendous disadvantage in a white society which is hostile to them" (page 81).

Ernesto made frequent references in his diary to the plight of the Indians and to the injustices and discrimination they suffered at the hands of the whites and mestizos. When he and Alberto visited the magnificent Incan ruins of Machu Picchu, he also noted how the North American tourists paid little or no attention to how the Indians lived. Although he and Alberto traveled to the ruins on the third-class train used only by the local Indians, he observed: "The tourists travelling in their comfortable railcars can only have the very vaguest idea of how the Indians live, gleaned from a quick glance as they whizz by our train which has to stop to let them pass" (page 101). And he later criticized how the wealthier people in Peru expected their Indian servants "to carry anything heavy and put up with any discomfort" (page 108).

Because of their interest in leprosy, they went to Lima, the capital city of Peru, to meet Dr. Hugo Pesce, a well-known expert in leprology and a university professor. Dr. Pesce put them up in the leper hospital he ran in Lima and invited them to eat dinner at his house, which they did just about every night while they stayed in Lima. They divided their time between the leper hospital and the National Museum of the Archaeology, Anthropology, and History of Peru, which presents the history of Peru from prehistoric times to the colonial era.

Ernesto also had long conversations about philosophy, politics, and critical health issues in Latin America with Dr. Pesce, who was a disciple of the Peruvian Marxist philosopher José Carlos Mariátegui and a prominent member of the Peruvian Communist Party. Pesce had been forced into political exile during the first years of the dictatorship of General Manuel Odría (1948–1956) and was probably the first man of medicine Ernesto and Alberto had met who was genuinely living a highly principled life and totally dedicated to serving the common good (Anderson 1997:85–86).

In Lima, Ernesto and Alberto decided to give up their original objective of traveling to the United States. They chose Venezuela as their ultimate destination after first visiting Dr. Pesce's largest treatment center for lepers in Peru's Amazonian region. When they were ready to leave, the patients of the leper hospital in Lima gave them an emotional send-off party. They were very touched by the affectionate farewell the patients gave them and by the small collection of money they presented them for their trip. Ernesto wrote in his diary that "some had tears in their eyes as they thanked us for coming, spending time with them, accepting their presents, sitting listening to football [soccer] on the radio with them," and he added that "if anything were to make us seriously specialize in leprosy, it would be the affection the patients show us wherever we go" (page 123).

Somewhat later, in a letter he wrote to his father from Iquitos, Peru, he observed that "their appreciation stemmed from the fact that we didn't wear overalls or gloves, that we shook hands with them as we would the next man, sat with them chatting about this and that, and played football with them." He added: "This may seem pointless bravado, but the psychological benefit to these people—usually treated like animals—of being treated as normal human beings is incalculable and the risk incredibly remote" (page 132).

Their destination when they set out from Lima was the San Pablo leper colony situated on the banks of the Amazon River. They hitchhiked from Lima to Pucallpa and then took a boat down the Ucayali River (one of the headwaters of the Amazon) to Iquitos. From Iquitos they took another boat down the Amazon to the San Pablo leper colony. Once there, they volunteered to work in the leprosarium's laboratory and endeared themselves to both the staff and the patients. They played soccer with the patients, took them on hikes, and even led them on hunting expeditions.

While they were at the colony, Ernesto turned 24 and the staff threw a birthday party for him. After he was given a touching toast by the director of the colony, Ernesto replied to the toast as expected under such circumstances. An excerpt from his account of this speech is worth quoting since it reveals his newfound Latin American identity and also what would become one of his deepest political convictions:

> In a few days we will be leaving Peru, so these words are also a farewell, and I'd like to stress my gratitude to all the people of this country, who over and over again since we arrived ... have shown us the warmth of their hospitality. And I would like to add another thought, nothing to do with this toast. Although we're too insignificant to be spokesmen for such a noble cause, we believe, and this journey has only served to confirm this belief, that the division of America into unstable and illusory nations is a complete fiction. We are one single mestizo race with remarkable ethnographical similarities, from Mexico down to the Magellan Straits. And so, in an attempt to break free from all narrow-minded provincialism, I propose a toast to Peru and to a United America. (page 135)

The speech received loud applause, and one can see in it the stirrings of his political oratory skills as well as his ultimate political mission—the political unification of Latin America.

When it came time for Ernesto and Alberto to leave, some of the patients gave them a very emotional farewell serenade, with a blind man singing local songs and a man with virtually no fingers playing an accordion. Alberto thanked them and said they were both deeply touched. The next day, Ernesto and Alberto went to see the patients and after taking some photographs with them came back with two large pineapples. After saying their final good-byes they cast off in a raft, named Mambo-Tango, built for them by one of the staff members so they could go down the river to Leticia, Colombia, where the borders of Colombia, Peru, and Brazil meet on the upper Amazon.

In Leticia, they got 50 percent off on the weekly flight to Bogotá and made some money coaching and playing for the town's soccer team. When they arrived in Bogotá they obtained permission to stay at a hospital where they were offered jobs in the leprosy service. However, they had a run-in with the local police over a knife Ernesto carried with him that was a present from his brother Roberto. They were harassed so badly by the police they decided to leave for Venezuela as soon as possible.

In reference to this encounter with the Colombian police in a letter Ernesto wrote to his mother from Bogotá, he observed: "There is more repression of individual freedom here than in any country we've been to, the police patrol the streets carrying rifles and demand your papers every few minutes, which some of them read upside down" (page 144). He also wrote that "the countryside is in open revolt and the army is powerless to put it down." Because of this situation, he said: "We're getting out of here as soon as we can." A few days later, the two harassed travelers left Bogotá on a bus headed for Venezuela.

They made their way to Caracas, the capital of Venezuela. Alberto looked up a doctor who was a specialist in leprology. Impressed by Alberto's interest in leprosy, the doctor offered him a position in his laboratory. At about the same time, Ernesto ran into an uncle who had an airplane that he used to transport race horses between Buenos Aires and Miami. The uncle told Ernesto that he could return with him to Buenos Aires if he wanted to resume his studies at medical school. Ernesto and Alberto made a pact: Alberto would accept the job offered him and stay in Venezuela, while Ernesto would go back to Buenos Aires to graduate from medical school and then return to Venezuela to work with Alberto. It was the end of July 1952 when they said good-bye in Caracas.

In one of the last entries in his diary, Ernesto commented on how much he missed Alberto. He said: "I'm always turning around to tell him something and then I realize he's not there." And he added: "All these months we've been together through thick and thin and the habit of dreaming the same dreams in similar situations has made us even closer." On the other hand, the same entry makes it clear he was looking forward to "going home to start my studies again and finally getting the degree which will enable me to practice [medicine]" (page 148).

When Ernesto left Caracas, the plane he took went to Miami, where it was scheduled to stop before returning to Buenos Aires. However, when they got to Miami the plane had mechanical problems, so it had to be repaired before it could leave for Buenos Aires. Ernesto took advantage of this opportunity to get to know the city (pages 153–54). As it turned out, he had to wait a whole month for the plane to be repaired. He had no money, but he was able to stay in a small hotel by promising to pay the bill from Buenos Aires as soon as he returned, which he did. During the month that he stayed in Miami, Ernesto visited the beaches and hung around with an Argentine student he met, who helped him find a job as a dishwasher in one of Miami's restaurants. When the plane was repaired, he flew back to Buenos Aires. It was September 1952.

In the prologue he wrote for Ernesto's *The Motorcycle Diaries*, his father says we can see in this written account of Ernesto's eight-month journey that he "had faith in himself as well as the will to succeed, and a tremendous determination to achieve what he set out to do" (page 4). He also recounts the observations made about Ernesto by a priest, Father Cuchetti, a friend of the family who was well known in Argentina for his liberal views. When he told him about Ernesto and Alberto's trip to the Amazon and their stay in the San Pablo leper colony, the priest said the following: "I take my hat off to your son and his friend's humanity and integrity, because to do what [they did] takes more than just guts: you need a will of iron and an enormously compassionate and charitable soul. Your son will go far" (page 2).

The Motorcycle Diaries reveal Ernesto's growing political consciousness and his early leanings toward socialism as he learned firsthand during his travels of the extreme conditions of social injustice and oppression that prevail throughout Latin America. However, what is most striking about *The Motorcycle Diaries* is that while they reveal he had a strong desire to help others less fortunate than himself, he did not possess the kind of self-righteousness or exaggerated piety that one often associates with zealous do-gooders and missionaries.

The legendary actor, producer, and director Robert Redford produced a popular film version of *The Motorcycle Diaries*, which was directed by the well-known Brazilian film director Walter Salles. The film was shown in cinemas around the world during 2004 and 2005. It provides a moving account of Ernesto's journey with his friend Alberto Granado throughout Latin America. It stars the popular Mexican actor Gael García Bernal as the young Ernesto, while Alberto is played by the Argentine actor Rodrigo de la Serna, who is related to Ernesto "Che" Guevara through his mother's side of the family. After making the film, García Bernal reportedly said: "He's a person that changed the world and he has really forced me to change the rules of what I am" (Osborne 2003).

Redford traveled to Havana to obtain permission to make the film from Che's widow, Aleida March, who maintains an archive of all his writings, official papers, and information written about him. When the production of the film was completed, Redford returned to Cuba to host a special screening, which was attended by Aleida, 84-year-old Alberto Granado, Che's sons and daughters, his former comrades, and people who had worked closely with him during the early years of the Cuban revolution. According to Redford, the film was well received by this audience, and he said later: "I could have probably died there in the seat. When I heard people sniffing and crying and I thought either they're so upset with me I'm not gonna get out of here, or they liked the film, which they did" (Smiley 2004).

The film was generally well received by critics and won various awards, including one Oscar. It was not widely distributed in the United States and earned only some $16 million in the United States, while it earned over $40 million at cinemas in other parts of the world. Gael García Bernal criticized the poor distribution of the film in the United States. According to the Internet Movie Database (IMDb), García Bernal told an interviewer for the *Detroit Free Press* that the Hollywood studio system relegates pictures like *The Motorcycle Diaries* to limited screenings in art film theatres. As a result, most people in the United States never even consider seeing them and they do not get the chance to compete with the well-funded, mainstream Hollywood films. He said: "They get tossed off as foreign and independent films like they are somehow not ready to compete with all that crap that Hollywood produces." Nevertheless, the film is available in DVD format and can be purchased or rented.

As his diaries and the film reveals, Ernesto learned a great deal about Latin America and himself through his travels. As a young man wandering around South America, he learned to take pleasure in traveling for days on end with little or no money, without the possibility of taking a bath and changing his clothes, and not even knowing when he would eat next or where he would stay the night. The knowledge he gained from this experience of surviving on his own wits and the personal traits he developed as a result of traveling from day to day in this manner helped prepare him for the life he would lead much later as a guerrilla fighter, when he often had to survive without food, water, bathing, or adequate clothing.

Chapter 3

A CALL TO ARMS IN GUATEMALA AND MEXICO

After he returned to Argentina, Ernesto undertook the remaining courses and exams to complete the requirements for his graduation from medical school. He met all the remaining requirements in less than a year and obtained his medical degree in March 1953. He still wanted to join Alberto Granado in Caracas as they had planned at the end of their trip together in July 1952, and he wanted at some point to visit Europe and maybe Asia. He did not want to settle down to a comfortable bourgeois life as a well-paid doctor in Argentina. Thus, at 25 years old with his medical degree in hand, Ernesto decided to set out on his second Latin American odyssey.

As his old friend Alberto Granado states in the foreword to the published version, *Back on the Road* (*Otra Vez*), of the diary Ernesto kept during this trip (Guevara 2001:vii):

> Whereas his first trip in South America served to deepen his ideas about social distinctions and made him see the importance of struggling against them, this second journey consolidates the political knowledge he has acquired and fuels a growing need for further

study to grasp why and how a struggle must be waged that will culminate in a genuine revolution.

His old friend is absolutely correct when he observes that while Ernesto is still motivated by a desire for travel and the study of archeology (particularly the Incan, Mayan, and Aztec civilizations), his political views were increasingly radicalized by the political, economic, and social conditions he witnessed in the countries he visited, especially Guatemala.

On this trip he is accompanied by another childhood friend, Carlos "Calica" Ferrer, whose political awareness, interests, and temperament are less compatible with those of Ernesto than were those of Alberto. While he starts the trip with a vague plan to join Alberto in Caracas and has some notion of later traveling to Europe and maybe Asia, he changes his travel plans in Ecuador, goes from there to Guatemala, and ends up in Mexico two years later. As Ricardo Gott notes in the introduction to Ernesto's diary of this trip (Guevara 2001:xv), the experiences he has in this lengthy journey change him from "a detached and cynical observer" to "a fully fledged revolutionary, seeking a theoretical framework through which to understand the world, and ardent in his desire to take immediate action to change it."

On July 7, 1953, Ernesto and Calica set out on the first leg of their journey—the 1,600-mile train trip from Buenos Aires to La Paz, Bolivia. As Ricardo Gott writes in *Back on the Road* (Guevara 2001:xiii): "His mother and father would not see him again for another six years," and "by that time their itinerate son had become famous throughout the world as 'Che' Guevara, the guerrilla fighter who had fought alongside Fidel Castro to bring revolutionary change to Cuba." And it would be another eight years (in 1961) before he would visit his homeland again, as one of the most important leaders of the new revolutionary government of Cuba. His outlook at the start of the trip is that of a Latin American (not just an Argentine), but by the time he visits Argentina again in 1961 it is that of a revolutionary internationalist.

Ernesto and Calica crossed from northern Argentina into southern Bolivia at La Quiaca, not far from where Ernesto would some 13 years later establish a base of operations for the revolutionary guerrilla movement he hoped would liberate the entire continent of South America.

A CALL TO ARMS IN GUATEMALA AND MEXICO

From La Quiaca, Ernesto and Calica traveled by rail to La Paz. They arrived in the Bolivian capital just a year after the country had undergone a dramatic popular revolution in which the major foreign-owned mines had been nationalized and the peasants had taken possession of the feudal estates on which they had formerly labored as unpaid serfs and tenant farmers. Thus, Ernesto found La Paz filled with revolutionary political fervor and excitement. In his diary, he wrote:

> The widest range of adventurers of all nationalities vegetate and prosper in the midst of a colorful mestiza city that is leading the country to its destiny. The "well-to-do" refined people are shocked at what has been happening and complain bitterly about the new importance conferred on Indians and mestizos, but in all of them I thought I could detect a spark of nationalist enthusiasm for some of what the government has done. (pages 4–5)

Soon after their arrival in La Paz, they met a group of Argentine exiles who had been forced to leave Argentina because of their opposition to the Perón regime. One of these exiles was a young lawyer named Ricardo Rojo. They meet again in Lima, Peru, and Ecuador and then again in Guatemala. Years later, Rojo wrote about his friendship with Ernesto and the experiences they had together in Latin America (Rojo 1968). Rojo recalls that when he met Ernesto in La Paz, he was living in a miserable rented room in one of the oldest parts of the city. Ernesto was spending most of his time visiting ancient Incan ruins or passing the day in the noisy cafés along the capital's main boulevard, Avenida 16 de Julio. From these cafés, Ernesto, Ricardo, and Calica were able to look out on the broad and sunny boulevard and watch the continuous parade of the Bolivian people as they stopped to look at the large signs propagandizing the revolutionary goals of the new regime.

On the basis of what he saw and learned while he was there, Ernesto developed a pessimistic view of the fate of the Bolivian revolution. He regarded the new regime as merely reformist and not truly revolutionary. On one occasion, Ernesto visited the Ministry of Peasant Affairs, where he saw long lines of peasants waiting to be given an audience. They were being methodically sprayed with DDT to rid them of lice.

As he saw things, this situation reflected the fact that the new government's leaders were not solving the root causes of Bolivia's problems. They were merely trying to ameliorate the effects of these problems and calm the country's discontented masses. Thus, in the case of the peasants, the government was spraying them to rid them of lice rather than pursuing policies that would genuinely improve the social and economic conditions that were the cause of their poverty and their lack of proper hygiene.

At this point in his political development, Ernesto was neither a Marxist nor a revolutionary. He was definitely a political nonconformist with a keen sense of social justice, but these traits had not yet led him to espouse any particular political cause or ideology. Rojo recalls that, when they first met, Ernesto was uncertain about what he wanted to do with his life, although he was very sure about what he did not want to do with it. According to Rojo, Ernesto demanded that his traveling companions be willing to walk interminably, be devoid of any concern for the condition of their clothing, and accept without anguish the state of being absolutely without money.

In September 1953, Ernesto and Calica left Bolivia for Peru. They went to visit Machu Picchu, the lost city of the Incas, and Cuzco, both of which Ernesto wanted to revisit. He noted in his diary that he missed Alberto. He wrote: "Despite Calica's enthusiasm for this place, I still miss Alberto's company," and, he added, "the way in which our characters were so suited to each other is becoming more obvious to me here in Machu-Picchu" (page 13). They went to Lima, where they visited Dr. Pesce and the people at the leprosarium, who received them very cordially.

They bumped into Rojo in Lima and made plans to meet up again in Guayaquil, Ecuador. While in Lima, Ernesto wrote his leftist friend from medical school in Buenos Aires, Tita Infante, an interesting letter on September 3, 1953, in which he described his visit to Bolivia. He wrote: "Bolivia is a country that has given a major example to the American continent," and "the fighting still goes on, and almost every night people are wounded by gunfire on one side or the other. But the government is supported by the armed people, so there is no possibility of liquidating an armed movement from outside; it can succumb only as a result of internal dissensions" (page 17).

As Richard Gott notes: "Guevara was intrigued by what he saw [in Bolivia], but he was far from impressed by the caliber of Bolivia's revolutionary leadership" and "he guessed rightly that this was not a revolution that would challenge the hegemony of the United States in Latin America" (page xvi). Gott also points out that in Ernesto's letter to Tita Infante (who had been a member of the Young Communists in their medical school in Buenos Aires) Ernesto reveals that his interest in the possibility of revolutionary change has been sparked by the revolution in Bolivia, but on the other hand he is also disappointed by what he has seen and is aware of the signs of corruption and internal conflicts within the leadership of the Bolivian government (page xvii).

When they arrived in Ecuador's port city of Guayaquil, Ernesto and Calica met up with Rojo, who was accompanied by three leftist Argentine law students. Rojo took Ernesto and Calica to the boardinghouse where they were staying, and according to Ernesto's diary the six of them formed a "student circle" and drank their last supply of maté. Rojo and his friends showed enthusiasm for the revolutionary government in Guatemala, which they said was more radical than anything they had witnessed in Bolivia. One of these students, Eduardo "Gualo" García, jokingly suggested that Ernesto and Calica should go with him to Guatemala to see for themselves what kind of revolution was taking place there.

Ernesto wrote in his diary: "The idea [of going to Guatemala] was lying there somewhere, it only needed that little push for me to make up my mind." Initially, Calica was planning to go with Ernesto to Guatemala by way of Panama, but after they started having problems obtaining visas for traveling by ship from Guayaquil to Panama, Calica took off for Quito, the capital of Ecuador, to wait for Ernesto there. Meanwhile, Ernesto, Gualo García, and one of the other Argentine students stayed in Guayaquil trying to arrange passage on a ship bound for Panama and obtain their visas from the Panamanian consulate. After much difficulty, they succeeded, Ernesto having to sell most of the items in his luggage to pay for his passage and his visa. By this time, Rojo and the other Argentine student had already left for Panama by air and Calica had left Quito for Colombia.

Ernesto and Gualo didn't reach Guatemala until the end of December 1953, having spent a number of weeks on the way there in Panama and Costa Rica, where Ernesto met Juan Bosch, the famous revolutionary nationalist leader of the Dominican Republic; the exiled Venezuelan political leader Rómulo Betancourt; and the Costa Rican Communist leader Manuel Mora Valverde. Along the way, they hitchhiked, took trains, walked, and bummed passage on a boat nicknamed the *Pachuca* (because it transported *pachucos*, or down-and-outs). When they stopped in the Costa Rican port of Golfito, which at the time belonged to the American-owned United Fruit Company, Ernesto noted in his diary: "The town is divided into clearly defined zones, with guards who can prevent anyone from moving across, and of course the best zone is for the gringos" (page 29). He also noted that in the hospital "the degree of comfort depends on the grade of the person working in the company" and "as always, the class spirit of the gringos makes itself felt."

After his discussion of Costa Rican politics with the Communist leader Mora Valverde, he wrote the following comments in his diary about the influence of the United Fruit Company and the U.S. government on the country's politics:

> Calderón Guardia [the former president of Costa Rica] is a rich man who came to power with the support of United Fruit and local landowners. He ruled for two years until the Second World War, when Cost Rica sided with the Allied powers. The first measure taken by the [U.S.] State Department was to demand the confiscation of lands in the hands of German owners, especially if coffee was grown on it. This was done, and the subsequent selling of the land led to obscure deals involving some of Calderón Guardia's ministers—deals which lost him the support of the country's landowners, but not of United Fruit. Those who work for the company are anti-Yankee, as a reaction against its exploitation. (page 31)

He also noted that the Costa Rican chief of police was "a Cuban colonel and FBI [Federal Bureau of Investigation] agent imposed by the United States."

With reference to José Figueres Ferrer, the three-time Costa Rican president, who was educated in the United States and backed by the U.S. government, Ernesto wrote: "In Mora's view, Figueres has a number of good ideas, but because they lack any scientific basis he keeps going astray. He divides the United States into two: the State Department (very just) and the capitalist trusts (the dangerous octopuses). Ernesto added a series of questions: 'What will happen when Figueres sees the light and stops having any illusions about the goodness of the United States? Will he fight or give up? This is the dilemma. We shall see'" (page 34).

As Ernesto and Gualo were hitchhiking in Costa Rica, a car with Boston University license plate holders stopped to pick them up. In the car were Rojo and two friends from Argentina who were on their way to Guatemala, where they planned to sell the car. After several minor incidents crossing borders, lots of tire punctures, difficulties from lack of money, and sleeping outdoors, they finally arrived in Guatemala City. They found lodgings in a boardinghouse where they didn't have to pay in advance since they had run out of money. They celebrated Christmas Eve at the house of a Guatemalan agronomist married to an Argentine woman, and Ernesto spent the next week suffering from an asthma attack that lasted until New Year's Eve.

Rojo introduced Ernesto and Gualo García to a Peruvian exile, Hilda Gadea (Ernesto's future wife), and asked her if she could help the two find a place to stay. Hilda had received political asylum in Guatemala and was working as an economist for the Guatemalan government. She was a militant member of Peru's leftist political party APRA (American Popular Revolutionary Alliance), and she had been forced to flee Peru because the dictatorial regime of General Manuel Odría had outlawed her party and persecuted its members. She was one of a group of Peruvians who had been offered political asylum and employment by the Guatemalan government. At this point, Guatemala was a refuge for leftist political exiles from all over Latin America.

Hilda's description of their first meeting is as follows:

> Guevara and [Gualo] García were both in their mid-twenties, thin, and taller than the average Latin American. Guevara had dark brown hair, framing a pale face and fair features that emphasized his striking black eyes. Both were good-natured and easy-going, and Guevara had a commanding voice but a fragile appearance. His movements were quick and agile, but he gave the impression of always being relaxed. I noticed his intelligent and penetrating look and the preciseness of his comments. (Gadea 2008:24)

Hilda also noted they were dressed in casual clothes and looked more like students than professional men, but as she talked with them she realized they were well educated. Nevertheless, her first impression of Ernesto was on balance negative since he seemed to her to be "superficial, egotistical and conceited." A few days later, she learned that his behavior when they first met was influenced by the fact that he did not like asking favors and he was suffering from an asthma attack. This information changed her opinion of him, and she "felt a special concern for him because of his condition."

Through Hilda and her friends in Guatemala City, Ernesto was introduced to a large circle of politically and intellectually interesting people. Some of them were Guatemalans who were government officials or political activists and some were members of the different Latin American political exile groups who were then living in Guatemala. Hilda and Ernesto soon became close friends and confidants. He told her about his original plan to join his friend Alberto Granado in Caracas but said that he had changed his mind about joining Alberto after he visited Bolivia because he wanted to learn more about revolutionary political conditions in Latin America, particularly the radical reforms being undertaken by the current government in Guatemala. (It is important to note here that his trip to Bolivia in 1953 changed his destiny and set him on a path that would ultimately return him to this country 13 years later to meet his death there in 1967.)

He also told Hilda about his childhood friends and his girlfriend Chichina Ferreyra in Córdoba, whom he said he had loved but could never marry because he could not live a bourgeois life in a provincial city of Argentina. He told Hilda about his family, and she was impressed by the fact that when he spoke of his family it was always with great warmth and affection. She noted "his tie with his mother was very deep." He told her in humorous terms that "the old lady liked to go around with a bunch of intellectual women" and "they may turn out to be lesbians," but she said he always spoke with "a tone of admiration and deep affection for the old lady," a term that he explained the Argentines commonly used for their mothers. Ernesto's love for his family, she said, made her appreciate his humanity since he was always "generous and tender" toward them despite the frequent cynicism and irony he used to describe them and himself (Gadea 2008:41). He also impressed her with his ideas about the proper role of doctors in Latin America, who he felt "should not be pampered professionals, taking care of only the privileged classes," but should instead dedicate their knowledge and skills to ending the malnutrition and the illnesses associated with the extreme poverty and filth in which the majority of the population of the region lived.

Among the various political exiles Ernesto met through Hilda were a group of Cubans who had been involved in the unsuccessful assault led by Fidel Castro on the Moncada military barracks in Santiago de Cuba on July 26, 1953. Both Hilda and Ernesto respected the Cuban exiles for their honest simplicity and the strength of their convictions. They were especially impressed by Antonio "Ñico" López. As Hilda later wrote, these Cubans "had hardly any political indoctrination—almost all of them were workers—yet they boasted the short but outstanding accomplishment of the Moncada attack." She said Ñico stood out not only on account of his tall and slender figure but also because of his deep conviction that "one had to make a revolution, and that in Cuba this revolution was going to be made by Fidel" (Gadea 2008:30). In fact, he told her: "Fidel is the greatest and most honest man born in Cuba since Martí [José Martí, famous leader of Cuba's struggle for independence from Spain]. He will make the revolution." As Hilda noted, political history subsequently proved Ñico right.

That Ñico and his comrades had taken part in the well-known attack on the Moncada army barracks gave them a special respected position among the other exiles, and they won Ernesto's admiration too. In his diary, Ernesto wrote that he felt small when he heard the Cubans making "grand assertions with total calmness" about making a revolution in their country. And after going to a political meeting with them where they had each taken turns speaking at the microphone, he wrote: "I can make a speech ten times more objective and without banalities: I can do it better and I can convince the public that I am saying something true. But I don't convince myself, whereas the Cubans do. Ñico left his heart and soul in the microphone and for that reason fired even a skeptic like myself with enthusiasm" (Guevara 2001:45).

Also in Hilda's circle of friends and acquaintances was a North American professor named Harold White. He had written a book on Marxism and was looking for someone who could help him translate it into Spanish. White asked Hilda to help him, but because she knew Ernesto needed some money to pay his bills, she convinced White to hire him. In reality, they translated the book together since she knew more English than Ernesto and he knew more about Marxism than she did (Gadea 2008:53–54).

Ernesto wrote in his dairy that through Hilda he had met a "strange gringo [North American] who writes stuff about Marxism and has it translated into Spanish" (Guevara 2001:38). He noted that he had made $25 helping him and that he was "giving English-Spanish lessons to the gringo." As the days passed, the three of them became close friends, and Hilda later wrote that White had a great deal of influence on Ernesto's thinking during this period. In her book about their life together, she wrote: "The three of us began going on Sunday picnics, during which time it became the custom to have long discussions between Ernesto, with his crude English, and White on subjects that ranged from the international situation to Marxism, Lenin, Engels, Stalin, Freud, science in the Soviet Union, and Pavlov's conditioned reflexes" (Gadea 2008:54). As their friendship developed, Ernesto told her: "This is a good gringo. He is tired of capitalism and wants to lead a new life." By this time he had developed a strong dislike for most of the gringos he had encountered and the United States' role in Latin America and the world, but Ernesto's friendship with White reveals that he was not prejudiced against all North Americans. In fact, several years later, after Che had become an important member of the new revolutionary government in Cuba, he invited White to come to Cuba, and White lived there until his death in 1968 (Guevara 2001:38).

In fact, according to Hilda their friendship with White "developed so well that at one point he, with his North American practicality, suggested that we should rent a house where the three of us could live, and very generously offered to pay the rent." Hilda said: "Ernesto was also enthusiastic about the idea [since] this would solve his lodging problem." However, Hilda didn't "share their enthusiasm because it would mean taking care of a house," and since she was working and involved in political activities she wanted to use her spare time to study rather than do housekeeping. In an effort to convince her to accept White's offer, Ernesto promised Hilda he would not make any advances toward her if the three of them lived together in the same house. At this point they were not yet lovers. Ernesto had hinted he was romantically interested in her, but she had not encouraged him.

In the book she wrote about her life with Ernesto, Hilda recounts a particular outing when they went with White to a picturesque town that was a considerable distance from Guatemala City. When they were ready to return to the city they found that because a religious celebration was being held in the town all the buses going back to the city were filled. White suggested they should stay overnight in a local hotel until the next day, but Hilda protested and Ernesto promised he would find some way for her to return to the city, which he did. She said this gesture heightened her opinion of him and made her remember he had warned her at the beginning of their friendship about how men often lie to women. He had noticed that one of her Peruvian friends was constantly flirting with her, so he took her aside and told her: "Be careful, he is married; you know men always lie" (Gadea 2008:55).

At the end of February 1954, Ricardo Rojo and Gualo García decided to leave Guatemala, but Ernesto chose to remain in Guatemala City because of his interest in Hilda and the revolutionary programs of the Guatemalan regime. During this period, Ernesto had almost no money and great difficulty paying for food and lodging since he couldn't find a job and had no income. He tried to obtain employment as a doctor in one of the government's public health programs. In particular, he was interested in working with a program that was being carried out among the indigenous (Indian) population in the remote El Petén region of Guatemala. One of the reasons he was interested in working in this area was his desire to explore the ancient Mayan ruins there. However, he was frustrated by the Ministry of Health not validating his medical credentials unless he took another year of medical studies in Guatemala. He also had difficulty getting a job because he was not officially a political exile, did not have a residence visa, had no affiliation with any of the political parties and organizations that were allied with the Guatemalan government, and was frequently confined to bed for days at a time because of his debilitating asthma attacks.

At one point, Hilda remembers he was offered a position in the government's department of statistics as a result of her introducing him to one of her friends, Herbert Zeissig, who was an influential member of the Guatemalan Communist Party, which had a number of members working in the department. She recalls that everything went fine until she informed Ernesto that Zeissig had told her that he would have to join the party if he wanted the job (Anderson:138). According to Hilda, Ernesto responded angrily that she should tell Zeissig "when I want to join the party I will do so on my own initiative, not out of any ulterior motive." She admired his reaction because even though he needed the job to survive he was incapable of doing anything that was contrary to his moral principles even if it hurt his own personal interests. He did not get the job, and he later told her: "It's not that I disagree with the Communist ideology, it's the method I don't like. They shouldn't get members this way. It's all false" (Gadea:62–63).

In mid-March 1954, Ernesto asked Hilda to be his girlfriend and suggested that later on they might get married. He said that if it was up to him, he would like to get married immediately. He gave her a handwritten poem that was a formal proposal of marriage. Hilda told him that she "also loved him, but not enough to marry him just yet," since the most important thing for her at that time was the political struggle in Guatemala and in her own country. In her book about her life with Che, she wrote: "The decision of marriage was a very difficult one for me; first, I had to accomplish something for society, and to do that I had to be free. He answered that those were *Aprista* [member of the APRA party] prejudices, and that it was wrong to think that political activists shouldn't marry, when in effect it was a path of greater fulfillment. He referred to Marx and Lenin, saying that marriage had not impeded them in their struggle. On the contrary, their wives supported them" (Gadea 2008:65–66). According to Hilda, Ernesto's poem was "beautiful and forceful." In it he told her "he did not desire beauty alone but, more than that, a comrade." While she did not accept his proposal for marriage at this point, they did become lovers.

Having failed to secure regular employment, apart from the occasional translating he did for Harold White, near the end of March Ernesto joined Ñico and the other Cubans selling small items door-to-door in the provinces. He also moved into the boardinghouse that the government had established for the Cuban exiles, but within a short time Ñico and most of the Cuban exiles left for Mexico City. Since he no longer could stay in the boardinghouse, Hilda arranged for him to stay in the house of their mutual friend Helena de Holst, a political exile from Honduras who was married to a German businessman. She had a great deal of knowledge about Marxism, had visited both the Soviet Union and

China, and treated Ernesto almost like a son. Helena offered to let him stay in her home without any compensation, but he gracefully refused the offer. Instead, he took his sleeping bag and started sleeping on the grounds of a nearby country club. Every morning he would come to the boardinghouse where Hilda lived to ask for hot water to make his maté. The landlady and Hilda always kept fresh fruit for him to eat, since he would not accept anything else. In the evenings he would usually return and eat only fruit or a salad, which was the strict diet he followed to avoid asthma attacks. About this time, he was offered employment as an intern in a teacher-training center run by the Ministry of Education, but he had to leave the country to renew his visa so that he could work legally in Guatemala (Gadea:67–70).

In a letter he wrote to his mother in April 1954 (Guevara 2001:61), he told her about his trip to neighboring El Salvador to obtain the visa that he needed to work in Guatemala. He wrote: "I went with a rucksack and a briefcase, half walking, half hitching, half (shame!) paying for shelter out of the $10 that the [Guatemalan] government itself had given me. I reached El Salvador and the police confiscated some books I had bought in Guatemala, but I got through, obtained a visa (the right one this time) to enter Guatemala again, and went off to see the ruins left behind by some Mexicans, a branch of Tlascaltecas, who once came south to conquer from their center in Mexico." He noted that these ruins "are in no way comparable to the Mayan structures, still less the Incan." He also said he tried to visit Honduras, but he wrote:

> The Hondurans refused me a visa just because I had residence in Guatemala, although I hardly need to tell you of my good intention to see something of a strike that has broken out there [in Honduras] and is supported by 25 percent of the whole working population (a high figure anywhere, but especially in a country where there is no right to strike and only underground trade unions). The fruit company [United Fruit Company] is in a fury, and of course [U.S. secretary of state John Foster] Dulles and the CIA [Central Intelligence Agency] want to intervene in Guatemala because of its terrible crime in buying weapons from wherever it wishes (the United States has not sold it a single cartridge for some time now).

Here we see the first mention in his writing of the confrontation that was brewing between the governments of the United States and Guatemala.

Finally, near the end of this letter to his mother he mentioned his relationship with Hilda. He wrote: "I drink maté when there is any, and I engage in endless discussions with the comrade Hilda Gadea, an *Aprista*, whom I try to persuade in my gentle way to leave that dump of a party. She has a heart of platinum, at least. Her help is felt in everything to do with my daily life" (page 61).

In a letter to his mother a month later, in May 1954, he wrote something quite revealing about his thoughts at the time. He said: "I could become very rich in Guatemala, but by the low method of ratifying my title [medical degree], opening a clinic and specializing in allergies (it's full of telltale colleagues here). To do that would be the most horrible betrayal of the two I's struggling inside me: the socialist and the traveler" (page 61). Here we see that he has no ambition to become a well-off physician and is increasingly developing an identity as a socialist, but he has not given up his desire to spend his foreseeable future as an adventurous traveler.

However, in June, the turn of events in Guatemala changed everything in his life and his plans. In his diary he wrote:

> A few days ago, some aircraft from Honduras crossed the border with Guatemala and flew over the city in broad daylight, machine-gunning people and military objectives. I enlisted in the health brigades to help on the medical side and in the youth brigades that patrol the streets by night. The course of events was [as] follows. After the aircraft had passed, troops under the command of Colonel Castillo Armas, a Guatemalan émigré in Honduras, crossed the frontier at several points and advanced on the town of Chiquimula. . . . The invaders thought that if they just gave a shout, the whole people would come out and follow them—and for this purpose they parachuted in weapons. But in fact the people immediately rallied under the command of Arbenz [the president]. The invading troops were checked and defeated on all fronts and driven back past Chiquimula, near the Honduran frontier. [But] pirate aircraft flying from bases in Honduras

and Nicaragua continued to machine-gun the fronts and towns. (pages 62–63)

In the letter he wrote his mother on June 20, 1954, he gave her a similar account of these events and again wrote something about his own reaction to these events. He said: "The incident served to unite all Guatemalans behind the government and all those who, like myself, came here attracted by the country." He explained the situation as follows:

> The danger does not come from the small number of troops that have entered the country so far, nor from the warplanes that have bombed civilian homes and machine-gunned a number of people; the danger lies in how the gringos (the Yankees) are manipulating their stooges in the United Nations, since even a vague declaration would be of great help to the attackers. The Yankees have fully dropped the good-guy mask that [President Franklin D.] Roosevelt gave them and are now committing outrages in these parts. If things reach the point where it is necessary to fight planes and modern troops sent by the fruit company or the USA, than that is what will be done. The people's spirits are very high, and the shameless attacks, together with the lies of the international press, have united behind the government all those who used to be politically indifferent. (page 63)

Then almost insignificantly he added: "I myself have been assigned to emergency medical service and have also enrolled in the youth brigades to receive military instruction for any eventuality."

However, only a few days later Ernesto wrote in his diary: "A terrible cold shower has fallen on all those who admire Guatemala. On the night of Sunday, 27 June, President Árbenz announced that he was resigning. He publicly denounced the fruit company and the United States as being directly behind all the bombing and strafing of the civilian population." Ernesto added: "Arbenz resigned under pressure from a North American military mission that was threatening massive bombing and a declaration of war by Honduras and Nicaragua provoking United States intervention." And with regard to how this turn of events had affected him, he wrote that he expected to be expelled the next day from the small hospital where he had been working, and that "repression is coming." He also noted that "Hilda has changed her address.... The top people in the Guatemalan [Communist] party are seeking asylum [and] Castillo will enter the city tomorrow."

How did this turn of events come to pass? Before 1944, Guatemala had been just another banana republic ruled by a series of dictators who served the interests of the local landed oligarchy and the United Fruit Company—the American-owned banana company that controlled vast landholdings, railways, and ports in Central America, the Caribbean, Colombia, and Ecuador (Schlesinger and Kinzer 1982). But in 1944 the ruling strongman, the dictator Jorge Ubico, was overthrown by a popular revolt led by junior army officers and students. On the surface, the revolt appeared to be aimed primarily at discarding Ubico's oppressive regime in favor of more democratic rule. But in reality, the groups who participated in the revolt demanded the complete reform of Guatemala's exploitative and highly unequal economic and social order.

Following the overthrow of the Ubico regime, elections were held and Juan José Arévalo became Guatemala's first popularly elected president. Under Arévalo's rule a major effort was made to bring Guatemala's majority Indian population into the 20th century and a large number of rural and urban workers were unionized. The revolutionary policies of Arévalo's government were continued and in fact accelerated by his successor, Colonel Jacobo Arbenz, who was democratically elected to the presidency in 1951. By the time Ernesto arrived in Guatemala, in late 1953, the Arbenz regime had distributed thousands of hectares of uncultivated land to over 100,000 landless peasants. This land was expropriated by the government from the country's large landed estates, and included 11,000 hectares of uncultivated land that belonged to the powerful United Fruit Company, which even distributed mail in Guatemala. The response from the U.S. government was almost immediate. The U.S. secretary of state at the time, John Foster Dulles, had close ties to the United Fruit Company, since his law firm had represented the company. Moreover, his brother Allen Dulles was the director of the CIA, and John Moors Cabot, who was in charge of Inter-American Affairs in the State Department, had a brother who was the former president of the United Fruit Company.

At the March 1954 foreign ministers' meeting of the Organization of American States (OAS), U.S. Secretary of State Dulles accused the Arbenz regime of being "Communist-infiltrated" and claimed Arbenz intended to align Guatemala with the Soviet bloc (Schlesinger and Kinzer 1982). He succeeded in having the OAS pass the famous Resolution 93, which expressed the right of the OAS members "to take the necessary measures to protect themselves against Communist intervention" in the hemisphere. As far as the U.S. government was concerned, the "necessary measures" in the case of Guatemala involved the clandestine preparation by the CIA of a mercenary force to invade Guatemala and overthrow the democratically elected government of President Arbenz. This force was assembled in the neighboring countries of Honduras and El Salvador and received the support of the dictatorial regimes in these two countries as well as the Somoza dictatorship in nearby Nicaragua—all three of these regimes were closely tied to Washington. The CIA supplied the invaders with arms and planes and also arranged for the betrayal of the higher echelons of the Guatemalan army.

On June 17, 1954, this force under the command of ex-army officer Carlos Castillo Armas crossed into Guatemala with the intent of marching on the capital. After an initial period in which the Arbenz government put up rather successful resistance, the U.S. ambassador and the high command of the army pressured Arbenz into resigning and turning over the government to several generals in the army high command. They in turn allowed Castillo Armas and his force to enter the capital unopposed. As a result, the democratically elected regime collapsed and Castillo Armas was flown into Guatemala from Honduras on the personal plane of U.S. Ambassador John Peurifoy. The new government led by Castillo Armas was backed by the Eisenhower administration, which gave it over $80 million over the next three years. It immediately suspended Guatemala's democratic constitution and instituted a campaign of political repression directed at all the individuals and groups that had supported the Arbenz government and its reforms. The police and a "liberation force" began rounding up, imprisoning, and executing many of the former government's officials and supporters as well as the political exiles from other Latin American countries that were in the country. The new government also issued a decree that returned the expropriated land given to the peasants to the large landowners and the United Fruit Company.

Once the invasion had begun, Ernesto and his friends watched in exasperation as President Arbenz naively relied on the army to repulse the invasion. He wrote the following about this situation in a letter to his mother on July 4, 1954: "Treason continues to be the birthright of the army, and once more the aphorism is confirmed that sees the liquidation of the army as the true principle of democracy." He also wrote: "The harsh truth is that Arbenz did not know how to rise to the occasion" and "we were completely defenseless, since there were no planes, no anti-aircraft guns and no shelters." As a result, Ernesto said: "Panic gripped the people, especially 'the brave and loyal army of Guatemala' [and] Arbenz did not think to himself that a people in arms is an invincible power." He concluded with the comment: "He could have given arms to the people but he did not want to—and now we see the result" (page 67).

In the repressive aftermath of the overthrow of the Arbenz government in Guatemala, Ernesto would almost certainly have been imprisoned, and perhaps executed, if he had not taken refuge in the Argentine embassy. All the Latin American embassies were immediately filled with asylum seekers, especially the Argentine and Mexican embassies. Ernesto asked for and was given asylum in the Argentine embassy, where he met a number of Guatemalan officials and Latin American political exiles who had also received asylum and were staying in the embassy. He told Hilda he wanted to go to Mexico and afterward to China and tried to convince her that she should go with him. He said they could get married in Mexico, but she said she wanted to return home to Peru or go to Argentina and asked him for his family's address there. According to Hilda: "Ernesto insisted, laughing, that we would one day meet again in Mexico and marry" (Gadea 2008:84).

During the first days that he was in the embassy they saw each other daily, but then one day he discovered she and the landlady at her boardinghouse had been arrested by the police. He also learned that the first question the police asked Hilda was whether she knew where he was. She said they should ask at the Argentine embassy and refused to give them a description of him or identify him in the photographs they had found among her things in the boardinghouse. The police confiscated her belongings and took her to the women's prison and placed her in a cell with common criminals (pages 85–88).

When Ernesto found out, he wanted to surrender himself in return for her release, but the chargé d'affaires of the Argentine embassy and all of the exiles there convinced him the police would merely put him in prison too and it would do her no good. Meanwhile, Hilda went on a hunger strike, claiming she had been given political asylum in Guatemala and the authorities had brought no charges against her. Because her hunger strike was picked up by the press and several Latin American ambassadors (but not the Peruvian ambassador) visited her in jail to make sure she was being treated properly, she was released but ordered to appear before the new attorney general. He accused her of being a Communist, which she vehemently denied, and then released her on condition she appear personally before President Castillo Armas. When she went to meet him he apologized for her imprisonment and agreed to give her a safe conduct so that she could leave the country without any further difficulties (pages 90–91).

While he was in the Argentine embassy, Ernesto received money and clothes from his family, but he refused to leave for Argentina on the planes that had been sent by the Argentine government to pick up people who had taken refuge in the embassy. Instead he asked the ambassador to obtain a safe-conduct pass for him so that he could leave the country and go to Mexico. While he was waiting for his safe-conduct pass and visa, he left the embassy to find Hilda. She was having difficulty leaving the country because the Peruvian embassy would not give her a valid passport.

They had a long discussion about what had happened and where they stood. Hilda wrote in her book: "On reviewing the events of that period it seemed to us that in trying to defend the goals of the Guatemalan people we had become closer than ever." She also wrote: "Our analysis of what we had experienced in Guatemala led us to the conclusion that the revolution there had failed because popular support was not sought to defend it," and "we also concluded that the right way for a revolution to maintain national sovereignty, free of the influence of imperialism, would be for it to arm the people to defend their gains" (page 97).

They also spoke about their plans, and Ernesto told Hilda: "I have not insisted lately . . . because things being the way they are, there is no possibility of starting a new life. But in Mexico we will get married. Have no doubt about it." Happily surprised by the strength of his conviction, she answered: "Do you really think so? I'm going south" (page 94). A few days later, Hilda saw Ernesto off on the train to Mexico. When she returned to the house where she had been staying, she was arrested again by the police. Much to her surprise, they told her that she was being deporting to Mexico! Unfortunately, her deportation from Guatemala was a harrowing experience, as opposed to Ernesto's relatively uneventful departure. She was taken under guard to the border and held prisoner there until she paid her captors to smuggle her across the river into Mexico (page 123).

When Ernesto arrived in Mexico City in mid-September 1954 he discovered that, like Guatemala during the Arbenz presidency, Mexico was a refuge for political exiles from all over Latin America. In addition to the latest influx of Guatemalan exiles, there were political refugees from the Dominican Republic, Cuba, Colombia, Peru, Venezuela, Haiti, and his own Argentina. Most of these exiles lived in the same neighborhoods of the city and frequented the same bars and cafés.

Since Hilda was granted political asylum by the Mexican authorities after she escaped from Guatemala, her status in the country allowed her to find employment without any difficulty. Ernesto, on the other hand, had entered the country on merely a visitor's visa and had the same difficulties finding employment as in Guatemala.

Ernesto initially made ends meet as a street photographer. He became a regular member of the exile community. Through mutual contacts in Mexico City, Ernesto and Hilda were reunited in late October shortly after she arrived in the city. Hilda's account of their meeting reveals they did not get off to a good start: "Again Ernesto spoke of the possibility of getting married. I said we should wait. I had just arrived in Mexico and wanted to adjust to the new environment and look for a job. I really was not yet certain. I think he realized this and seemed somewhat bothered by it. I had the feeling that my ambiguous answer had created a certain tension, because he then said we would just be friends. I was a little surprised: I was only asking him to wait. But I accepted his decision. I had just arrived, and here we were, already quarreling" (page 125).

However, over the next few months they did see each other frequently and they discussed their Guatemalan experiences often. They both had developed a deep sense of disdain for the U.S. government, which they blamed for the overthrow of the Arbenz regime, the political repression that followed in Guatemala, and most of Latin America's economic and political ills. Ernesto told Hilda he had obtained a position as an assistant in the allergy ward of the general hospital in Mexico City, which paid very little but allowed him to practice medicine. He also told her he was in touch with Ñico López, who had by chance come into the allergy ward at the hospital one day with another Cuban. He said they embraced each other as old friends reunited. Ñico told him that he and his Cuban friends in Mexico were in constant contact with the revolutionary 26th of July Movement in Cuba, and they expected Fidel Castro and his brother Raúl would soon be released from prison there and might come to Mexico.

In a letter he wrote his mother in November 1954, it is possible to get a sense of what Ernesto was thinking at this period in his life. He told her he enjoyed being in Mexico but still hoped to go to Europe. He also said that while he had not "lost a bit of contempt for the United States" he wanted "to get to know New York at least," but then added he felt sure he would "leave just as anti-Yankee" as when he arrived there (Guevara 2001:87). At the end of the letter he also said that "in the hecatomb that Guatemala became after the fall [of President Arbenz]—where everyone expected to fend only for himself—the Communists kept their faith and comradeship alive and are the only group still working there." And then he said: "I think they deserve respect and sooner or later I will join the Party myself. What most prevents me from doing it right now is that I have a huge desire to travel in Europe, and I would not be able to do that if I was subject to rigid discipline [as a member of the party]."

Ernesto and Hilda grew closer and toward the end of December became lovers again. As a New Year's present, he gave her a copy of the Argentine writer José Hernández's epic poem about a gaucho called "Martin Fierro," which he had frequently recited and applied to the reality of their own lives since they first met. In the flyleaf he wrote the following inscription: "To Hilda, so that on the day we part the substance of my hopes for the future and my predestined struggle will remain with you" (Gadea 2008:134). She tried to hide her emotion, but confessed she was deeply moved by this inscription.

He continued to insist they should get married. She resisted at first, but within a few months realized she really did want to marry him, so they made plans to marry in May 1955. However, they had difficulty obtaining permission from the Mexican government since they were not Mexican citizens and had different nationalities. They decided to live together until they could get married officially. They rented a small flat in a section of the city where most of the Latin American political exiles were living. One night, Ernesto brought Raúl Castro home with him. Ñico had introduced them shortly after Raúl arrived in Mexico. Hilda's account of this meeting provides an invaluable description of him: "Despite his youth—he was twenty-three or twenty-four years old at the time—and even younger appearance, blond and beardless and looking like a university student, his ideas were very clear as to how the revolution was to be made and, more important, for what purpose and for whom. He had great faith in Fidel, not because he was his brother but because of his political leadership. It was his faith in Fidel that had led him to participate in the Moncada attack" (page 143).

He told Hilda that he was convinced that an armed struggle was necessary since one could not expect to take power through elections in Cuba and most of Latin America. However, he said this armed struggle would have to be carried out in close association with the populace, since it would only succeed with the support of the people. Once power had been taken with the support of the people, he said it would then be possible to transform Cuba's capitalist society into a socialist society. According to Hilda, Raúl had Communist ideas and was an admirer of the Soviet Union. She said: "He firmly believed that the power struggle must benefit the people" and this struggle would have to be against U.S. imperialism, not only for Cuba but in all of Latin America (page 143).

Thereafter, Hilda noticed that Ernesto saw Raúl almost every day, and they learned Fidel was coming to Mexico. Raúl told them about how they had begun to organize the 26th of July Movement. She said "it was spirit lifting just to talk to him," since he was always "joyful, communicative, sure of himself, and very clear in his ideas." For this reason, she said, he and Ernesto got along very well. Early in July, Fidel arrived in Mexico, and Ernesto met him at the home of a Cuban woman married to a Mexican. They ended up talking for almost 10 hours straight through the night, exchanging ideas about Latin American and international affairs. According to Hilda, Ernesto said Fidel had a deep faith in Latin America and that he was a new type of political leader who was modest, knew where he wanted to go, and had great tenacity and firmness. She said Ernesto discovered that he was a "true Latin American" and "he

A CALL TO ARMS IN GUATEMALA AND MEXICO 59

also found in Fidel a deep conviction that in fighting against [the Cuban dictator Fulgencio] Batista, he was fighting the imperialist monster that kept Batista in power" (page 144). In the journal he was keeping at the time, Ernesto wrote: "I met Fidel Castro, the Cuban revolutionary. He is a young, intelligent guy, very sure of himself and extraordinarily audacious; I think we hit it off well" (Guevara 2001:99).

Later, Ernesto told Hilda: "Ñico was right in Guatemala when he told us that if Cuba had produced anything good since Martí it was Fidel Castro. He will make the revolution. We are in complete agreement. . . . I could only fully support someone like him." She said that after the first day they met, Ernesto and Fidel began meeting together three or four times a week, but they had to be secretive because the Cuban exiles in Mexico were being watched and might be jailed since it was not only Batista's police but also the FBI who were watching them. Hilda met Fidel for the first time when he came to a dinner party that she and Ernesto arranged for him. Again, her account of this meeting provides an invaluable description of this important figure at an early stage in his political career: "He was young, only thirty, fair-skinned, and tall, about six foot two, and solidly built. . . . He did not look like the leader one knew him to be. He could very well have been a handsome bourgeois tourist. When he talked, however, his eyes shone with passion and revolutionary zeal, and one could see why he could command the attention of listeners. He had the charm and personality of a great leader, and at the same time an admirable simplicity and naturalness. . . . We were all in awe of him, except Ernesto, who had already spoken with him at length" (page 145).

Hilda asked Fidel why he had come to Mexico. He told her that he had come there to organize and train a group of fighters that would invade Cuba and confront Batista's army, which was backed by the Yankees. He said that his invading group of fighters would call on the Cuban people to help them overthrow the corrupt Batista dictatorship and that they were organizing clandestine support committees in the country as well as overseas to help them. At the end of his explanation he told her: "The struggle in Cuba was part of the continental fight against the Yankees, a fight that [Simón] Bolívar and Martí had foreseen." After he finished, Hilda said she was absolutely convinced and ready to accompany them. Afterward, she asked Ernesto if Fidel would take women in his invasion force, and he said: "Perhaps women like you—but it would be very difficult." A few days later, he asked her what she thought of "this crazy idea of the Cubans, invading an island completely defended by coastal artillery?" She realized that he was asking her opinion about whether he should join the expedition. Even though it would mean their separation and would be very dangerous, she said: "It is crazy, but one must go along." He embraced her and said the reason he asked her this question was because he wanted to know what she would say, since he had decided to join Fidel's force as their doctor (page 147). Hilda said that from this point on, Ernesto spoke of nothing but the Cuban Revolution and that in the end she lost her husband to this cause.

According to Fidel, Ernesto joined the 26th of July Movement the night they first met in Mexico City. The following is Fidel's account of this meeting: "Because of his state of mind when he left Guatemala, because of the extremely bitter experience he'd lived through there—that cowardly aggression against the country, the interruption of a process that had awakened the hopes of the people—because of his revolutionary avocation, his spirit of struggle . . . in a matter of minutes Che decided to join [our] small group of Cubans who were working on organizing a new phase of the struggle in our country" (Deutschmann 1994:99).

In early August, Hilda realized that she was pregnant. When she told Ernesto, he was very happy and said that they needed to hurry up and get married and let their parents know. They made arrangements to get married at the Argentine embassy but at the last minute Ernesto asked a doctor at the hospital where he was working to marry them since he was also the mayor of the beautiful little town of Tepotzotlán outside Mexico City. On August 18, 1955, they were married in Tepotzotlán. Raúl Castro accompanied them as well as a Venezuelan poet named Lucila Velasquez, a friend of Hilda's, and Jesús Montané, a member of the 26th of July Movement who had just arrived from Cuba to serve as treasurer of the movement and aide to Fidel.

Hilda recalled years later in her book about her life with Ernesto that their marriage ceremony in Tepotzotlán was simple, intimate, and full of warm comradeship. When they all returned from the wedding, Ernesto prepared an Argentine-style roast dinner, which Fidel attended. Over the next few days, they told their friends about their wedding and sent cables to their parents in Argentina and Peru. Hilda's parents sent them some money and a letter scolding them for not having invited them to the wedding. Ernesto wrote to Hilda's parents and thanked them for their generous gift and described their future plans as follows: "First we will wait for 'Don Ernesto.' (If it's not a boy, there's going to be trouble.) Then we'll consider a couple of firm propositions I have, one in Cuba, the other a fellowship in France, depending upon Hilda's ability to travel around. Our wandering life isn't over yet and before we definitely settle in Peru, a country that I admire in many ways, or in Argentina, we want to see a bit of Europe and two fascinating countries, India and China. I am particularly interested in New China because it reflects my own political ideals" (Gadea 2008:153–54). In another section of this rather lengthy letter, Ernesto wrote about their relationship as equals: "Our married life probably won't be like yours. Hilda works eight hours a day and I, somewhat irregularly, around twelve. I'm in research, the toughest branch (and poorest paid). But our routines work harmoniously together and have turned our home into a free association between two equals."

Fidel left Mexico for a time to seek support from Cubans living in the United States who opposed the Batista dictatorship. From these Cuban exiles he collected funds and recruits for his planned invasion, and when he returned to Mexico he obtained the services of a Colonel Alberto Bayo to train his group in the tactics of guerrilla warfare. Colonel Bayo had been born in Cuba and had served as an officer in the Spanish Republican Army. During the Spanish Civil War, he had gained a great deal of experience in guerrilla warfare and later he had collaborated in Latin American efforts to launch an armed popular struggle.

Toward the end of 1955, the meetings between Ernesto, Raúl, Fidel, and the other Cubans became more frequent, and they often met at the apartment where Ernesto and Hilda lived. Fidel arranged to have all his mail sent to their address under Hilda's maiden name. Consequently, Ernesto warned Hilda to be careful with the mail addressed to her, especially if it came from Cuba or the United States. On Christmas Eve 1955, they attended a dinner prepared by Fidel, who spoke at some length about the projects that would be carried out in Cuba once the revolution had succeeded. According to Hilda: "He spoke with such certainty and ease that one had the feeling we were already in Cuba, carrying out the process of construction. . . . Suddenly as if by design, there was silence. Fidel's last words still echoed in my mind. I looked at Ernesto and he returned the glance. In his eyes I could read the same thoughts that were going through my mind. In order to carry out all these plans, it was first necessary to get to Cuba.... This meant many difficulties, great efforts, and sacrifices—all the dangers that must be undergone to achieve the power for revolutionary change" (page 168).

In the silence, Hilda said it was possible to sense the thoughts of everyone in the room. They all wanted Fidel's plans to come true, but they were painfully aware of the enormous costs in pain, suffering, and death that would be necessary for these plans to be realized. For Hilda, the sacrifice would be, in her own words, "terribly painful" since it would mean separation from her new husband and the father of her child and waiting with "agonized awareness" of the constant dangers he would face. She also worried about the "marvelous group of comrades" whom she had grown to love and what could happen to them. But at the same time she said that she "felt proud of them and what they were about to do for the liberation of Cuba, the first stage in the liberation of [the] continent" (page 168).

In January 1956, they began almost daily preparations for their expedition to Cuba. Ernesto started eating lightly to keep his weight down—just meat, salad, and fruit, which was his favorite diet anyway. He gave up his allergy research and turned down a lectureship in physiology so that he had more time to go with the Cubans to a gymnasium where they practiced judo, wrestling, and karate. In addition, he started reading extensively about economics. Each week he would read a book and then discuss it with Hilda, since she was an economist and knew most of the books he was reading. He also asked her to teach him to type, which she did. They discussed seriously the implications of his commitment to participate in the mission to invade Cuba. It would mean giving up their plans to go to Africa on the fellowship, which he had previously applied for from the Pan American Health Office. In fact, it meant abandoning all their plans.

For Hilda, it was now completely clear that he was going to participate in the expedition to create a popular revolution in Cuba. She accepted this commitment and realized it was part of a larger commitment to "fight against Yankee imperialism" in all of Latin America. She saw it as only the first stage of the liberation of the continent, and realized that "afterward, the struggle would have to be continued in the other countries." She was in total accord with this commitment on the part of Ernesto, even though she knew that it would not be possible for her to participate in the Cuban expedition because she had to take care of their child. She was willing to help as best she could—"by supporting the movement and carrying on propaganda activities" (page 172).

On February 15, 1956, Hilda gave birth to their child, a girl. Ernesto was with her the entire time, including in the delivery room. They had agreed that if the baby was a boy, she would choose his name, but if it was a girl, he would choose her name. He chose the name Hilda Beatriz. The first name, Hilda, was in his wife's honor, and the second name was in honor of his favorite aunt, Beatriz Guevara. Fidel was their first visitor in the hospital and like Ernesto he was enchanted with the baby. He held her in his arms and said: "This girl is going to be educated in Cuba," and he said it with such conviction that Hilda felt sure it would happen (page 173).

Ernesto became a doting father and rushed home every day to watch and play with her. When the baby was only a few weeks old, Hilda came down with a bad cold and a high fever. Ernesto stayed home and immediately took over the care of Hildita (little Hilda). According to Hilda, he always showed great concern for both her and Hildita and consistently gave them tender and affectionate care. During this period, they read books together about wars of liberation and the Chinese revolution, and Russian novels about the struggle against the Nazis in Russia and Eastern Europe during World War II. On the basis of their readings, they concluded that guerrilla warfare might be the best way for a popular revolution to succeed in Latin America.

With Colonel Bayo's assistance, Fidel established a secret training camp for his group at a large ranch in the mountainous Chalco district outside of Mexico City. Fidel brought 80 men to this training camp, including Ernesto. Within a short time, Colonel Bayo singled out Ernesto as his best student. It was during this training period that Ernesto's Cuban comrades gave him the nickname "Che." They called him Che because like most Argentines he used the word *che* constantly, which is similar to "Hey, buddy!" in English and is used by most Argentines at the beginning of a sentence to catch someone's attention or express familiarity. Ernesto accepted this nickname with pride.

In April 1956, after their military training the group began studying Marxist literature and discussing the problems of Cuba and Latin America. Che (Ernesto) came home only on the weekends. In late May, he told Hilda they were going somewhere for field training and they might depart from there for the invasion of Cuba. About a week afterward, she saw an article in the Mexico City newspapers about the arrest of Fidel and four of his Cuban companions because their immigration papers were not in order. Hilda suspected that trouble was brewing, so she collected all their papers and books in their apartment and took them to a friend's house. Shortly thereafter, two men came to her door and asked her if she was Hilda Gadea. She answered that she was Hilda Gadea Guevara. They asked her about the mail she received and told her she had received a telegram that was compromising. They wanted her to come with them, but when she said she was nursing a four-month-old child and she would have to bring the baby with her, they told her she did not have to go with them at that moment. They said she should wait until they came back. When they left, she immediately sent word through one of the Cubans to warn the others that she was under police surveillance (Gadea 2008:185–86).

Later that evening, the same two men returned and took her and the baby to the federal police office in the center of the city. There she was questioned about a telegram from Cuba that had been sent to her address. One of the interrogators was a Cuban who said he had sent the telegram. They asked her where her husband was, who were the visitors to her house, and whether she was involved in politics. She told them she was a political exile and they should notify the Mexican senator who had signed her asylum papers. She also complained they were violating her rights, asked for a lawyer, and said her daughter's health was being endangered by detaining them both in uncomfortable conditions. They took her into a dark interrogation room where she was forced to sit, with the baby in her arms, looking into a bright light. They asked her a series of questions intended to prove that her husband and the Cubans were Communists. She had the impression one of the people in the room was a CIA or an FBI agent. They finally let her return to her apartment after they failed to get the information they wanted from her and saw that they could not intimidate her.

The two policemen who took her back to the apartment stayed there with her all night. The next morning they took her and the baby back to the federal police headquarters and she was again interrogated. They tried to convince her she should save herself and the baby by telling them everything they wanted to know about her husband and his Cuban friends. She refused to give them any information and asked again for a lawyer. Fidel and his four companions were in the same building, and they discovered she was being detained there too. Later in the day she was taken to the police chief's office and found Fidel there. He greeted her affectionately and told her: "I can't allow you to be here with the baby. Please tell them that you receive letters for me—being a political exile, I had no permanent address and had asked you to receive mail for me, addressed to you." She hesitated, but he said: "You make this statement so that you'll be freed, because I can't let you and the baby go through these discomforts and dangers" (page 186). After he insisted, she signed the statement and they let her go.

Later she discovered that the former president of Mexico Lázaro Cárdenas had intervened on Fidel's behalf. She also learned that Fidel had agreed to take the police to the ranch where Ernesto and the others were hiding in order to avoid a gunfight and bloodshed. Fidel arranged with the federal police to go in first and prepare the group to surrender without a fight. Fortunately, when Fidel went to the ranch with the police, Raúl and half the group were not at the ranch and escaped being taken by the police. They also hid the group's weapons so that the police were not able to find them.

Fidel and the group (including Che) that were captured at the ranch were all taken to the Immigration Detention Center in Mexico City, where they were interrogated and held as prisoners. When Hilda discovered where he was being held prisoner and went to visit him, he told her: "There is no doubt the FBI is mixed up in this, to defend Batista. He represents for them the control of the sugar industry and commerce [in Cuba]. The Mexicans can't be that interested in hunting down Cuban revolutionaries. Not only that, they have made their own revolution and they know what it is to take up arms. It's those Yankee *hijos de la chingada*, sons of bitches, as they say here who are behind this whole affair" (page 193).

Fidel, Che, and the rest of the group being detained by the Mexican authorities banded together and became a close-knit circle of comrades under the stressful conditions of their confinement. In a letter he wrote to his mother dated July 15, 1956, Che had the following to say about the effect his imprisonment had on his feelings toward his Cuban comrades:

> During these prison days and the period of training that preceded them, I have identified totally with my comrades in the cause. I remember a phrase that once seemed to me idiotic or at least bizarre, referring to such a total identification among the members of a fighting body that the very concept of the "I" disappeared and gave way to the concept of "we." It was a Communist morality and may, of course, appear to be a doctrinaire exaggeration, but in reality it was (and is) a beautiful thing to be able to feel that stirring of "we."

He also said the following in response to his mother's advice that he pursue a more moderate path and look out for himself: "You are profoundly mistaken in believing that great inventions or works of art arise out of moderation or 'moderate egoism'. Any great work requires passion, and the revolution requires passion and audacity in large doses—things that humanity as a whole does have." Near the end of this letter, he referred to his future plans. He said that after Cuba he planned to go somewhere else to carry on the revolutionary struggle against imperialism and that he would really be done for if he were to choose a career in which he would be "shut up in some bureaucratic office or allergy clinic" (Guevara 2001:110–11).

After several weeks, the group of detainees decided to go on a hunger strike. In a few days, all of the group, including Fidel, were released—but not Ernesto and Calixto García, a Cuban, since the federal police claimed their immigration papers were not in order. Fidel gave the Mexican authorities a large sum of money to resolve their immigration problems and told Hilda they would have to wait a while before the federal police would release the two remaining detainees. Ernesto and Calixto were released after spending almost two months in detention.

During this period, Hilda visited him regularly with Hildita, and she later wrote that one of her fondest memories was of Che playing with their daughter during those visits. She wrote: "We met in a large patio where the prisoners could play football to keep in shape. There I would spread out a blanket and put Hildita under an umbrella. Che played for long periods of time with Hildita until she fell asleep, then he would watch her, observing every gesture the baby made in her sleep. At other times he would pick her up and carry her proudly around the patio" (Gadea 2008:195). She said that it was during this time that Che took to calling Hildita "love's petal most profound."

Hildita was four months old when he was arrested but almost six months old when he was released. He went to their apartment and surprised both Hilda and Hildita. He told them he could spend only a short time at home since he had to go finish his training and go into hiding to do so, but he promised he would visit them as often as he could. When he did come home it was usually for just a few days and he would always spend as much time taking care of Hildita as he could. He started calling her "my little Mao," and he would recite poetry to her while he carried her around in his arms. According to Hilda, one day he looked at Hildita tenderly and said: "My dear daughter, my little Mao, you don't know what a difficult world you're going to have to live in. When you grow up, this whole continent, and maybe the whole world, will be fighting against the great enemy, Yankee imperialism. You will have to go fight. I may not be here anymore, but the struggle will enflame the continent." Hilda was overwhelmed by his words and embraced him (page 203).

The last time Hilda saw Che before he left for Cuba, he returned for a weekend and they made plans to take a short trip to the beach resort of Acapulco. One of the Cubans came to the house early on Sunday morning and asked for Che. He said the police were on the hunt for them again and they would have to leave right away. Hilda had the feeling something serious was going on and asked him to tell her if something was going to happen. He told her they were only taking precautions and calmly gathered his things. When he kissed her good-bye she trembled without knowing why and drew closer to him. Later she remembered how hard he had tried to remain natural so as not to alarm her, but he never came back after that weekend.

In a letter he wrote his mother in November 1956, he said: "Still here in Mexico, I am answering your last letters. I can't give you much news about my life, because I am only doing a little gymnastics and reading a huge amount (especially things you can imagine). I see Hilda some weekends." He added: "I've given up trying to get my case resolved through legal channels, so my residence in Mexico will be only temporary. In any event, Hilda is going with the little girl to spend New Year with her family. She'll be there for a month, then we'll see what happens. My long-term aim is to see something of Europe, if possible live there, but that is getting more and more difficult. . . . I had a project for my life which involved ten years of wandering, then some years of medical studies and, if any time was left, the great adventure of physics. Now that is all over. The only clear thing is that the ten years of wandering look like being more (unless unforeseen circumstances put an end to my wandering), but it will be very different from the kind I imagined. Now, when I get to a new country, it won't be to look around and visit museums and ruins, but also (because that still interests me) to join the people's struggle" (Guevara 2001:111–12).

Che was one of the 82 members of the 26th of July Movement who left Mexico for Cuba the last week of November 1956. Fidel was able to obtain only one boat for this expedition. It was an old 60-foot cabin cruiser–type yacht named *Granma* that had a normal carrying capacity of only 20 persons. Some of the men who had trained for the expedition had to be left behind because Fidel could not fit all of them on the boat. The 82 men who did get on the boat left from the Mexican port of Tuxpan under the cover of darkness shortly after midnight on November 25, 1956. After a series of difficulties, bad weather, and mishaps that slowed their trip across the Gulf of Mexico, they disembarked on the southeastern shoreline of Cuba on December 2, 1956. The general location of this landing was the same as where Cuba's national hero José Martí had landed 61 years earlier during the struggle to liberate Cuba from Spanish colonial domination.

Chapter 4

EL CHE: THE HEROIC GUERRILLA WARRIOR

When they finally reached the Cuban coastline near Cape Cruz, it was beginning to get light. The landing spot they had chosen was near the coastal town of Niquero in what was then called Oriente Province. Waiting for them there was Celia Sánchez, who was one of the founders of the 26th of July Movement and a key member of the clandestine network in Santiago de Cuba, the main city of Oriente Province. She was waiting for them with some vehicles, food, weapons, and about 50 men who were ready to join with Fidel Castro's group to attack and capture Niquero and then the neighboring town of Manzanillo.

A few days earlier, on November 30, 1956, the naval station and police station in Santiago de Cuba, the largest city in the region, had been attacked by the 26th of July Movement. This attack was a diversionary tactic to draw the army and police away from the area where the *Granma* expedition was supposed to land. But when the *Granma* arrived off the coast of Oriente Province on the morning of December 2, 1956, it was running out of fuel and was two days behind schedule. Fidel and his men were forced to beach the ship at a spot called Playa de los Colorados, near the village of Las Coloradas, about 15 miles south of the designated landing spot. The exact spot where they beached the boat was a muddy mangrove swamp, and they were unable to unload most of their heavy weapons.

The guerrillas were forced to abandon their heavy equipment and most of their supplies and make their way to land by wading through the muddy marsh. The following is Fidel Castro's account of this critical moment in the history of the Cuban revolution:

> On two occasions, the skipper at the helm of the *Granma*, a former Cuban Navy commander who had joined our movement, tried to follow the correct route through the labyrinth marked by the buoys, and on two occasions he came back to the point of departure. He was trying a third time. It was impossible to keep up this exasperating search. There were only a few liters of fuel left. It was already broad daylight. The enemy was relentlessly searching by sea and by air. The boat was in grave danger of being destroyed a few kilometers off the coast, with all of the forces on board. We could see the coast nearby, and the waters were apparently shallow. The skipper was ordered to head straight for this spot, full steam ahead. The *Granma* ran into mud and stopped 60 meters from shore. The men disembarked with their weapons, and struggled through the water over soft mud that threatened to swallow them up as they were overloaded. (Castro 2001:21)

But as soon as they reached what had seemed to be the solid shore they encountered mud again.

They found themselves in a long, swampy coastal lagoon that stretched between their point of arrival and the solid land beyond. According to Castro: "It took almost two hours to cross that hellish swamp. Having just reached solid ground, the first heavy weaponry shots were heard firing at the landing point, near the now solitary *Granma*. Its presence had been sighted and communicated to the enemy command, which immediately responded with a sea attack on the expedition and machine gunning from the air of the area to which the small expeditionary force of 82 men was headed" (Castro 2001:22). Fortunately, the mangrove thickets through which they were making their way protected them from being seen from the air. For several days they marched toward the neighboring Sierra Maestra (Cuba's largest mountain range) by hiding during the day and marching during the night. At first they did not encounter any resistance, but on December 5, they were surprised by a large detachment of the army near a sugarcane field at a place called Alegría de Pío, where they had stopped to rest. Because they had eaten and drunk very little since their departure from Mexico and were exhausted from the ordeal of their landing and several days of nighttime marching, they were completely unprepared to defend themselves and ran in all directions to try and save themselves.

The tragic outcome of this encounter with Batista's forces is described by Fidel Castro as follows: "A surprise enemy attack in a light forest where we were waiting for nightfall to continue the march to the Sierra Maestra. A terrible setback, total dispersion; a tenacious search and persecution of the scattered men; an enormous cost in the lives of combatants, the vast majority of them murdered after falling prisoner; almost all the weapons lost." Only Guevara, Fidel and Raúl Castro, and 12 others escaped and made their way to the Sierra Maestra. Guevara was wounded in the neck, but his wound was not serious since the bullet ricocheted off a cartridge case in his chest pocket. He survived, but with only the most rudimentary medical treatment because he had left his medical knapsack at Alegría de Pío.

In one of the essays he later wrote and published in *Pasajes de la Guerra Revolucionaria* (*Episodes of the Revolutionary War*), Guevara described his baptism of fire at Alegría de Pío as follows: "Perhaps this was the first time I was faced with the dilemma of choosing between my devotion to medicine and my duty as a revolutionary soldier. There at my feet was a knapsack full of medicine and a box of ammunition, I couldn't possibly carry both of them; they were too heavy. I picked up the box of ammunition, leaving the medicine, and started to cross the clearing, heading toward the cane field. I remember Faustino Pérez, kneeling and firing his submachine gun. Near me, a compañero named Emilio Albentosa was walking toward the cane field. A burst of gunfire hit us both. I felt a sharp blow on my chest and a wound in my neck, and I thought for certain I was dead. Albentosa, vomiting blood and bleeding profusely from a deep wound made by a .45-caliber bullet, shouted: 'They've killed me' and began to fire his rifle at no one in particular" (Deutschmann 1997:26).

While he was lying alone on the ground waiting to die, Guevara was approached by one of members of the group who urged him to get up and go with him into the nearby cane field, where they encountered two other men. According to Guevara's account of this situation: "[Juan] Almeida approached, urging me to go on, and despite the intense pain I dragged myself into the cane field. . . . Then everything became a blur of airplanes flying low and strafing the field. . . . With Almeida leading, we crossed the last path among the rows of cane and reached the safety of the woods. The first shouts of 'Fire' were heard in the cane field and columns of flame and smoke began to rise. . . . We walked until the darkness made it impossible to go on, and decided to lie down and go to sleep all huddled together in a heap. We were starving and thirsty, and the mosquitoes added to our misery. This was our baptism of fire on December 5, 1956, in the outskirts of Niquero. Such was the beginning of forging what would become the Rebel Army" (page 27).

Meanwhile back in Mexico, Hilda and Hildita had moved out of their apartment and into the home of one of Hilda's friends. According to the plans she and Che had made before his departure, as soon as she saw news of the expedition's invasion of Cuba in the newspapers she and Hildita were to leave for Peru, where they would await the outcome of the revolutionary struggle. If this struggle succeeded, they were to join him in Cuba, stay there for a while, and "then decide whether to go to Peru or Argentina to continue the fight," since it was "Che's intention to continue fighting in other countries of Latin America" (Gadea 2008:208).

On December 2, 1956, the news of Fidel Castro's expedition was published in all the Mexico City newspapers. The first headline Hilda saw read "INVASION OF CUBA BY BOAT—FIDEL CASTRO, ERNESTO GUEVARA, RAUL CASTRO AND ALL OTHER MEMBERS OF THE EXPEDITION DEAD" (page 209). She was shocked and overwhelmed with grief, but some of her friends cautioned her to wait for confirmation of this bad news; they said both the Cuban and Mexican government authorities were most likely spreading false information to the press to discourage people from supporting Castro's cause. General Bayo visited Hilda and told her he didn't believe what the newspapers were reporting. In fact, he told her he was sure Guevara was alive. He said: "I can tell you this: he's the most intelligent, the cleverest—the one who most profited from my instruction. I am sure nothing has happened to him" (page 210).

Then Guevara's father called Hilda from Argentina to say he had contacted one of his cousins, who was the Argentine ambassador in Cuba. He said his cousin told him his son was not among the dead, the wounded, or the prisoners taken by the Cuban authorities. Still not knowing for sure whether he was alive or dead, Hilda followed the plan they had made before the departure of the expedition. She left Mexico with Hildita to go stay with her parents in Lima, Peru. Bur after staying there for a few weeks, they both went to Argentina at the invitation of Guevara's parents. Just before they left for Argentina, she received a call from his father, who informed her they had received word that Ernesto was alive.

The first letter that Hilda received from Guevara was dated January 28, 1957 (Gadea 2008:216). It provides an excellent summary of his baptism of fire and his first days on Cuban soil. In this letter, he wrote: "As you probably know, after seven days of being packed like sardines in the now famous *Granma*, we landed at a dense, rotting mangrove jungle through the pilot's error. Our misfortunes continued until finally we were surprised in the also now famous Alegría [de Pío] and scattered like pigeons." He said he had been wounded in the neck, but he survived "due to my cat's lives." He explained to her that "a machine-gun bullet hit a cartridge case in my chest pocket, and the bullet ricocheted and nicked my neck. For a few days I walked through those hills thinking I was seriously wounded because the bullet had banged my chest so hard." He also described in this letter how his group managed to survive: "Our group, including Almeida and Ramirito, whom you know, spent seven days of hunger and terrible thirst until we were able to slip through the cordon and, with help from the peasants, get back to rejoin Fidel."

What he undoubtedly knew (but did not want to reveal to his wife) when he wrote this letter was that of the 82 members of the *Granma* expedition, most were killed or caught and then murdered by the Cuban army in the first days after the guerrilla force landed in Oriente Province. Besides Guevara and the Castro brothers, there were only 12 other survivors. As he hinted in his letter to Hilda, among those who were killed was Ñico López, his friend since Guatemala days.

The survivors of the *Granma* expedition were joined by six discontented peasants in January 1957, and this minuscule group began operating as a guerrilla force from hiding places in the Sierra Maestra. Their first victory was an attack on a small army garrison on the coast where the La Plata River comes down out of the Sierra Maestra to the ocean. As Guevara later wrote about this attack: "The effect of our victory was electrifying and went far beyond that craggy region. It was like a clarion call, proving that the Rebel Army really existed and was ready to fight" (Deutschmann 1997:28). At this time, they had only 22 weapons and they were short of ammunition. He wrote they had to take the garrison "at all costs, for a failure would have meant expending all our ammunition, leaving us practically defenseless."

On January 16, 1957, they observed the garrison from the distance and took prisoner the drunken foreman of a local plantation who gave them information about the garrison. Under the cover of darkness, they attacked the garrison's small buildings from the left, center, and right. Guevara was in the group that attacked from the center. At great risk and under heavy fire, he and another man got close enough to set one of the three buildings on fire. Intimidated by the fire, the soldiers gave up the fight and surrendered. As a result, the guerrillas were able to seize their weapons, ammunition, fuel, food, and clothing. While none of the guerrillas received even a scratch in the fighting, they killed two of the soldiers, wounded five, and took three prisoners. The rest of the soldiers fled into the night. After attending to the wounded, the guerrillas set fire to the barracks and withdrew into the Sierra Maestra (page 32).

According to Guevara, their humane treatment of prisoners "was in open contrast to that of Batista's army." He wrote: "Not only did they kill our wounded; they abandoned their own. This difference made a great impact on the enemy over time and it was a factor in our victory."

As the months went by, the guerrillas carried out a number of daring attacks against small military outposts in the region. They were able to do this with the help they received from the 26th of July Movement's clandestine urban network of supporters in Santiago de Cuba led by Frank País and Celia Sánchez. This network sent men, arms, ammunition, and food to the Rebel Army. Castro assigned Guevara to be the liaison between this urban underground network and the guerrilla force. In March 1957, Guevara guided a group of over 50 men that Frank País had recruited and sent to join the guerrilla force in the Sierra Maestra. By April 1957, the guerrilla force totaled some 80 men.

The news of their actions began to attract the support of local peasants and the members of other political groups that were opposed to the Batista dictatorship all over the country. The ranks of the guerrilla force began to swell with recruits from these groups, the local peasantry, and the urban supporters of the 26th of July Movement in the cities of Santiago, Bayamo, Guantánamo, and Manzanillo.

Guevara was to have been the medical officer of the revolutionary guerrilla force, but his value as a guerrilla leader soon became evident. According to Fidel Castro, Che distinguished himself and won the admiration of his comrades at the second encounter their small guerrilla force had with the army on May 28, 1957. This battle took place in El Uvero, a small village along the road from Niquero to Santiago de Cuba.

In this battle, the guerrillas actually outnumbered the army by 80 to 53 (Bonachea and San Martín 1974:95). They took the army unit by surprise, and in an exchange of gunfire that lasted almost three hours, they killed 14 soldiers and wounded 19 before the remaining soldiers surrendered. Their own losses were 7 dead and 9 wounded. Guevara considered this battle to be one of the most important of the revolutionary war. He wrote later that "for us, it was a victory that meant our guerrillas had reached full maturity. From this moment on, our morale increased enormously, our determination and hope for victory also increased, and though the months that followed were a hard test, we now had the key to the secret of how to beat the enemy" (Guevara 1963:72). Using the element of surprise, they were now strong enough to encircle most enemy units and force them to surrender or flee under the threat of complete annihilation.

According to Guevara, after El Uvero "the relationship of forces in the Sierra Maestra began to shift greatly" in favor of the Rebel Army, and the government's forced evacuation of peasants from the area resulted "in a thousand crimes, robberies, and abuses against them." However, as he noted, "the peasants responded with renewed support to the cause of the July 26 Movement" and the guerrilla's "fair treatment toward the peasantry—respecting their property, paying for what we consumed, tending their sick, helping those most in need—was the total opposite of the government's bestial policy."

By this point, Guevara's bravery and military prowess had impressed and won over his Cuban comrades. As Castro later wrote: "From the very first moment, he was absolutely willing to give his life, regardless of whether it was in the first battle or the second or the third. Here we had a person born in a place thousands of kilometers from our country . . . but for that country and that cause, he was the first at every moment to volunteer for something dangerous, for a mission with great risks" (page 105). Castro described Guevara's role in El Uvero as follows: "In a practically individual battle with an enemy soldier, in the midst of general combat, he shot the adversary and crawled forward under a hail of bullets to take his weapon . . . and it earned him the admiration of all" (Deutschmann 1994:102).

According to Castro: "Che was one of those people who was liked immediately, for his simplicity, his character, his naturalness, his comradely attitude, his personality, his originality, even when one had not yet learned of his other unique qualities" (Castro 1994:68). Initially, as the guerrilla force's only doctor, he established a special bond with the other members of the small force. But in the force's second victorious battle, as Castro has stated, he became "the most outstanding soldier in that battle, carrying out for the first time one of those singular feats that characterized him in all military action" (page 69). In subsequent battles, according to Castro, he was outstanding as both combatant and doctor, caring for wounded comrades as well as wounded enemy soldiers.

In one case during the early months of the guerrilla force's campaign in the Sierra Maestra, Guevara stayed behind with the wounded after the rest of force abandoned the scene of a bloody encounter with the army. Castro's account of this occasion is as follows: "After all the weapons had been captured and it became necessary to abandon that position, undertaking a long return march under the harassment of various enemy forces, someone had to stay behind with the wounded, and it was Che who did so. Aided by a small group of our soldiers, he took care of them, saved their lives, and later rejoined the column with them" (page 70). As Castro's account reveals: "From this time forward, he stood out as a capable and valiant leader, one of those who, when a difficult mission is pending, do not wait to be asked to carry it out." Indeed, his willingness to instantly volunteer for the most difficult missions "aroused admiration—twice the usual admiration," according to Castro, since he "was so altruistic, so selfless, so willing to always do the most difficult things" and "to constantly risk his life."

Because of how he distinguished himself in combat and because he had won the respect and admiration of his comrades, Castro gave Guevara increasingly greater military responsibilities. In March 1957, he appointed him, along with Ramiro Valdes, Ciro Redondo, and Camilo Cienfuegos, to the rank of captain. And a few months later, on July 21, 1957, Castro appointed Guevara as *comandante* (commander or major), the highest rank in the guerrilla army, which was held at the time only by Fidel Castro himself (page 70). In addition, Fidel placed Guevara at the head of a new guerrilla column with instructions to operate apart from the main force. It was called the Dispossessed Peasants and consisted of three platoons. This force numbered close to 75 men who, Guevara said, made him feel "very proud," despite their being "heterogeneously dressed and armed" (page 38).

Guevara's own account of how Castro appointed him commander and how he received his commander's star is worth noting here. In *Episodes of the Revolutionary War,* he wrote the following account: "We wrote a letter of congratulations and appreciation to 'Carlos,' the underground name of Frank País, who was living his final days. It was signed by all the officers of the guerrilla army who knew how to write. (Many of the Sierra peasants were not very skilled in this art but were already an important component of the guerrillas.) The signatures appeared in two columns, and as we were writing down the ranks on the second one, when my turn came, Fidel simply said: 'Make it commander.' Thus, in a most informal manner, almost in passing, I was promoted to commander of the second column of the guerrilla army." Guevara also noted in this account: "There is a bit of vanity hiding somewhere within every one of us. It made me feel like the proudest man in the world that day." And he added: "My insignia, a small star, was given to me by Celia Sánchez," who was present on this important occasion (page 38). This star, which he wore on the front of his black beret, soon became an important feature of his now legendary iconic image.

A few days later, on July 30, 1957, Frank País, who was only 23 years old at the time, was killed by Batista's police as he left the house where he was hiding in Santiago. Unaware that País had been killed, the next day Guevara's column attacked a small army post in the Sierra Maestra town of Bueycito (Bonachea and San Martín 1974:96). In this attack, they again caught soldiers at a post by surprise and wounded six of them. However, one of the members of Guevara's column was killed and three others were wounded in the attack. As they left the town, one of the local miners decided to join them. He later became a well-known comandante in the Rebel Army.

When they returned to their base in the mountains, they heard the news of Frank País's death. Guevara later wrote that the death of País "represented an enormous loss to the Revolution," since he was "one of the purest, most brilliant figures of the Cuban Revolution." As a result of País's death, there were mass public protests in both Santiago and Havana, and the government responded with complete censorship of the press as well as the arrest and murder of a large number of the urban supporters of the 26th of July Movement. Guevara wrote: "When Frank País was murdered, we lost one of our most valuable fighters, but the people's reaction to the crime showed that additional forces were joining the struggle and the people's fighting spirit had increased" (Guevara 1963:96).

In 1957 Guevara's column spent August in a small valley called El Hombrito near the summit of the Sierra Maestra. Since his column was composed of a large number of new recruits, they had to be trained, but they also had to be ready for battle at any moment. According to Guevara, it was their duty to attack any enemy units that dared invade what they called the "free territory of Cuba," which at this time was a relatively small section of the Sierra Maestra (page 97).

On August 29, a local peasant informed them that a large number of soldiers were headed their way on the trail that led to the valley where they were camped. Guevara had his men take up positions along the trail so they could ambush the soldiers when they reached a curve where the trail made an almost 90-degree turn around a rock. His plan was to let 10 or 12 soldiers go by the rock and then open fire on them. His men were supposed to then take the dead soldiers' weapons and withdraw while they were being covered by their rear guard. However, when the soldiers came to the rock, one of his men opened fire too soon and they succeeded in wounding only one of the soldiers at the head of the army column. Nevertheless, in the exchange of gunfire that followed they managed to force the soldiers, who were equipped with bazookas, to retreat.

As Guevara noted in his *Episodes of the Revolutionary War* (page 100), this encounter with a large army unit of some 180 men proved that it was relatively easy for the guerrillas to attack large enemy columns on the march, since they could ambush and fire on the head of the enemy's approaching column and immobilize the rest of the column. In his account of this battle, Guevara wrote: "We continued this practice until it became an established system, so efficient that the soldiers stopped coming to the Sierra Maestra and even refused to be part of the advance guard." He added that, "of course, it took more than one battle for our system to materialize." Moreover, he noted his guerrilla force was quite satisfied with these small victories at the time this battle took place, since they were still a poorly prepared, small guerrilla force that had only light weapons to confront well-equipped army units.

On November 4, 1957, the first issue of *El Cubano Libre* (*The Free Cuban*), the newspaper of the Rebel Army, was published by Guevara in the Sierra Maestra. The choice of this name for the newspaper had considerable historical significance, since *El Cubano Libre* was the name of the paper published by Cuban patriots during the independence wars against Spanish colonialism in the 19th century. A few months later, Guevara was also instrumental in creating the Rebel Army's clandestine radio station Radio Rebelde, which began its transmissions in February 1958 by stating it was broadcasting from "the free territory of Cuba." Soon, Radio Rebelde began regularly broadcasting news of the Rebel Army's actions as well as the declarations of the 26th of July Movement, speeches by Castro, Cuban political news, and coded messages from the movement's members to their loved ones. It subsequently also provided radio communications between the rebel columns operating in different parts of the island.

Guevara was the main proponent of establishing this clandestine radio station. He had been impressed by the role that the CIA-backed radio station La Voz de la Liberación (The Voice of Liberation) had played in the overthrow of the Árbenz government in Guatemala (Moore 1993). Radio Rebelde, with its trademark salutation "Aquí Radio Rebelde" (Radio Rebelde here), still broadcasts today in Cuba.

During April and early May 1958, Castro had Guevara take charge of creating a training school for the new recruits that were joining the Rebel Army in increasing numbers. They were put through a lengthy political, physical, and military training program similar to the training the *Granma* group underwent in Mexico. Castro and Guevara wanted only the toughest and most dedicated recruits to join the Rebel Army, and they used the training program to weed out the weaker recruits.

Castro also gave Guevara the responsibility for defending the western sector of the territory held by the Rebel Army against the full-scale offensive launched against it by the Batista government's armed forces at the end of May 1958. This offensive was undertaken by a force of some 15,000 troops. They were armed with mortars and bazookas and supported by tanks and aircraft. Their strategy was to encircle and annihilate the Rebel Army. They divided into three combat battalions, which attacked Castro's guerrilla forces from three different directions. The guerrillas fell back to the defensive positions they had prepared in the Sierra Maestra and ambushed the army battalions as they tried to advance.

The fighting was intense, and the guerrillas had to give up much territory, but the government forces failed to defeat the Rebel Army. The government forces launched their last major attack on the Rebel Army on June 28, 1958, using two battalions of troops that were camped at the Estrada Palma Sugar Mill at the base of the Sierra Maestra (Bockman 1984). As these troops advanced into the mountain using a single road, they were attacked by units of the Rebel Army under Guevara's command when they had gone only a few miles. Guevara's units ambushed and pinned down the lead battalion, which called up armored cars to clear the way ahead of them. As the armored cars advanced, they ran into minefields Guevara's troops had planted on both sides of the road. Several armored cars were destroyed or disabled by the mines, and soldiers began to panic and retreat as they came under increasing sniper fire from Guevara's sharpshooters.

The retreat of the troops in the first battalion turned into a rout when they saw that the second battalion was not coming to their relief. As both of the army battalions withdrew in a disorganized manner, Guevara's guerrillas moved in on them from the sides and cut them to ribbons. In total, the army suffered 86 casualties, whereas Guevara's force had only 3 casualties. Guevara's force also captured a large number of weapons and 18,000 rounds of ammunition (Bockman 1984).

By mid-July 1958, the guerrilla forces of the Rebel Army had taken the initiative away from Batista's increasingly demoralized and battered troops. In fact, during the first 11 days of combat in July, the guerrillas captured over 200 of Batista's soldiers, who were no match for the guerrilla fighters of the Rebel Army in the rugged terrain of the Sierra Maestra. By this point, it was clear the offensive was a failure and it became a tremendous propaganda victory for Castro's forces. Over 1,000 of the government's soldiers were killed, wounded, or taken prisoner. The Rebel Army turned over approximately 450 prisoners to the Red Cross. As Guevara later wrote: "Batista's army came out of that last offensive in the Sierra Maestra with its spine broken" (Deutschmann:51).

The Battle of Las Mercedes at the end of July and the beginning of August 1958 was the last significant battle of the Batista government's summer 1958 offensive against the Rebel Army (Bockman 1984). This battle started out as a trap designed to lure the columns under Castro's command into a place where they could be surrounded and destroyed by a much larger force. As the battle began, the Cuban army general in charge of the offensive called on special reinforcements that he had stationed nearby to move into the area and trap Castro's guerrilla columns (Bockman 1984). The reinforcements, a force of some 1,500 troops, started heading toward the area where Castro's columns were engaged in Las Mercedes with other units under the general's command. Castro realized his forces were in a precarious position, and he called on Guevara's column to come to their aid.

Guevara had the ability to see in his mind's eye the whole battlefield in any given encounter. He quickly figured out the army's plan and saw that Castro's columns could be saved from disaster only if the army reinforcements heading toward the area were prevented from reaching the scene. As result, Guevara ordered his men to ambush these troops and keep them from reaching the scene of the battle. His men succeeded in blocking the advance of the army reinforcements. They inflicted serious casualties on the advancing troops and took about 50 prisoners. This action allowed Castro's columns to slip out of the trap set for them by the army. Years later, Major Larry Bockman of the U.S. Marine Corps Command and Staff College analyzed Guevara's tactics during this battle, and he concluded they were brilliant (Bockman 1984). The action taken by

Guevara's column kept the Las Mercedes battle from resulting in Castro's death or capture by the government's forces.

Having turned Batista's offensive into a guerrilla victory and a major propaganda success, the Rebel Army was able to attract widespread political support. On July 20, the leaders of the Cuban political parties opposing the Batista regime, both moderates and conservatives, signed a declaration in Caracas, called the Caracas Pact, in which they threw their support behind the 26th of July Movement and the Rebel Army.

Now the Rebel Army went on the offensive with the strategy of carrying out a three-pronged attack on Santiago de Cuba in the east, the cities in Las Villas Province in the center of the country, and the province of Pinar del Rio at the western end of the island. The key to the success of this strategy was the campaign to divide the country in two by taking control of Las Villas Province. In August 1958, Castro gave Guevara instructions to lead two columns down from the Sierra Maestra to the plains of Camaguey and then march toward Las Villas, where they would cut the country in half and block the movement of troops from Havana to the eastern half of the island.

Guevara took the lead of one of the two columns and Camilo Cienfuegos headed the other. They took separate routes through Camaguey Province toward Las Villas. Cienfuegos's column headed for the northern portion of Las Villas with instructions to establish a base of operations around the small town of Yaguajay. From there, his column was to head toward Pinar del Rio at the western end of the island. Guevara's column had instructions to establish a base of operations in the Escambray Mountains in the southern portion of Las Villas. The mission of his column was to convince the various small guerrilla groups operating there to join forces with his column and tie down the government troops in the central portion of the island so they could not reinforce the army units that were being attacked by the Rebel Army's on two fronts (led by Fidel and Raúl Castro) in Oriente Province.

Guevara and his men made the march from the Sierra Maestra in Oriente Province on foot and on horses over difficult terrain, crossing flooded rivers and streams caused by a hurricane at the beginning of September. He described this march as follows: "Days of tiring marches through desolate expanses where there was only water and mud. We were hungry, thirsty and could hardly advance because our legs were as heavy as lead and the weapons were enormously heavy" (Deutschmann:53).

As Guevara's column moved across the plains of Camaguey toward Las Villas, it was subjected to constant attacks from Batista's army and air force. Guevara wrote: "Despite the difficulties we were never without the encouragement of the peasants," who served as their guides or gave them food, without which they could not have had the strength to go on (page 54). They escaped the ambushes and airstrikes and won one battle after another. Moreover, the almost suicidal character of their maneuvers against the regular army units they encountered seriously demoralized the government's forces. Meanwhile, Cienfuegos's column outmaneuvered and slipped past the army units in their path and made its way to Yaguajay.

Guevara's column made its way through Camaguey Province, and on October 16, 1958, they swam across the Júcaro River, which divides the provinces of Camaguey and Las Villas, in order to slip through the encirclement the army had set up to trap them. Within a few days, they arrived safely in the Escambray Mountains, thanks to the tactical skills and leadership provided by Guevara.

He convinced the five groups of guerrillas already operating in the Escambray Mountains to join with his men in attacking the army garrisons in the center of the province. To achieve this objective, Guevara had to convince the leaders of these independent organizations to join forces with his column. In referring to this accomplishment, he later wrote: "After laborious talks I had with their respective leaders, we reached a series of agreements and it was possible to go on to form a more or less common front" (Deutschmann:57). This common front was an extremely important achievement in the struggle to create revolutionary unity among the various groups fighting the Batista government. From the Escambray Mountains, they were able to harass the Batista dictatorship's armed forces and their communications network in Las Villas Province.

In a desperate attempt to shore up his shaky regime, Batista tried to stage a rigged national election in November 1958. But Castro called on the population to abstain from participating in the elections and ordered his forces to disrupt the elections. The election was boycotted by a majority of the citizenry and by all the political parties that had signed the Caracas Pact. The public's repudiation of the rigged election so infuriated Batista that he launched an unprecedented reign of police terror against the general populace. The guerrillas took this as the cue to begin their general offensive to bring down the dictatorship.

It was in the Escambray Mountains that Guevara met Aleida March, whom he later married (after divorcing Hilda Gadea). March was a schoolteacher in Santa Clara who joined the local branch of the 26th of July Movement in 1956 (March 2008:37). She subsequently served as a clandestine arms courier, saboteur, and messenger for the movement throughout Las Villas Province. In late October 1958, the leadership of the movement in the province gave her money to take to Guevara's guerrilla force in the Escambray Mountains. She had orders to stay on with Guevara's force because it would be too dangerous for her to return to her previous activities.

In her first meeting with Guevara, she gave him 50,000 pesos that she had strapped to her body (page 59). She told him she had been ordered to place herself under his command because the Batista authorities were hunting for her and she knew too much about the movement's clandestine network to be captured by the authorities. At first, Guevara refused to grant her request to join his column as a combatant and suggested she stay at the column's base camp as a nurse. She argued that she had spent the last two years working clandestinely for the movement and that this experience gave her the right to be a guerrilla fighter and not a nurse (pages 60–61). He compromised by asking her to serve as his personal secretary (page 71). After his column had fought its way across the province to the provincial capital in Santa Clara, he gave her an M1 rifle and told her she had earned it. This gesture made her feel that he regarded her as a true combatant—no different in this respect than any of the other members of his column (page 85).

During November and December 1958, Guevara's column and Cienfuegos's column, aided by their allies from the Escambray Mountains, carried out a series of lightning attacks that captured most of the towns, closed the highways, and blocked the railroad lines throughout Las Villas Province. Although they were subjected to constant aerial attacks from Batista's air force and they often faced much larger forces with tanks and heavy weapons, they managed to outmaneuver, demoralize, and defeat their opponents in almost every encounter. As a result of their successful campaign to rapidly seize most of the towns and strategic points in the province, they ended up in control of over 3,000 square miles of territory in a period of a few weeks, and they prevented the government from sending troops to Oriente Province except by air and sea.

They followed a strategy of launching surprise attacks on the garrisons of the army and Rural Guard units in the towns and smaller cities of the province. They would surround barracks or forts and then force them to surrender after cutting off their supplies and threatening to set fire to, or in some cases actually setting fire to, the buildings government forces occupied. The guerrillas promised to release them after they surrendered if they would hand over all their weapons and ammunition, would listen to a lecture about the goals of the revolution, and agreed to leave the province immediately. In some cases, the guerrillas released them to the Red Cross, which then escorted them out of the province. As the news of these surrenders spread throughout the province, the local population offered them increasing support and assistance.

At the end of December 1958, the decisive battle of the revolutionary war was fought by Guevara's column and his allies in Santa Clara, the largest city in Las Villas Province. Santa Clara was the transportation and communications hub of Las Villas and possessed approximately 150,000 inhabitants at the time. It had a railroad station, an airport, and television and radio stations.

Guevara's force, outnumbered nine to one, faced a force of some 3,200 soldiers, Rural Guards, and police (Taibo 1996:304). This force had superior weaponry (tanks, armored personnel carriers, mortars, bazookas, canons, and an armored train), was supported by the air force, and occupied the hills surrounding the city as well as its tallest buildings. Guevara, on the other hand, had a force under his command that totaled only 214 combatants. They were organized into seven platoons with light weapons. The heaviest weapons they possessed were .30-caliber machine guns. They did have one bazooka, but they did not have any rockets for it. In fact, they were low on ammunition and had had very little sleep, since they had been fighting constantly over the preceding 10 days.

On the night of December 27, 1958, the advance unit of Guevara's force arrived at the outskirts of the city. They were followed by a convoy of confiscated trucks and jeeps filled with Guevara's experienced guerrillas from the Sierra Maestra, the guerrillas of the rebel organization called the Revolutionary Directorate, which had joined forces with him in the

Escambray Mountains, and new recruits (students and peasants) who had been recently trained at Guevara's base camp in the mountains. The convoy took a little used back road that brought them to the provincial university campus on the edge of the city. Guevara initially established his command center there and later moved it into the center. On the 28th, he sent his units to capture strategic points in the city while the Revolutionary Directorate's units laid siege to the garrison of the Rural Guards.

Aleida March was constantly at Guevara's side. She knew the city's street pattern well and was able to guide him and his men through the city as they attacked one after another of the positions held by the army units and the police defending the city. She also was able to help him gain support from the local population. As they moved toward the center of Santa Clara, they often had to dodge bullets as they ran from building to building (March:85). Both of them later recalled how frightened they were the other one would be harmed when at one particularly dangerous moment they had to run across a street in front of an army tank that was shooting in their direction.

Guevara was concerned about both the army units stationed on a hill called El Cápiro overlooking the city and the armored train with some 400 soldiers and heavy weapons that was stationed on the railway tracks below them. Thus, the units on the hill and the armored train were strategic targets for Guevara's units. He had his men bring a bulldozer from the school of agronomy at the university to remove 30 feet of rails from the railway line so that the train would be derailed if it attempted to move from its position below the hill.

Guevara ordered his suicide squad, led by 18-year-old Roberto Rodríguez—nicknamed the "Cowboy Kid"—to capture the hill. They succeeded in dislodging the soldiers from the hill and started to attack the train, which withdrew toward the middle of town in the direction where the rails had been removed. As Guevara planned, the train was derailed as it attempted to flee with its cargo of troops, weapons, and ammunition. According to his account, at this point "a very interesting battle ensued: the men in the armored train had been dislodged by our Molotov cocktails [but] in spite of their excellent protection they were prepared to fight only at long range. . . . Harassed by our men who from nearby train carriages and other close-range positions were hurling bottles of flaming gasoline, the train—thanks to its armor plate—became a veritable oven for its soldiers. After several hours, the entire crew surrendered, with their twenty-two armored cars, their anti-aircraft guns, their DCA machine guns, and their fabulous quantities of ammunition (fabulous, that is, to us)" (Guevara 1968:252). Actually, Guevara's account is too modest since it was he who personally negotiated the surrender of the soldiers on the train by meeting unarmed with their commander and assuring them he would allow them to return to Havana escorted by the Red Cross after they laid down their arms (Taibo:244).

As word went through the city of the surrender of the troops on the train, the citizenry began barricading the streets with cars and buses in order to obstruct the movement of the army's tanks and armored cars. Batista ordered the air force to bomb and strafe the city, which it did repeatedly. But even though many buildings were reduced to rubble and the civilian population was terrorized by the air force's indiscriminate bombing and strafing of the city, the situation could not be reversed.

After the troops on the train surrendered, the large number of police and four army tanks that were defending the main police station were persuaded to surrender by one of Guevara's officers. In the fighting leading up to the surrender of the police station, the Cowboy Kid was killed. The Rural Guards garrison capitulated to the Revolutionary Directorate fighters with the aid of some of Guevara's units which used some of the heavy weapons confiscated from the armored train, and then, according to Guevara: "The prison, the courthouse, and the provincial government headquarters fell to us, as well as the Grand Hotel where the besieged men continued their fire from the tenth floor almost until the cessation of hostilities" (page 253).

By New Year's Day 1959, Guevara's forces had gained control of the city except for some 1,000 soldiers inside the Leoncio Vidal Army Garrison, the largest military installation in central Cuba. Guevara had been concerned they might attempt to mount a counterattack on his forces, and he had directed most of his units to concentrate on the garrison and begin to assault it. However, as the news of the surrenders in Santa Clara reached Havana, the dictator Batista and his immediate family fled the country. Informed of this, the commander of the garrison contacted Guevara about negotiating an indefinite truce. After consulting with Castro, Guevara met with the commander of the garrison and told him the following: "It's either unconditional surrender or fire, but real fire, and with no quarter. The city is already in our hands. At 12:30 P.M. I will give the order to resume the attack using all our forces. We will take the barracks at all costs. You will be responsible for the bloodshed" (Taibo:253). The commander went back to talk to his officers, but the soldiers were already deserting their positions and fraternizing with Guevara's men. They began to throw their weapons down and walk unarmed over to the rebel lines. The battle for Santa Clara was over. Guevara's troops allowed the surrendered soldiers to leave Santa Clara unarmed and return to Havana via the port city of Caibarién.

Over Radio Rebelde, Castro demanded the surrender of the besieged garrison in Santiago and he ordered Guevara and Cienfuegos to march their columns immediately to Havana. He gave Guevara orders to take over La Cabaña fortress, which dominates the entrance to Havana and its harbor, and he gave Cienfuegos orders to occupy the Camp Columbia barracks, which was the most important garrison of Batista's army. On January 2, 1959, they left in a convoy of trucks and jeeps for Havana. On the way to Havana, Guevara made his first declaration of love for Aleida when the convoy stopped for gas and they found themselves alone for a moment. He told her that he realized he was in love with her in Santa Clara when they had to cross the street almost directly in front of the tank that was firing in their direction. He told her he couldn't bear the thought of something happening to her (March 2008:85).

In the early morning hours of January 3, 1959, Guevara and Cienfuegos arrived with their columns in Havana. According to Aleida's account of their arrival at the imposing La Cabaña fortress overlooking the city: "In such a fortress it was strange to observe how the mass of soldiers subordinated themselves to the rebel command without any kind of opposition. This fact revealed a great deal about the moral breakdown of the dictatorship, but above all else about the trust and respect for the new Rebel Army, which had the unconditional support of the people" (page 95).

Meanwhile, Castro marched with his troops to Santiago de Cuba to capture the Moncada, the fortress where he had made an abortive attempt six years earlier to bring down the Batista regime. On January 5, five Latin American countries recognized Castro's provisional government. Great Britain and a number of other nations soon followed. On

January 7, the United States recognized the new government, and recalled Ambassador Earl Smith, who was unanimously condemned by Cuban public opinion for having supported Batista. On January 8, Castro's column arrived in Havana, where Guevara and Cienfuegos awaited him.

As Fidel triumphantly rode into the city, his brother Raúl was at his right and Guevara was at his left. In less than three years, the young Argentine had risen from the obscure existence of a roving young adventurer to become one of the most popular and important leaders in the Cuban Revolution. Three years earlier he had only begun to think seriously about his political convictions and commitments, but now, at the age of 31, he found himself an accomplished military commander and one of the three most powerful leaders in the new government of Cuba.

While historical circumstances, destiny, or fate—call it what you will—must be given some of the credit for Guevara's meteoric rise to fame and power, the importance of the man's personality must not be underrated. By the time he arrived in Havana, Che seems to have acquired all the characteristics of a true revolutionary and charismatic leader. He demonstrated an amazing capacity for personal sacrifice, and he never compromised his ideals. From the time he became a guerrilla, he appears to have lived according to the motto *todo o nada* (all or nothing). In fact, he was so demanding of himself that he did not permit himself a single indulgence. This, of course, made it possible for him to demand a great deal from those around him.

Che had that quality of personal magnetism that attracts and inspires the loyalty and devotion of others. In the Sierra Maestra, his bravery, boldness, and determination invoked the enthusiasm of his comrades, and it soon became clear to Castro that Guevara was a natural leader. Once having elevated him to a position of leadership, Castro found that Che was an extremely capable and resourceful military commander. He gave him increasingly greater responsibilities, and in the end entrusted him with the most important and crucial campaign of the revolutionary war.

Castro had complete confidence in Guevara, since he knew that he had no personal political ambitions. He recognized that as an Argentine, Guevara felt it was not his place to question the basic political objectives chosen by his Cuban comrades. Castro knew that he could count on Guevara's loyalty and unquestioning devotion to the goals of the revolutionary movement. Their relationship was very close, largely because of the similarity of their thinking, and he soon gave Guevara some of the most important positions of leadership in the new revolutionary regime.

Chapter 5
CHE'S ROLE IN CUBA'S REVOLUTIONARY GOVERNMENT

When the 26th of July Movement and its allies seized political power in January 1959, they quickly formed a new revolutionary government in Havana. It was led by a coalition of the top leaders of the revolutionary insurrection, Fidel Castro as well as prominent political figures who had opposed the Batista dictatorship but had not taken part in the revolutionary armed struggle that overthrew it. This new coalition government suffered a series of strains and internal conflicts almost immediately. Within a short time, Fidel Castro, other key revolutionary leaders, and the more militant supporters of the 26th of July Movement gained firm control over both the new government and the post-insurrectionary political situation in the country.

The fortress of La Cabaña, which overlooks Old Havana and was occupied under the command of Che Guevara, soon became one of the bastions of the new revolutionary regime, and "El Che" almost overnight became one of the regime's most capable and charismatic leaders. He immediately transformed the La Cabaña fortress into a large training school for the men under his command, and he established a series of small factories in the huge fortress like those he had created in the Sierra Maestra (March 2008:99).

He told Aleida and his closest companions that although the insurrectionary war against the Batista dictatorship had ended, the real revolution had just begun, along with a new life for everyone involved. He said their task was to reestablish order out of chaos and organize themselves to accomplish this task. He began to dictate notes to Aleida about the tasks of the Rebel Army as the vanguard of the revolution, and she assumed the duties of his personal secretary.

CHE AND THE REVOLUTIONARY TRIBUNALS

During January 1959 the Rebel Army organized a series of revolutionary tribunals in La Cabaña that were held to publicly prosecute and punish the torturers, thugs, and murderers of the Batista dictatorship. A commission headed by a captain of the Rebel Army who had been a lawyer took responsibility for investigating and prosecuting government officials, members of the armed forces, and police accused by the public of the worst crimes and abuses under the Batista dictatorship.

Although Guevara, as the garrison commander of La Cabaña, received some of the appeals and interviewed some of the family members who pleaded for clemency in the case of some of the prisoners, he did not participate in any of the trials or the executions (March:101). Nevertheless, the U.S. government and news media, and later the Cuban exile community in Miami (many of whom were sympathizers or former officials of the Batista dictatorship), accused Guevara of being in charge of the trials and executions since many of them took place in La Cabaña (Taibo:344). As time went by, the leaders of the Cuban exile community in Miami conducted a slanderous campaign to smear the popular image of Che by calling him "the Butcher of La Cabaña."

In response to the U.S. campaign against the revolutionary tribunals, Fidel Castro launched a media counterattack on January 21, 1959, in which he compared the revolutionary tribunals with the famous Nuremberg trials held by the U.S. military at the end of World War II in Germany to punish top Nazi leaders and officials for the war crimes and crimes against humanity they had committed in Europe. Castro said the nature of the crimes committed by members of the Batista army and police was no different than that of those committed by the Nazis during their reign of terror in Europe, and thus the revolutionary tribunals in

Cuba and execution by firing squad of the torturers and murderers of the Batista regime were a legitimate form of popular justice (Taibo:344).

Television, radio, magazines, and newspapers throughout Cuba were filled with accounts of the horrible acts of torture, rape, and murder committed by Batista military and police officials; the discovery of secret graves with the mutilated bodies of young men and women taken prisoner by the Batista authorities; and the testimonials of eyewitnesses to the massacres of peasants carried out by the Batista forces during the offensives against the Rebel Army in the Sierra Maestra (page 343). A private national survey carried out at this time in Cuba indicated that over 90 percent of the respondents supported the trials and the executions (page 343).

CHE'S MOTHER AND FATHER VISIT CUBA

On January 18, 1959, Guevara's mother and father arrived from Argentina. He met them at the airport with Aleida and his bodyguard. When his father asked who Aleida was, he told him she was the woman he was going to marry. A few days later, on January 21, Hilda Gadea and Che's three-year-old daughter, Hildita, arrived and were met by one of their mutual friends from their days together in Mexico City. When Gadea met Che, she said: "Ernesto, with his frankness of always, told me he had another woman that he had met in the battle for Santa Clara" (Gadea 2008:179; Taibo 344–45). She agreed to a divorce so that he could marry Aleida. She also decided to remain in Cuba so that Hildita could be educated there and spend time with her father. Shortly afterward, the new government publicly proclaimed Che Guevara to be a Cuban citizen with the same rights as every citizen born in Cuba.

On May 17, 1959, Prime Minister Castro put into effect a new agrarian-reform law, which allowed the government to take over Cuba's large estates and give them to the formerly landless peasants who worked them, but through the creation of a form of collective rather than individual private ownership. This was immediately denounced by top government officials in the United States and the media there as a dangerous threat to the private ownership of property in Cuba, particularly the large landholdings of U.S. citizens and companies. As a consequence, the value of shares in Cuba's U.S.-owned sugar companies dropped to an all-time

Major Ernesto "Che" Guevara, age 34, and his bride Aleida stand before the wedding cake following their marriage at a civil ceremony at La Cabana Military fortress, March 23, 1959. At the extreme left is Major Raul Castro, commander in chief of the armed forces and brother of Prime Minister Fidel Castro. Next to Major Castro stands his wife, Vilma Esping. AP Images.

low on the New York Stock Exchange, and relations between the U.S. government and the new Cuban government became quite hostile. Significantly, Che played an important role in the agrarian reform and the Cuban government's seizure of U.S.-owned companies.

CHE BECOMES CLOSE CONFIDANT OF FIDEL CASTRO

During the first six months of the new government, Che became one of Fidel Castro's closest confidants and advisers. On June 2, 1959, he married Aleida March. She continued to serve as his personal secretary, and she accompanied him nearly everywhere he went in Cuba. However, he refused to take her on a two-month-long international trip he undertook only two weeks after their wedding. He told her he could not take her with him because she was now his wife and it would not be fair to the others accompanying him on the trip who were not able to bring their partners with them.

On June 12, 1959, Guevara left Cuba for the first time since his arrival three years earlier on the *Granma*. The purpose of the trip was to establish friendly relations between the new government in Cuba and the governments of socialist Yugoslavia, the Arab states in the Middle East, and various countries in Asia. He had suggested this trip to Castro in May because he felt it was important for Cuba to establish close relations with the governments of these countries as soon as possible. Castro agreed with him that it was important to strengthen Cuba's relations with these countries. They both felt that in the event of U.S. military aggression against the new revolutionary regime the support of these countries would be decisive in gaining a favorable response from the General Assembly of the United Nations. In addition, they both thought close relations with these countries would permit Cuba's leaders to consult and collaborate with some of the most capable and important statesmen in the world at the time—internationally famous leaders such as Joseph Tito of Yugoslavia, Abdel Nasser of Egypt, Ahmed Ben Bella of Algeria, Jawaharlal Nehru of India, and Mao Tse-tung of the People's Republic of China. Indeed, during this trip Guevara met all of these leaders.

Castro trusted Che with this important mission and subsequent missions of a similar nature because he was confident Che would be an effective representative of Cuba's new revolutionary government. Over the next few years, these missions became one of Guevara's most important responsibilities, and they contributed greatly to the survival and international influence of Cuba's revolutionary regime.

Guevara returned to Cuba in August 1959. Shortly after his return, Castro presided over a meeting of the new National Institute of Agrarian Reform (its acronym in Spanish was INRA) and announced that he was appointing Guevara as head of the Department of Industrialization in that organization. As Guevara saw it, the new government's first big battle to transform Cuba's neocolonial economy was the agrarian-reform program. This program confiscated the *latifundia* (big estates) in Cuba in order to give free land to the country's large number of poor peasants, made up of sharecroppers, tenant farmers, squatters, and small-scale sugarcane growers who had previously rented small plots of land. Later (1961), Che was appointed Minister of Industry.

Che Guevara as Minister of Industry, Cuba, 1963. Library of Congress.

Castro wanted Guevara to lead the effort to persuade the peasantry to increase the country's agricultural production so that it could finance the industrialization of the economy. He believed Guevara was the right person to do this since he had acquired a great deal of experience working closely with the peasantry during the guerrilla war against the Batista dictatorship. Moreover, he had been responsible for the small industries established in the Sierra Maestra by the Rebel Army that produced soap, boots, land mines, and other basic items needed by its members.

CHE TAKES CHARGE OF THE INDUSTRIALIZATION OF CUBA

As head of INRA's Department of Industrialization, Guevara became responsible for the increasing number of industries that were taken over by the revolutionary government, including the petroleum, nickel, sugar-refining, and tobacco industries. He also was responsible for developing the first plans for the industrialization of the country, with the fundamental goal of creating industrial enterprises that would save the country valuable foreign exchange earnings by producing necessary products that previously had to be imported from abroad.

According to his wife, Aleida: "One of the most emotional moments of this stage was when Che had contact for the first time with the miners and learned the extent of exploitation to which they had been submitted in the years of the neocolony, during which time their standard of life was exceedingly low in spite of the enormous effort they made, their nutrition was scarce and they didn't have any schooling." In her book about their life, she recounts how Che made sure "measures were taken to humanize not only their work, but also to dignify these human beings." She said, right from the start, "they were given an adequate diet, and workers dining halls and decorous housing" (March 2008:123).

At the end of November 1959, Castro appointed Guevara to the important post of president of the Central Bank of Cuba, which placed him in charge of the country's financial affairs. Shortly after Guevara assumed this position, he made a public declaration in which he said Cuba would not give any special guarantees to foreign corporations and that the country would seek close trade and financial ties with the then existing socialist bloc of countries led by the Soviet Union.

Throughout the early sixties, Guevara became second only to Raúl Castro in his proximity to Fidel Castro and was Cuba's unofficial foreign relations minister (Guevara 2001:xiv). In addition to his political responsibilities, he wrote what has now become a classic work on revolutionary guerrilla warfare, *La Guerra de Guerrillas* (Guerrilla Warfare) (Guevara 1961), plus books and articles on various other subjects. One of the most famous of these books was *Reminiscences of the Cuban Revolutionary War* (Guevara 1968).

CHE'S ROLE IN SHAPING REVOLUTIONARY CUBA'S FOREIGN RELATIONS

Che played a major role in shaping the new Cuban government's relations with socialist countries, Latin American countries, the United States, and the newly independent nations in Africa, Asia, and the Middle East. He also played a major role in the secret negotiations that took place between the government of the Soviet Union and the Cuban government that allowed the Soviet Union to station nuclear missiles in Cuba (Anderson 1997:526–28). This fateful decision led to the infamous Cuban Missile Crisis of October 1962, in which the United States threatened the Soviet Union with nuclear war if it did not remove all its missiles from Cuba. This crisis brought the world closer to a devastating intercontinental nuclear war than any other incident during the four decades of the cold war between the United States and the Soviet Union.

Che also played a key role in placing Cuba at the forefront of what became known as the Third World, a loose anti-imperialist coalition of African, Asian, Middle Eastern, and Latin American countries—most of which had been previously conquered and colonized by one or more of the major Western countries. The political leaders of these Third World countries sought to increase their national independence and socioeconomic development by steering a middle course between the First World industrial-capitalist countries headed by the United States and the Second World socialist countries headed by the Soviet Union.

Che's speech at the United Nations in December 1964 provides an excellent example of the role he played in projecting Cuba's solidarity with Third World countries. In early December 1964, he traveled to New York City as head of the Cuban delegation to the United Nations General Assembly. While he was in New York he became an instant celebrity. For example, he appeared on the CBS Sunday news program *Face the Nation* and was invited by Malcolm X, one of the most famous African American political activists at the time, to appear with him at an important public rally in Harlem. Although Che was not able to attend this event in person, he sent Malcolm X a letter to read to the participants. Before Malcolm X read the letter, he told the crowd how much he admired Guevara, who he said was "one of the most revolutionary men in this country right now" (Anderson 1997:618).

In Che's speech to the General Assembly entitled, "Colonialism is doomed," he vociferously denounced the United States as an imperialist and warmongering world power. He particularly condemned the U.S. government's military involvement in Vietnam, Cambodia, and Laos and the imperialist role he said the U.S. government was playing in Africa through its military intervention and support of neocolonial leaders in the Congo and its backing of the white racist regime in South Africa.

The following is an excerpt from his speech to the General Assembly on December 11, 1964 (Deutschmann 1997:283–84):

Of all the burning problems to be dealt with by this Assembly, one of special significance for us, and one whose solution we feel must be found first—so as to leave no doubt in the minds of anyone—is that of peaceful coexistence among states with different economic and social systems. Much progress has been made in the world in this field. But imperialism, particularly U.S. imperialism, has attempted to make the world believe that peaceful coexistence is the exclusive right of the earth's great powers. . . . At present, the type of peaceful coexistence to which we aspire is often violated. Merely because the Kingdom of Cambodia maintained a neutral attitude and did not bow to the machinations of U.S. imperialism, it has been subjected to all kinds of treacherous and brutal attacks from the Yankee bases in South Vietnam. Laos, a divided country, has also been the object of imperialist aggression of every kind. Its people have been massacred from the air. The conventions concluded at Geneva have been violated, and part of its territory is in constant danger of cowardly attacks by imperialist forces. The Democratic Republic of Vietnam knows all these histories of aggression as do few nations on earth. It has once again seen its frontier violated, has seen enemy bombers and fighter planes attack its installations and U.S. warships, violating territorial waters, attack its naval posts. At this time, the threat hangs over the Democratic Republic of Vietnam that the U.S. war makers may openly extend into its territory the war that for many years they have been waging against the people of South Vietnam.

Che made it clear in this speech that Cuba wanted to build socialism and it supported the socialist bloc of countries, but he said Cuba was also a member of the "nonaligned, Third World countries" because they were all fighting against imperialism to secure their national sovereignty. In this regard, he said:

We want to build socialism. We have declared that we are supporters of those who strive for peace. We have declared ourselves to be within the group of Nonaligned countries, although we are Marxist-Leninists, because the Nonaligned countries, like ourselves, fight imperialism. We want peace. We want to build a better life for our people. That is why we avoid, insofar as possible, falling into the provocations manufactured by the Yankees. But we know the mentality of those who govern them. They want to make us pay a very high price for that peace.

He also made it clear that while Cuba rejected "accusations against us of interference in the internal affairs of other countries, we cannot deny that we sympathize with those people who strive for their freedom." And he stated that "we must fulfill the obligation of our government and people to state clearly and categorically to the world that we morally support and stand in solidarity with peoples who struggle anywhere in the world to make a reality of the rights of full sovereignty proclaimed in the UN Charter."

To most of those who knew and observed him during the years he served at Castro's side, Che was a model revolutionary leader. He was dedicated to his duties, absolutely convinced of the rightness of his cause, and devoted to Castro. In the opinion of many, he was the most intelligent and persuasive member of Castro's cabinet. But he was also clearly dissatisfied with the routine and bureaucratic aspects of his ministerial responsibilities. On a number of occasions he told his friends of his desire to return to the revolutionary armed struggle. As time went by, he spoke increasingly of the possibility of leaving his ministerial post and devoting his future efforts to the revolution against imperialism in Latin America and in other parts of the world.

Che's personal austerity and disregard for flattery and personal gain presented a sharp contrast to the self-indulgent lifestyles, womanizing, and personal excesses of many of the people around him (Anderson 1997:571–72). In this regard, it is interesting to note that even though he was one of the most important and high-ranking members of the Cuban revolutionary government, he was famous for his careless appearance—he always wore his uniform shirt out of his pants and open at the throat and his boots were never laced to the top. Moreover, when he visited Cuba's industries, he always entered first the workshops to talk with the workers, and only later would he go to the offices of the managers (Taibo 1996:467).

His casual dress and unconventional behavior can be traced to his vagabond trips around South America as a young man, when he seems to have taken delight in traveling for days without bathing or changing his clothes, and he was not distressed by traveling with little or no money or having no idea where he would stay the night. All of these traits helped him when he became a guerrilla fighter and he had to go without bathing, food, water, or a roof over his head.

Che had an ironic and sarcastic wit and a sharp tongue, but he could also laugh at himself. He practiced a curious blend of romanticism and pragmatism; and while he did demand a great deal of those around him, he demanded even more of himself (Anderson 1997:572).

In his lifestyle and personal conduct, he exemplified the principles of individual sacrifice, honesty, loyalty, and dedication. Women were attracted to him, and he was constantly approached by people who wanted to do him favors, but he spurned all attempts at flattery and pandering, hated brownnosers, and remained monogamous throughout his days in Cuba.

In the fall of 1960, Che was asked by a reporter from *Look* magazine if he was an orthodox Communist. His answer was no, he preferred to call himself a "pragmatic revolutionary." In fact, he was neither a pragmatic revolutionary nor an orthodox Communist. To be sure, his outlook, his values, and the events in which he participated generally placed him in the Communist ranks. But as *New York Times* correspondent Herbert Matthews said after interviewing him in 1960, Che would have had no emotional or intellectual problem in opposing the Communists if the circumstances had been otherwise (Matthews 1961).

He made common cause with most Communists because they were opposed to the same things in contemporary Latin American society he opposed. But Che differed from the more orthodox Communists, who tended to rigidly follow the ideological leadership and foreign policy goals of the Soviet Union. He particularly refused to accept their rigid ideological position that the proper conditions for a socialist revolution in Latin America and the rest of the Third World did not yet exist. Che firmly believed the Cuban Revolution demonstrated that socialist revolutions in the Third World could be launched successfully and without the direction and control of an orthodox Communist party. It was heretical views such as these that earned him the disfavor of the pro-Soviet and orthodox Communists.

Che's unorthodox political views and his distrust of the Soviet Union made him a prime target of the pro-Soviet Communists in Cuba. This group, led by Anibal Escalante, was in constant conflict with Che right up to the time of his resignation from the cabinet in 1965. According to them, Cuba's economic instability and its strained relations with the Soviet Union were a direct result of Che's impractical projects and his "pathological" revolutionary adventurism.

The assertion by this group that Che was a pathological adventurer must be discounted as an obvious attempt on their part to discredit a man who stood in the way of the policies advocated by this group of pro-Soviet Communists. Nevertheless, Che was a dreamer and an adventurer. He was prone to dreaming up grandiose plans and projects, especially when he was confined to bed by his asthma. One of his dreams was to lead a revolution in his native Argentina. And only a dreamer could have believed, as he did, that the revolutionary liberation of Latin America was an objective capable of realization in the mid-1960s.

As for the assertion that Che was an adventurer, this he admitted himself in his farewell letter to his parents (Gerassi 1968a:412), which he wrote in the spring of 1965, shortly before he departed Cuba on a secret mission to help the rebel forces in the Congo.

Ernesto "Che" Guevara speaks before the United Nations General Assembly in New York, December 11, 1964. He charged the United States with violating Cuba's territory and attacked U.S. actions in the Congo, Vietnam, Cambodia, and Laos. AP Images.

Dear Parents:

Once again I feel below my heels the ribs of Rosinante [Don Quixote's scrawny horse]. I return to the road with my shield on my arm.

Almost ten years ago, I wrote you another farewell letter. As I remember, I lamented not being a better soldier and a better doctor. The second doesn't interest me any longer. As a soldier I am not so bad.

Nothing in essence has changed, except that I am much more conscious, and my Marxism has taken root and become pure. I believe in the armed struggle as the only solution for those peoples who fight to free themselves, and I am consistent with my beliefs. Many will call me an adventurer, and that I am; only one of a different kind—one of those who risks his skin to prove his beliefs.

It could be that this may be the end. Not that I look for it, but it is within the logical calculus of probabilities. If it is so, I send you a last embrace. I have loved you very much, only I have not known how to express my love. I am extremely rigid in my actions and I believe that at times you did not understand me. It was not easy to understand me. On the other hand, I ask only that you believe in me today.

Now, a will that I have polished with the delight of an artist will sustain my pair of flaccid legs and tired lungs. I will do it!

Remember from time to time this little condottiere [Italian term for the captain of a band of soldiers of fortune] of the twentieth century. A kiss to Celia, to Roberto, Juan Martín and Pototín, to Beatriz, to everyone. A large embrace from your recalcitrant prodigal son.

Ernesto

Che knew full well that his life might well come to a violent end. In addition to his reference to this in his farewell letter to his parents in the spring of 1965, he also acknowledged the possibility in a letter that he sent at about the same time to his old friend and traveling partner Alberto Granados. In this letter he prophetically wrote: "My rolling house has two legs once again and my dreams will have no frontier—at least until the bullets speak."

Che was not a fanatic, and he did not have a pathological love of bloodshed or human cruelty. However, he was not a conventional and contented man. If he had been, he would never have become a revolutionary. He was a dreamer, an adventurer, and an unrelenting rebel against the established order of things. He was a man deeply incensed by the social injustices that he saw in the world all around him, and he was motivated by a sincere desire to rectify them.

He was the personification of the true revolutionary—a superidealist who insists on bringing heaven immediately to earth. Moreover, his willingness to die for his ideals is proof that he possessed far more courage and conviction than the ordinary man or woman. Indeed, the fact that he fought and died for what he believed in makes him stand in sharp contrast to the vast majority of Latin America's political leaders, whose opportunism and lack of conviction have left the poor majority of the region's population with little hope that their condition will ever be improved by the existing political order.

Chapter 6

CHE'S CONTRIBUTION TO REVOLUTIONARY GUERRILLA WARFARE

Che Guevara's ideas about revolution and guerrilla warfare are required reading for all those interested in understanding the nature of both topics. His book *La Guerra de Guerrillas* (*Guerrilla Warfare* in the 1985 English translation), which was first published in 1961, is one of the most important publications on guerrilla warfare in the world. This book, along with certain articles he wrote, in particular his "Guerra de Guerrillas: Un Metodo" ("Guerrilla Warfare: A Method," published in Gerassi 1968a:266–79), provide a complete theory of revolutionary guerrilla warfare, largely based on the Cuban experience. This theory has influenced revolutionary movements throughout Latin America and the rest of the world and has inspired many radical groups to start a revolutionary guerrilla *foco* (focal point or center of guerrilla operations) like the one established by Fidel Castro, Che, and their comrades in the Sierra Maestra of Cuba.

During his days as a guerrilla leader in the Sierra Maestra, Che made it a habit to write down his daily observations in a personal campaign diary. At the end of a long day's march or after an engagement with the enemy, he always sat down somewhere apart from the others to write about the events of the day. On the basis of these notes he was later able to formulate his theories about guerrilla warfare and to write an excellent historical account of the Cuban revolutionary war, *Pasajes de la Guerra Revolucionaria* (*Episodes of the Revolutionary War*, 1996).

It was Che's belief that the Cuban Revolution clearly demonstrated that the people of Latin America can liberate themselves from dictatorial rule if they resort to guerrilla warfare. In *La Guerra de Guerrillas* (*Guerrilla Warfare*), Che wrote that the Cuban Revolution had made three fundamental contributions to revolutionary thought in Latin America. First, the Cuban experience proved that popular, irregular forces could win a war against a professional army. Second, it proved that it is not necessary to wait until all the conditions for revolution are present. According to Che, the insurrectional guerrilla foco can itself create the necessary conditions.

Third, Che believed Cuba demonstrated that, in Latin America, which has a large rural population, a successful revolutionary struggle must initially concentrate on the rural areas and not the cities if it is to succeed. Che claimed that the first two of these contributions refuted the arguments of those who claimed to be revolutionaries but refused to take any revolutionary action because of the pretext that they could not defeat a professional army or because the necessary "objective conditions" for revolution did not exist in Latin America.

He believed a nucleus of 30 to 50 men could establish and consolidate a revolutionary guerrilla foco in any country of Latin America, providing they were determined, had the cooperation of the people, and had perfect knowledge of the terrain where they would be operating. Che also stressed that the people must believe it is impossible for them to obtain social and economic reforms through peaceful means before they will be inclined to support an insurrectionary guerrilla foco. Moreover, he argued that where a government has risen to power by some form of popular consent, including fraudulent elections, and maintains at least the appearance of constitutional legality, it is impossible to establish and consolidate a guerrilla foco because many of the people will believe that there is some possibility of improving their social and economic conditions through legal means.

Che disagreed with those who argued that the revolutionary struggle in Latin America depended primarily on the political mobilization of the discontented urban masses in the cities. He felt that it was far more difficult to carry out a successful insurrection in the cities, where the armed forces and police can be effectively concentrated and utilized, than in the rural areas, where regular troops are at the mercy of a highly mobile guerrilla force supported by the rural population. The support of the rural population, according to Che, is the sine qua non of guerrilla warfare. In fact, he defined guerrilla war as a war of the people, led by a fighting vanguard (the nuclear guerrilla force) against the forces of the ruling oligarchies (elites) and their foreign backers (the U.S. government and the transnational corporations with investments in the Third World). Thus, in Che's view, the guerrilla force does not seize power by itself; rather, it serves as a catalyst that inspires the people themselves to take up arms and overthrow the established regime.

In *La Guerra de Guerrillas*, Che wrote that without the support of the people a guerrilla force is nothing more than a roving gang of bandits. He noted that both have the same characteristics: homogeneous membership, respect for their leaders, courage, knowledge of the terrain, and appreciation of the correct tactics to employ against numerically superior forces. However, they differ in one fundamental respect: one has the support of the people and the other does not. Consequently, bandits are inevitably hunted down and eliminated, whereas guerrilla forces, which count on the support of the people, can defeat a professional army and bring about the downfall of the most oppressive regime.

A guerrilla force, according to Che, wins the support of the masses in rural areas largely by championing their grievances. This means that the guerrillas must present themselves as crusaders intent on righting the injustices of the prevailing social order. Che believed that the major grievances shared by the rural masses throughout Latin America arose from the concentration of land ownership in the hands of a small, wealthy, landed elite. Thus, the great majority of the peasantry do not own the land on which they live and work. Consequently, he saw land reform as the key issue to be used by guerrilla forces in their effort to win the support of the rural masses. In other words, Che argued that the guerrilla fighter must be an agrarian revolutionary who uses the peasantry's hunger for land as the basis for mobilizing its support.

He also believed that any revolutionary guerrilla force must be the conscience of the people, and that the moral behavior of the guerrillas must be such that the people regard them as true priests of the social reforms that they advocate. According to Che, guerrilla fighters must always exercise rigid self-control and never permit themselves a single excess or weakness. This means guerrillas must be ascetics whose moral behavior earns them the respect and admiration of the local population. In addition, Che wrote it is the duty of guerrillas to give technical, economic, and social assistance to the peasantry. In this way, they develop a close relationship with the peasantry, which allows them to win their trust and confidence. Once this relationship has been achieved, it then becomes the task of the guerrillas to indoctrinate the peasantry about the fundamental importance of the armed struggle as the only way they can liberate themselves from their present state of exploitation and oppression. Che believed that the successful execution of this task brings into existence a true people's war and the inevitable destruction of the existing regime.

One of Che's most original contributions to the literature on guerrilla warfare is his discussion of the qualities of the guerrilla fighter. According to him, the ideal guerrilla soldier is an inhabitant of the zone where the nuclear guerrilla foco is established. This is because the two most important prerequisites of successful guerrilla warfare are a thorough knowledge of the terrain and the cooperation of the local population. The guerrilla who inhabits the region where he or she operates knows the terrain and has friends in the area to turn to for help. It follows, therefore, that in Latin America the local campesino (peasant) makes the best guerrilla soldier, although Che emphasized that a guerrilla force should not be composed exclusively of campesinos.

Che seems to have been describing himself without knowing it when he listed the personal qualities that the ideal guerrilla soldier should have. He stressed audacity and a readiness to take an optimistic attitude at times when an analysis of existing conditions does not warrant it. He also believed that the guerrilla fighter must be ready to risk his or her life almost daily and to voluntarily give it up if the circumstances require it. This of course demands a high degree of devotion to the cause for which the guerrillas are fighting, and according to Che, such devotion can be sustained only if the guerrilla movement is based on ideals that are meaningful to each guerrilla fighter. He concluded that among nearly all campesinos such an ideal is the right to have a piece of land of their own, while the ideal of adequate wages and better social conditions plays a comparable role among guerrillas from the urban working classes and more abstract ideals, such as political freedom and social equality, motivate students and intellectuals.

In addition to the moral and psychological qualities that make a good guerrilla fighter, Che stressed that guerrillas must also have certain important physical qualities and be able to adapt to the most difficult environmental conditions. As Che knew well from his own experience, the conditions of guerrilla life require enduring severe privations, including the lack of food, water, proper clothing, shelter, and medical attention. Moreover, guerrillas must be able to adapt to a life of almost constant movement, in which they are required to march long distances and traverse areas no ordinary man or woman would ever venture.

Che wrote that in terms of the general pattern of a guerrilla's day-to-day life, combat is the most interesting event. Combat, therefore, is both the climax and the greatest joy in that life, only combat provides the means to fulfill the purpose for which the guerrilla exists. Che emphasized that guerrillas must perform their role as combatants without any reluctance or weakness, since they must give the enemy no quarter and expect none in return. On the other hand, Che also made the point that wounded and captured enemy soldiers must be treated benevolently by guerrilla soldiers, unless they have committed criminal acts that require they be tried and perhaps executed.

The final objective of a revolutionary guerrilla war according to Che's perspective is the defeat of the enemy's army and the seizure of political power in the name of the people. However, he made it quite clear that guerrilla warfare cannot in itself bring about victory. He emphasized that it is important to remember that guerrilla warfare is only the first phase of a war of national liberation and that, unless it develops into a conventional war, the enemy cannot be completely defeated.

Che wrote that in a revolutionary guerrilla war's earliest stages the primary strategy of the revolutionary guerrilla force is to assure its own survival. This means that it must flee from and avoid the enemy forces sent to destroy it. During this phase, it must restrict its offensive activities to lightning attacks on unsuspecting enemy posts or units and in each case retreat to a secure hiding place before the enemy has a chance to react with its superior forces and weapons. If the guerrilla force succeeded in eluding the enemy forces sent to destroy it, Che assumed it would increasingly attract recruits from the rural population and gradually enlarge the scale of its operations, striking more frequently at the enemy troops in the zone surrounding the guerrilla foco. In this way, the guerrillas begin to weaken and demoralize the enemy's forces. By systematically harassing the enemy through surprise attacks, they also disrupt communications and force the enemy onto the defensive.

The next phase involves extending the territory of guerrilla activity by sending small groups deep into enemy territory to sabotage and terrorize the enemy's key centers of supply and communications. Meanwhile, the original base of guerrilla operations must be continually strengthened and measures must be taken to indoctrinate the inhabitants of the guerrilla zone. Later, when more fighters and arms have been obtained and the circumstances appear to warrant an expansion of the conflict, new guerrilla columns are formed and sent to operate in areas behind the enemy's lines.

The final phase of the struggle begins, according to Che, when the guerrilla columns unite and engage the enemy's forces in a conventional war of fixed fronts. It is at this moment that the people's army comes into existence and the drive toward the cities begins. The death knell of the old order comes as the urban masses turn on the defending troops and the last strongholds of enemy resistance surrender to the people's army. This clears the way for the revolutionary leaders to seize power and begin the building of a new society. "Above all it must be made clear that this type of struggle is a method: a method for achieving a purpose. That purpose, indispensable and unavoidable for every revolutionary, is the conquest of political power" (Guevara 1963).

Che warned that a people's army does not emerge spontaneously and that victory is obtained only after a long and difficult struggle in which the people's forces and their leaders are exposed to repeated attacks by superior forces intent on annihilating them. He also pointed out that the guerrillas must expect to suffer greatly at the hands of the enemy. Che made this point most effectively in the following passage from his article "Guerrilla Warfare: A Method," which prophetically describes the situation his guerrilla force encountered in Bolivia:

> The enemy army will punish them severely. At times they will be split up into groups, and those who fall prisoner will be tortured.

They will be hounded relentlessly like hunted animals in the areas they have chosen for their operation. They will suffer the constant uneasiness of having enemies at their heels, and they will constantly have to suspect all they encounter, since the frightened peasants will in some instances hand them over to the repressive troops in order to rid themselves of the latter by removing the reason for their presence. Their only alternative will be death or victory, at times when death is a thousand times present and victory is a myth about which only a revolutionary can dream. (in Gerassi 1968:276)

However, Che argued that even if only a fragment of the original guerrilla nucleus survives, it can continue to spark the revolutionary spirit of the masses and can organize anew to carry on the struggle.

Che believed that war is subject to a series of scientific laws and that those who disregard these laws are destined to be defeated. Since guerrilla warfare is merely one type of war, he claimed that it was governed by the same laws. However, because of its special aspects, Che argued that guerrilla warfare is also governed by a series of accessory laws or principles that must be recognized by a guerrilla force hoping to succeed.

Since one of the precepts of guerrilla warfare is the enemy's vast superiority in troops as well as in equipment, Che stressed that the guerrillas must utilize special tactics that allow them to offset the enemy's superiority in troops and equipment. These tactics are based, as already mentioned, on two essential preconditions: (1) the guerrillas must be highly mobile, and (2) they must possess a much greater knowledge of the terrain than the enemy.

Extreme mobility and a detailed knowledge of the terrain of operations make it possible, in Che's opinion, for the guerrillas to outmaneuver and surprise the numerically superior and better-equipped forces sent against them. With these capabilities, they can strike when the enemy is off guard and then quickly disappear before retaliation, thus inflicting heavy casualties on the enemy with very few or no losses of their own. "Strike and run, wait, watch carefully, and then again strike and run" (Guevara 1963). This, in Che's words, is the primary tactic of guerrilla warfare, to be repeated over and over until the enemy is demoralized and forced to take a static and essentially defensive posture.

The basic characteristics of this tactic are the element of surprise and the rapidity of the guerrillas' attacking and withdrawal maneuvers. The speed and surprise inherent in this tactic give the guerrillas a great advantage over the enemy's larger and better-equipped forces. Moreover, Che noted that it is particularly effective when used at night and that, for this reason, one of the basic features of guerrilla warfare is night fighting.

Somewhat more static than the hit-and-run technique, but just as effective, is the ambush. This tactic is, of course, as old as war itself and has always been used by the weak against the strong. It requires that the enemy be on the move, ideally marching in file through a ravine, canyon, or pass, where the forces can be caught in a devastating crossfire. However, Che made an original contribution to this age-old tactic. In his writings, Che mentions the psychological damage inflicted on the enemy if the guerrillas always concentrate their fire on the advance elements of the army units they ambush. The enemy's soldiers realize they can expect almost certain death if they are in the advance positions of a column. This tactic, Che claimed, creates panic among the soldiers and may even lead them to mutiny if they are ordered to take the lead positions in a column marching through a suspected guerrilla area.

In addition to the ambush and the rapid hit-and-run type of attack, Che also wrote about what is called the "minuet tactic." Somewhat analogous to the dance of the same name, this tactic involves surrounding an enemy column with several small groups. These groups alternately engage the enemy from different points. As soon as one group retreats, another one initiates an attack from a different direction. As a result, the enemy column is constantly kept off balance and demoralized. In fact, if the guerrillas have enough men and ammunition and there is no possibility of the surrounded enemy column receiving outside aid, the guerrillas can annihilate the entire column.

Che emphasized that a guerrilla force must never allow itself to be encircled, for experience had shown, he said, that the only really effective way of stamping out a guerrilla force is to encircle the guerrillas in a given area, concentrate as many troops in the circle as possible, and progressively close in around the guerrillas until they are liquidated. For this reason, guerrilla warfare is a war without any fixed front or battle lines. According to Che, the guerrillas must appear and disappear at the enemy's rear, at the flanks, and in its midst. In the initial stages, guerrillas should rarely attempt to hold a given position, since their concern is to avoid encirclement or a frontal encounter with the enemy's superior forces. Instead, their aim should be to inflict as many casualties on the enemy's forces as possible without jeopardizing themselves. Confronted with this type of irregular warfare, Che claimed that the enemy's regular army is rendered powerless. Since the army is equipped and trained to fight a conventional war or control the street demonstrations of students and workers, it becomes frightened and demoralized when faced with the tactics of the guerrillas.

Since one of the most important aspects of guerrilla warfare is the relationship between the guerrillas and the local population, Che believed that the guerrillas should conduct themselves at all times in the most respectful manner toward civilians. For this reason, he advocated that they always pay for any goods taken, or at least give a certificate of debt to be paid at some future date. He also emphasized that the zone of guerrilla operations must never be impoverished by the direct action of the guerrillas and that the local inhabitants must be permitted to sell their products outside the guerrilla zone, except under extreme circumstances. As the guerrilla effort progresses and whole areas of a country come under their control, then, according to Che, the guerrillas must assume responsibility for governing the civilian population and regulating economic activity in the areas under their control.

Although Che believed sabotage was one of the most effective tactics available to a revolutionary guerrilla movement, he was opposed to terrorism per se. He believed that terrorism is a negative weapon that can turn the people against a revolutionary movement. Moreover, in his opinion, the results of terrorist attacks are not worth the cost in lives that they entail. On the other hand, he distinguished sabotage (the destruction of essential industries and public works) from terrorism (the systematic use of violence to coerce the population) and advocated the destruction of nearly everything necessary for normal, modern life, for example, telephone lines, electrical power stations, water mains, sewers, gas pipelines, railroads, and radio and television stations. Yet even in the case of sabotage, Che pointed out that a guerrilla force must consider the social consequences of each act of destruction so as not to cause unnecessary suffering among the urban and rural masses.

For Che, one of the most important characteristics of guerrilla warfare is the difference between the information possessed by the guerrillas and that possessed by the enemy. He saw the situation as one in which the enemy's regular forces must constantly operate in areas where they encounter the sullen silence of the local inhabitants, while the guerrillas can count on a friend in every house who will pass information about the enemy's movements along to the guerrilla headquarters or the guerrilla force operating in the area. Che believed that this is one of the greatest advantages enjoyed by guerrillas and that it should be utilized to the fullest extent.

However, in Che's opinion, a guerrilla force should never confide too much in the local peasantry, since peasants have a natural tendency to talk to their friends and relatives about everything they see and hear. Moreover, in view of the brutal way the regular troops treat the local population in an area where guerrillas are known to be operating, he warned that it is to be expected that some will give the enemy information about the guerrillas in order to escape torture or mistreatment.

Since Che conceived of guerrilla warfare as a revolutionary war of the people in which the guerrillas serve as the revolutionary vanguard, he repeatedly emphasized throughout his writings that the support of the masses was crucial to the success of any guerrilla insurgency. Therefore, he was preoccupied with treating in detail how a guerrilla force secures and develops popular support. For this reason, his writings on revolutionary guerrilla war come closer to being a manual on how to organize and successfully execute a popular revolution than a theoretical work on military strategy and tactics.

Most revolutionary movements in Latin America following the Cuban revolution were based on Che's contention that a small band of from 30 to 50 guerrillas can create the conditions required for a revolutionary victory in any country of Latin America. Most of these movements, including the one directed by Che himself, failed to demonstrate that an insurrectionary guerrilla foco located in a rural area could, by itself, produce a successful popular revolution.

The Cuban revolution was not purely a peasant revolution, mounted by a small guerrilla force that came down out of the mountains to liberate the cities. Che knew this. There is much more to the story of the Cuban Revolution than this. To be sure, the guerrillas were the symbol of the revolution, and they played a crucial role in its development. However, Cuba's urban working and middle classes, who threw their weight behind the guerrillas because of their hatred of the corrupt Batista regime, and the weakness of the Cuban army, which was not enthusiastic about defending the unpopular regime, played decisive roles. Moreover, if Castro had put forward a more radical program of social and economic reforms prior to his seizure of power, the revolutionary movement against Batista would not have been able to acquire the magnitude of popular support that made its victory possible.

Ironically, the international importance and historical significance of the Cuban Revolution may well have made another Cuban-style revolution in Latin America very difficult to achieve. It is hard to imagine a similar revolutionary guerrilla movement today either (1) deceiving the upper and middle classes into believing it has moderate political aims, or (2) winning the support of U.S. and international public opinion as romantic freedom fighters combating a tyrannical regime. The political elites in Latin America have learned a lot from the Cuban Revolution and subsequent attempts to replicate it. They now know that a revolutionary guerrilla force must be eliminated as soon as it appears, that the army must be effectively trained in counterinsurgency warfare, and that serious efforts must be made to win the support of the peasantry or at least to forestall their giving support to a revolutionary movement.

However, Che's theory of revolutionary guerrilla warfare overemphasized the importance of the rural population as the popular base for a successful revolutionary movement in Latin America. The armies of a number of Latin American countries, using modern counterinsurgency tactics that their officers have learned from U.S. advisors and training programs, have shown that they can defeat or at least contain Cuban-style revolutionary guerrilla movements that rely principally on a rural base of support.

But even more important is the obvious fact, recognized by most Latin Americans interested in revolution, that the main breeding grounds for any kind of radical popular movement in Latin America are the cities and towns. The cities are inundated with migrants from the rural areas. Hoping to break away from the poverty and misery of rural Latin America, they generally find waiting for them in the cities unemployment and worse living conditions than they had in the rural areas. The frustration and discontent that derive from this situation provide a fertile soil for radical political groups. Thus, today and in the future, the exploding urban centers offer an important base of potential popular support for radical political movements in Latin America and in other parts of the world with similar social and economic conditions.

Nevertheless, it is important to note that in a modified form Che's ideas on guerrilla warfare and the Cuban model of the catalytic guerrilla foco were adopted with some success by armed revolutionary movements in Central America in the 1970s and the 1980s. The success of the Sandinista Front for National Liberation (Frente Sandinista de Liberación Nacional, or FSLN) in overthrowing the Somoza dictatorship in Nicaragua at the end of the 1970s is perhaps the best example of a successful revolutionary movement in Latin America that began with a rural-based guerrilla force similar to that recommended by Che. However, the FSLN, which was backed by Che and the Cubans in the sixties, succeeded in overthrowing the Somoza regime in the 1970s because it combined guerrilla warfare in the countryside with a successful campaign of urban guerrilla warfare and the development of a multiclass, multiparty political alliance—not that different from what occurred in Cuba. This broad-based political alliance helped the FSLN mobilize a nationwide popular insurrection that toppled the Somoza regime (Harris and Vilas 1995).

For those who believe a rural-based armed insurrection is no longer viable, with the end of the cold war and modern military methods, the surprise appearance on the contemporary scene of the Zapatista revolutionary movement in southern Mexico in the mid-1990s provides clear evidence that guerrilla movements similar to the type advocated by Che Guevara continue to arise in Latin America and other parts of the world where extreme social injustices persist. And the striking resemblance of the Zapatistas' charismatic spokesperson, Subcomandante Marcos, to Che is certainly no accident of history. Not only does Marcos project a revolutionary persona modeled to a large degree on Che's iconic revolutionary image but he mentions him frequently in his speeches and interviews. The Zapatista movement has more modest political goals and has used less aggressive military tactics than Che and his comrades, but this revolutionary movement, which has emerged from the largely rural, indigenous peasant population of the state of Chiapas clearly reflects the legacy of Che's revolutionary example. Many of his ideas about imperialism, revolution, socialism, and guerrilla warfare have clearly influenced the ideology and tactics of this revolutionary movement (Anderson 1997:753). The relative success and international attention given to this movement have also helped to create renewed interest in Che's ideas about revolutionary guerrilla warfare.

Chapter 7
CHE'S IDEAS ABOUT IMPERIALISM AND SOCIALISM

Che silently resigned his cabinet post in Fidel Castro's government and disappeared from public view in 1965 (Deutschmann 1994:27–31). There was a great deal of speculation at the time about his disappearance. Some believed Che and Castro had had a serious disagreement and Che had been imprisoned or secretly executed. There were also reports that Che had been killed in the Dominican Republic during the civil war that took place there in the spring of 1965. Later on, there was speculation that Castro or elements within the Cuban regime had eliminated Che because of his opposition to certain policies advocated by the political faction within the Cuban Communist Party that believed Cuba should follow the advice of Cuba's advisors from the Soviet Union and the socialist Eastern European countries (such as Czechoslovakia, Poland, and East Germany) closely tied to the Soviet Union.

By the beginning of 1964, it was evident even to Che that his four-year plan initiated in 1961 to industrialize Cuba was having great difficulties. He realized he and many of his comrades had underestimated the difficulties involved in transforming Cuba from a largely agrarian economy dominated by the production and exportation of sugar into an industrialized economy based on the production of a wide range of agricultural as well as manufactured products and the extensive application of modern technology (Taibo 1996:482–500). He made Herculean efforts in his posts as head of the national bank and minister of industry. He worked 16–18 hours a day and drove those around him to do the same. He had a genius for finding innovative solutions to the country's problems associated with its lack of technology and the technical skills needed for industrial development. However, his exemplary leadership and commitment to his responsibilities and ideals could not overcome the many organizational deficiencies, widespread lack of technology, shortage of replacement parts (caused largely by the U.S. economic blockade of Cuba), and the lack of trained cadres. All of these problems obstructed the expansion of both Cuba's agricultural production and the development of its underdeveloped manufacturing sector.

On the basis of what Che told his friends, it is possible to ascertain what his thinking was during this period. In the first place, it is clear that Che was forced to admit that Cuba would have to return to its historical mode of livelihood, that is, the production of sugar for export. Yet he was not willing to accept the advice of Cuba's Soviet and Eastern European advisors that the revolutionary government should abandon the goal of industrializing the country. He felt strongly that Cuba's economic relations with the socialist bloc of nations led by the Soviet Union should not be the same as those between capitalist countries. If Cuba could not industrialize by itself, as a result of its neocolonial legacy and the underdeveloped character of its economy, then, Che argued, the more developed socialist countries such as the Soviet Union had an obligation to help Cuba. He thought the Soviet Union should finance Cuba's long-term efforts to industrialize instead of expecting Cuba to serve primarily as the sugar mill for the socialist bloc.

Che found little sympathy for his ideas among the Soviet Union's leaders and the Soviet advisors in Cuba. They regarded his plans to industrialize Cuba as unrealistic and impractical. Even if Cuba were to succeed in transforming its economy with Soviet assistance, they argued that there would be an insufficient market for Cuba's manufactured goods. Moreover, they pointed out the island lacked most of the raw materials needed for heavy industries (Anderson 1997:488–89). They argued the size of Cuba's internal market was not large enough to make the production of its own manufactured items economically justifiable and that, in view of Cuba's political isolation, it could not expect to export manufactured products to any of its neighbors in the Western Hemisphere. When Che countered that Cuba would have an export market in Latin America as soon as the revolution was carried to other countries of Central and South America, the Soviets made it quite clear that they were not willing to risk basing their economic assistance to Cuba on this eventuality.

Che was also critical of the Soviet Union's state capitalist economic system and its reliance on what he regarded as basically capitalist methods of organization, management, and investment. In particular, Che felt that the Soviet system's reliance on material incentives and a system of decentralized financial management in its state industries were contradictory to the development of a genuine socialist economy and the development of a socialist consciousness on the part of the workers (Gerassi 1968a:292–316). Moreover, he suspected Moscow and Washington had entered into a tacit agreement to respect each other's international spheres of influence, and as part of this agreement Moscow had promised to restrain Havana from promoting revolution throughout Latin America and the Caribbean.

Che felt strongly that Cuba should firmly align itself with the newly independent Third World nations of Africa, the Middle East, and Asia and assist national liberation struggles and socialist revolutions throughout the still colonized parts of the Third World. This idea motivated him to travel extensively throughout Africa and Asia during early 1965.

He went on an extended state visit to Africa, China, and then back to Africa during the first three months of 1965. In Africa, Che visited Algeria, Mali, Congo-Brazzaville, Guinea, Ghana, Dahomey (Benin), Tanzania, and Egypt, where he met with important African and Arab leaders such as presidents Ahmed Ben Bella of Algeria, Kwame Nkrumah of Ghana, Julius Nyerere of Tanzania, and Abdel Nasser of Egypt (Anderson 1997:620–21).

Che also made a trip to the People's Republic of China with the official purpose of explaining Cuba's position with regard to the growing international conflict between the Soviet Union and China. The Chinese were upset over what they considered to be Cuba's increasing support for the Soviet Union. Because of the growing tension between Cuba and China at the time, Che had only a brief, formal meeting with China's famous leader Mao Tse-tung, but he was able to meet at length with other top Chinese officials and discussed with them his ideas about a united anti-imperialist front to liberate the Third World from Western (U.S., British, French, Belgian, and Portuguese) imperialism.

Actually, Che's views were closer to those held at the time by the Chinese leadership than to the Soviet Union's, since he had become increasingly critical of the Soviet Union's international relations. He considered the course adopted by the Soviet Union under Premier Nikita Khrushchev to be a "rightist" deviation from socialism. He also considered the emphasis placed by the Soviet advisors in Cuba on continuing the country's specialization in sugar production, the use of material incentives to increase labor productivity, and allowing Cuba's state enterprises to adopt financial self-management as contrary to the Cuban revolutionary regime's commitment to the rapid industrialization of the economy and the replacement of capitalist material incentives and methods of organization with communist moral incentives and methods of organization. He predicted (correctly as it turned out) the Soviet Union and the Soviet bloc of socialist countries would return to capitalism if they continued to rely on capitalist market mechanisms, material incentives, and enterprise self-management (Anderson 1997:697).

Following his visit to China, he returned to Africa via Paris, where he learned definitively of the death of his friend Masetti in Argentina and his abortive effort to start a guerrilla foco there. From Paris he flew to Dar es Salaam, Tanzania, where he met with President Nyerere and with the representatives in Dar es Salaam of the armed guerrilla movements fighting for national independence at that time in the Portuguese colonies of Angola and Mozambique, white-settler-controlled Rhodesia (Zimbabwe), and the former Belgian Congo (Taibo 1996:514–15). Among the representatives whom he met in Dar es Salaam were Gaston Soumaliot and Laurent Kabila, two of the leaders of the Congolese rebel movement that was then in control of the eastern portion of the Congo. Although he was not impressed by Soumaliot and most of the other representatives he met, he was favorably impressed by Kabila's leftist views, which he found similar to his own, and acting on the authority that he had previously received from Fidel Castro, Che offered to send to Kabila's forces Cuban arms and military advisors.

From Tanzania he went to Egypt, where he told President Nasser of his desire to go to the Congo at the head of the contingent of Cuban advisors he had promised Kabila. In February 1965, Che appeared as an observer at the second conference of the Organization of Afro-Asian Solidarity in Algeria, where he initiated a personal crusade to create an anti-imperialist front among the neutral nations of the Third World. In the speech he delivered at this conference, he criticized the socialist countries for being the "accomplices of imperialist exploitation" and called on them to support popular revolutions in the neocolonial and colonial countries of the Third World, instead of pursuing their own selfish foreign policy (Gerassi 1968:378–86).

The Soviet observers who were in attendance were outraged. Following the conference, both Ben Bella of Algeria and Nasser of Egypt tried to talk Che out of the idea of heading a Cuban contingent to the Congo. Nasser warned him that if he went to the Congo he would be considered a white man and that his involvement there could only turn out badly (Taibo 1996:517). Ben Bella was more supportive and allowed Che to establish a base in the hills overlooking Algiers, which he and representatives of other Latin American revolutionary groups, supported by the Cuban government, used for training purposes and maintained as a sanctuary until Ben Bella was overthrown by a military coupe in June 1965.

When Che returned to Cuba in March 1965, he was ready to resign his position in the Cuban government in order to devote all his efforts to furthering the armed struggle against imperialism. Since he had played such an important role in the Cuban Revolution although not Cuban, he assumed be would be able to do the same elsewhere, not only in Latin America but this time in Africa.

Shortly after Che returned to Havana, he met with Fidel Castro to discuss the results of his travels and his views regarding the position Cuba should take in international affairs. At this meeting, it appears that Castro reproached Che for criticizing the Soviet Union and the other socialist countries in his speech at the Organization of Afro-Asian Solidarity in Algiers (Taibo 1996:522). Castro also made it clear that he was under both external and internal pressure to move Cuba closer to the Soviet Union in the growing split between the Soviet Union and revolutionary China. In fact, the Soviets and the old-guard members of the Cuban Communist Party within the Cuban regime were pressing him to come out openly in favor of the ideological position held by the leaders of the Soviet Union and against the more radical ideological line taken by the leaders of the People's Republic of China. These former allies were now locked in an international struggle for the leadership of the international socialist movement.

Che's radical brand of revolutionary socialist internationalism was not shared by the leadership of the Soviet Union and by the leaders of most of the pro-Soviet Communist parties in Latin America. The Soviet leadership regarded what they considered Che's radical leftist adventurism to be a threat to their own international strategy of peaceful competition and coexistence with the United States and its allies. However, there appears to have been some sympathy for Che among the Soviet leaders, especially since his influence had been decisive in convincing Fidel Castro to align Cuba with the Soviet Union shortly after the revolutionary government was formed in Cuba.

According to Feder Burlatsky, a former advisor to Soviet premier Khrushchev, the Soviet leadership disliked Che's revolutionary adventurism and they were afraid his example would lead the Cubans and other leftists in Latin America into taking actions that would provoke a major military confrontation between the Soviet Union and the United States (Anderson:581). But in an interview he gave to the journalist Jon Lee Anderson in 1995, Burlatsky claimed: "Even though Che was against our interests, there was still some sympathy for him. . . . There was a romantic aura around him; he reminded people of the Russian Revolution" (Anderson:581).

Anderson also interviewed Nikolai Metutsov, who was responsible for maintaining relations between the Communist Party of the Soviet Union and the Communist parties in the non-European socialist states such as Cuba and Vietnam. Metutsov told Anderson he "fell in love" with Che upon meeting him, because of his "very beautiful eyes," and because his stare was "so generous, so honest," and because he was impressed by the way he spoke with such impetus, "as if his words were squeezing you" (Anderson:585). According to Anderson, Metutsov's appraisal was that Che's views could not be easily classified.

> Externally one could truly say that, yes, Che Guevara was contaminated by Maoism because of his Maoist slogan that the rifle can cre-

ate power. And certainly he can be considered a Trotskyite because he went to Latin America to stimulate the revolutionary movement there . . . but in any case I think these are external signs, superficial ones, and that deep down, what was most profound in him was his aspiration to help man on the basis of Marxism-Leninism. (Anderson:585)

Metutsov told Anderson that he thought that Che's personal commitment to the cause of revolution was his "peculiarity." He said Che's dedication to armed struggle, while a source of worry for some members of the leadership of the Soviet Communist Party, was not perceived by the Soviet leadership as a whole to be a cause of significant concern. Whether this last statement about their lack of concern was true is hard to assess now.

Che was committed to both fomenting revolution on a truly international scale and personally putting into practice his thesis that it was possible for a small, if committed, guerrilla force to ignite a full-scale popular revolution in countries under the control of oppressive regimes backed by U.S. imperialism. His so-called peculiar commitment to these beliefs was shared by most of his closest friends and comrades as well as many admirers and sympathizers around the world. His commitment threatened the positions of the pro-Soviet leaders of the orthodox Communist parties in Cuba and elsewhere as well as many other leftist political parties and governments not aligned with the Soviet Union. Che openly criticized these parties and movements for their unwillingness to fight U.S. imperialism and to engage in an armed revolution to bring down the capitalist regimes in their countries and build socialist societies in their place.

Che realized, however, Cuba had no other alternative but to side with the Soviet Union. Che also knew his continued presence in the government was a liability. This was because of several reasons: his disagreements with the Soviets over their ideological line and their foreign policy, Cuba's growing dependence on Soviet military aid and trade, and his desire to involve himself directly in the revolutionary struggles against imperialism taking place in Latin America and around the world.

He realized that it would be impossible for him to involve himself directly in a revolutionary struggle in Latin America or Africa if he continued to hold a high position in the Cuban government. The international repercussions would have been too great for Cuba. In view of these circumstances, Che decided to resign his positions in the Cuban government and leave Cuba. His main interest was carrying the revolution to South America, particularly his homeland Argentina. He had established ties with revolutionary groups throughout Latin America and in other parts of the world while he held his important positions in the Cuban government, and he now planned to use some of these connections to carry out his plans of taking an active leadership role in creating or aiding armed revolutionary movements in South America and Africa.

His friend and confidant Fidel Castro encouraged him to go to Africa and assist the revolutionary movement in the Congo, since he felt the conditions were not yet ready for him to go to South America. Castro knew that he had become increasingly restless in his governmental posts in Cuba and was anxious to carry out what he considered to be his historic mission of liberating the Third World countries from Western imperialism and capitalist exploitation (Anderson 1997:628).

Of course, this meant resigning from his important positions in the Cuban government, and it meant leaving behind all that Che had accomplished in Cuba as well as his wife and five children and most of his Cuban comrades (except for those who would accompany him first to the Congo and later to Bolivia). It was an extremely difficult and courageous decision for him to make. However, Che was a man who was totally committed to carrying out his convictions. His wife, Aleida March, knew this well. She had learned this by his side during the revolutionary war against the Batista dictatorship, and she always knew that one day he would leave her and their children to fulfill his chosen destiny—to fight to the death if necessary against imperialism and for the establishment of socialism.

In her book about their life together (March 2008), she discusses the tremendous sacrifices they both endured as a result of his total commitment to live by his revolutionary ideals—ideals that she shared wholeheartedly with him. The separations were almost unbearable for both of them, since they never knew when or whether they would see each other again. Indeed, she tried repeatedly to convince him to take her with him—both on his mission to the Congo and to Bolivia. But he convinced her the time was not right for her to join him and their young children needed her to stay with them until they were much older.

Che was very close to his five children even though they were very young when he left them—to his first child Hildita (Hilda Beatriz Guevara Gadea), who lived with her mother (his first wife, Hilda Gadea) in Havana, and to his four children with Aleida March: Aleida, Camilo, Celia, and Ernesto, who lived with him in Havana. He was also very much in love with Aleida. Therefore, his separation from Aleida and his children was very painful and he missed them deeply while he was in the Congo and Bolivia.

The personal side of Che and his many admirable personal traits are revealed beautifully in Aleida March's book on their life together. She describes many intimate moments of touching tenderness and romantic love between them. In general, her account of their life together reveals both his continuing devotion to her and the sincere concern he always showed for her feelings and her personal welfare. During his long absences from Cuba, he would write love letters and poems for her and make tape recordings to be given to her and the children. In the letters and poems he wrote for her, he nearly always referred to her as *mi única*, (my only one), and they all display great affection and longing for her.

For example, here is a fragment of a poem he wrote for Aleida upon his departure for Bolivia (March 2008:221):

Adiós, my only one,
do not tremble before the hungry wolves
nor in the cold steppe of absence;
by my heart I carry you
and together we will continue until the road fades away . . .

And in the last message she received from him in Bolivia, he wrote the following:

My only one:
I am taking advantage of the trip of a friend to send you these words, which could go by mail, but a "semi-official" road seems more intimate. I could tell you that I miss you to the point of losing sleep, but I know you would not believe me, so I will abstain.

> But there are days in which the homesickness becomes uncontrollable and possesses me. On Christmas and New Years, above all, you don't know how much I miss your ritual tears, below a sky of new stars that remind me of how little of my life I have devoted to personal affairs. (March 2008:225)

In this last communication with his wife, one can sense his homesickness and longing for her as well as the sadness he felt over how little of his life he had spent with her and their children. He ended this message with a "kiss for the little pieces of flesh [his children], all the rest" and a kiss for her that he said was "pregnant with sighs and anguish."

This romantic personal side of Che's life was little known to all but his inner circle of family and friends until Hilda Gadea published her book in the late seventies on her relationship with Che and more recently Aleida March published her book on their life together. In this regard, it is also important to recognize that the ideological cornerstone of Che's revolutionary thinking and practice was not guerrilla warfare or armed revolution but his almost utopian concept of *el hombre nuevo* (the new man or human being). He used this concept to express the almost spiritual belief he held in the development of new socialist human being for the 21st century. In fact, he believed the development of this new type of human being was an essential aspect of the construction of a genuine socialist society. His belief in this ideal human being was an important source of inspiration for him and for those who adopted or were influenced by his views on socialism and the future development of humanity (Siles del Valle 1996:47–92).

Che was dedicated to living his life in accordance with his ideal concept of the new type of human being that would come into existence in the revolutionary struggle to build a new socialist world order for humanity. Che believed this new type of human being would arise out of the revolutionary struggle to liberate humanity from the egoistic individualism, dehumanizing exploitation, and social alienation associated with capitalism.

Che felt the struggle against capitalism and the construction of a new socialist order required a new type of human being who would always be committed to making personal sacrifices for the good of others. Nowhere is this concept of *el hombre nuevo* presented more explicitly than in Che's essay "Socialism and Man in Cuba," written early in 1965 while he was traveling as a Cuban statesman in Africa. What follows are some brief excerpts from this essay (in Gerassi 1968:398–400).

He describes the characteristics of revolutionary 21st-century men and women who he hoped would arise out of the struggle to build a socialist society. First and foremost, he believed they would be guided by "strong feelings of love" for humanity. He wrote:

> Let me say, at the risk of appearing ridiculous, that the true revolutionary is guided by strong feelings of love. It is impossible to think of a true revolutionary without this quality.

While he felt that there could be "no life outside of the revolution" for the men and women of the new socialist society, he also believed the revolutionary leaders of the 21st century would have to avoid falling into "dogmatic extremes" and "have a highly developed sense of justice and truth." Thus, he wrote:

> There is no life outside the revolution. In these conditions the revolutionary leaders must have a large dose of humanity, a large dose of a sense of justice and truth, to avoid falling into dogmatic extremes, into cold scholasticism, into isolation from the masses.

As for the level of social commitment required of the new human being, he believed very strongly that this commitment would require a great deal of personal sacrifice. In this regard, he seems to have been writing as much about himself as the new socialist human being when he wrote the following lines:

> Each and every one of us punctually pays his share of sacrifice, aware of being rewarded by the satisfaction of fulfilling our duty, aware of advancing with everyone toward the new human being who is to be glimpsed on the horizon.

Che firmly believed this ideal new human being would develop in the future, despite the difficulties of achieving the level of social consciousness and social commitment required for this human development to take place. Thus, he wrote: "the road is long and in part unknown," but "we are aware of our limitations" and "we will make the twenty-first century human being, we ourselves!"

His widow, Aleida March, recounts in her book about their life together how Che's closest friends and comrades felt that he was the best example of the new human being he wrote and spoke about so frequently. As Fidel Castro says in his memoir of Che (Deutschmann 1994:108–9):

> He was a living example. It was his style to be the example, to set the example. He was a person with a great spirit of self-sacrifice, with a truly spartan nature, capable of any kind of self-denial. His policy was to set an example. We could say that his entire life was an example in every sphere. He was a person of absolute moral integrity, of remarkably firm principles, a complete revolutionary who looked toward the future, toward the humanity of the future, and who above all stressed human values, humanity's moral values. . . . None of the words I use about him involve the slightest exaggeration, the slightest overestimation. They simply describe the man we knew.

Chapter 8

THE SECRET MISSION IN AFRICA

Fidel Castro supported Che's recommendations about providing Cuban support to the rebels in the Congo (later called Zaire), other liberation movements, and the new leftist governments in Africa. According to Castro, the rebels in the eastern Congo requested Cuban military assistance in 1964. In a 1987 interview with the Italian journalist Gianni Minà (Deutschmann 1994:118), which took place on the 20th anniversary of Che's death, Castro said the following about Che's involvement in the Congo:

> At the time, white mercenaries had intervened in the former Belgian Congo, now Zaire. [President] Lumumba had been killed, a neocolonial regime was established, and a movement of armed struggle emerged in Zaire. We never made this public, but the revolutionary movement asked us for help and we sent instructors and combatants on an internationalist mission.

He also told Minà it was his idea that Che go with the Cuban force sent to the eastern Congo. In this regard, he said:

I myself suggested the idea to Che. He had time on his hands, he had to wait [before the conditions were more favorable for his long-hoped-for mission to South America]. . . . So we put him in charge of the group that was going to help the revolutionaries in what is today Zaire. . . . In all, about 100 Cubans went and stayed there several months. He followed the approach of teaching Zairians how to fight. Cuban and Zairian patriots fought white mercenaries and the forces sent by the government. . . . In the end the revolutionary leaders of the former Belgian colony decided to halt the struggle, and our personnel were withdrawn.

As Che's wife, Aleida March, wrote in the foreword to his Congo diary: "Che, together with the group he led, aimed to strengthen as much as possible the liberation movement in the Congo, to achieve a united front, to select the best men and those prepared to continue the struggle for the final liberation of Africa" (Guevara 2000:xlv). And according to Che's second in command in the Congo, Víctor Emilio Dreke, Che decided to participate in the Congo project after his African trip, even though this project went against his original idea of going to fight in Argentina (page xxiv).

I suppose Che decided to participate in the project after his African trip. It went against his original idea to go to fight in Argentina. The assassination of Lumumba and the general situation in the Congo led him to take an interest in the guerrilla struggle there. It enabled him to follow a double objective: to prepare a group for Latin America, and to create a third front [against imperialism], in Vietnam, Latin America, and Africa. These were the ideas he wished to bring to fruition. Africa seemed easier than Latin America. . . . The moment had come to act in Africa.

Moreover, according to Pablo Rivalta, the Cuban ambassador in Tanzania who assisted Che's Congo mission, Che saw the Congo as a good site for a training base for liberation movements that would revolutionize all the African countries and in particular, bring down the infamous white supremacist regime in South Africa.

Despite the rumors at the time, Che's disagreement with Castro regarding Cuba's relationship with the Soviet Union was not the reason for his departure from Cuba, and this disagreement did not end the long-standing friendship between them. Nor did Cuba's relationship with the Soviet Union lead Castro to abandon his desire to see Cuba play an active role in the international struggle against U.S. and European imperialism. Castro was quite willing to send a contingent of Cubans, headed by Che, to assist the left-wing rebels in the Congo, who were then fighting against the pro-Western regime of Prime Minister Moise Tshombe.

The Congo became the scene of a bloody civil war following its independence from Belgium in 1960. The country's first elected prime minister, Patrice Lumumba, was overthrown and then murdered by a U.S.-backed coup d'état in December 1960. When Tshombe, who was involved in Lumumba's assassination, subsequently became the country's head of state in 1964 with U.S. support, Lumumba's followers launched an armed uprising against him. In November 1964, with the intent of crushing this uprising, the U.S. government provided planes to transport Belgian troops and white mercenaries to the Congo.

Because of the cold war conflict at the time between the United States and its allies and the Soviet Union and its allies, the situation in the Congo became a major international political crisis. In December 1964, Fidel Castro sent Che to represent Cuba at the United Nations General Assembly in New York. In the well-publicized speech he gave at the General Assembly, Che denounced the involvement of the U.S. government and its allies in the Congo and other parts of Africa (Deutschmann 1997:286–88).

In this speech, Che reminded the members of the General Assembly that Lumumba was murdered following the occupation of the country by a United Nations force that Lumumba had requested. He said this force had allowed his opponents to capture and kill Lumumba with impunity. He claimed the United States and other Western imperialist countries used the United Nations to depose Lumumba and kill thousands of Congolese, and their purpose was to defend the superiority of the white race in Africa and to continue Western imperialist control over the Congo's vast mineral resources. And if this was not enough, he said, "the latest acts have filled the world with indignation" because they allowed one of Lumumba's murderers, Tshombe, to come to power illegally with the help of "Belgian paratroopers, carried by US planes, who took off from British bases" (Deutschmann:287).

Che went on to state: "Our free eyes open now on new horizons and can see what yesterday, in our condition as colonial slaves, we could not observe," namely, that so-called Western civilization uses "a showy façade" to disguise an ugly "picture of hyenas and jackals." He ended his comments on the Congo crisis by saying: "All free men of the world must be prepared to avenge the crime of the Congo." Only a few months later, in April 1965, Che led a secret contingent of 100 Cuban volunteers to assist the Congolese rebels, who were fighting both the Tshombe regime and what they considered its Western imperialist backers.

The idea of going to the Congo to assist the leftist rebels fighting the neocolonial regime there appealed to Che largely because of his fascination with the idea of linking the nations of Africa, Asia, and Latin America together in a common struggle against Western imperialism. And despite the lack of enthusiasm for the idea among many of the African leaders he met on his previous his trip to Africa, Che wanted to establish a Cuban-led military training center in the eastern Congo. He hoped revolutionaries from all over the African continent would come to this base to train and gain valuable fighting skills and experience that they would then take back to their respective countries (Anderson:623).

To prepare for the Congo expedition, Che removed himself from public view at the end of March 1965. By the end of April, his disappearance from public view had begun to cause a great deal of speculation both inside and outside Cuba about what had happened to him. On April 30, Fidel Castro was interviewed by a number of reporters, and in response to their questions about Che, he answered that he could say only that Che would always be where he could be of most use to the revolution. This statement, however, only served to intensify the speculation and rumors about Che's disappearance.

Che wrote a confidential and rather personal letter of resignation to Castro when he left for the Congo. This letter (Gerassi 1968a:410–11), which Castro made public in October 1965, appears to have been designed among other purposes to absolve the Cuban government of all responsibility for Che's actions in the Congo in the event he was discovered, captured, or killed there.

Fidel:

I remember at this hour many things, when we met at Maria Antonia's house in Mexico, when you suggested that I come to Cuba, and the tension of the last minute preparations. One day they came around asking who to advise in case of death, and its real possibility struck us all. Afterward, we knew that it was certain, that in a revolution you die or triumph (if the revolution is a true one). Many of our comrades were left behind on the long road to victory. Today everything has a less dramatic tone because we are all more mature, but the same thing is repeating itself. I feel I have completed that part of my duty that has tied me to the Cuban revolution and so I say good-bye to you, our comrades, and to your people, who are now mine too.

I formally renounce my post in the directorate of the party, my post as minister, my rank of comandante, and my status as a Cuban. There is nothing legal that ties me to Cuba, only ties of another type that cannot be broken as in the case of offices. Making a summary of my past life, I think that I have worked with sufficient honesty and dedication to consolidate the success of the revolution. My only fault of any gravity is that I did not confide in you at the beginning in the Sierra Maestra and have not understood with sufficient clarity your qualities as a leader and revolutionary.

I have lived magnificent days at your side and I have felt the pride of belonging to our people in the dark and bright days of the Caribbean crisis [Bay of Pigs invasion by U.S.-backed Cuban exiles]. Rarely has a statesman shone as brightly as you in those days. I feel proud of having followed you without hesitation, identifying myself with your way of thinking, seeing and appreciating both the dangers and principles. Other lands of the world now claim the assistance of my modest efforts. I can do what you now are prevented from doing because of your responsibility at the helm of Cuba, and so the time has come to separate. Let it be known that I do this both in pleasure and sorrow: here I leave the purest of my hopes as a builder and the most cherished of my loved ones and I leave a people who admitted me as one of their sons; this lacerates part of my spirit. To new fields of battle I will take the faith that you have given me, the revolutionary spirit of my people, and the feeling of carrying out the most sacred of duties: to fight against imperialism wherever it exists; this comforts and cures my pain abundantly.

Once again I say that I free Cuba of all responsibility, except that which comes from her example. If my last hour should come under other skies, my last thought will be for the Cuban people and especially for you. I am grateful for your teaching and example, and I will be faithful to you until my last act. I have always identified myself with the foreign policies of our revolution and will continue to do so. Wherever I go I will feel the responsibility of being a Cuban revolutionary, and I will act as one. I leave nothing material to my wife and children; and this doesn't bother me for I am happy that it is this way. I ask nothing for them, since the state will provide them enough to live and will educate them. There are many things I could tell you and our people, but I feel that this is not necessary. Words cannot express what I want to say, and it is not worth while to fill sheets of paper. Victory always! Country or death! My embrace with all revolutionary fervor.

Che

When Che left for the Congo in April 1965, he led a handpicked group of mostly black Cubans who had fought with him and Castro in the Sierra Maestra. Their clandestine mission was carefully planned by Cuban intelligence, which planted a false report in the Dominican Republic that Che had arrived in the capital of Santo Domingo in April and had been killed shortly thereafter in the civil war going on in that country at the time (Anderson 1997:638). Thus, while the CIA was looking for evidence of Che's presence in the Dominican Republic, he and his companions were able to leave Cuba, travel to Africa, and enter the Congo with complete secrecy.

Che's reasons for leaving Cuba in 1965 to go fight in the Congo and later in 1966 to establish a guerrilla training base in Bolivia were twofold. He felt his mission in life was to carry out the struggle for the liberation of Latin America and the rest of the Third World from imperialist domination and capitalist exploitation. Moreover, he felt he would soon be too old to be able to physically carry out this kind of mission. Furthermore, to carry out this kind of mission, he needed the freedom of action that he could gain only if he was no longer a high-profile official in the Cuban government. His official responsibilities required him to speak in the name of this government and to act in accordance with its policies and diplomatic relations (Taibo:530).

He felt it was necessary to free himself from the constraints imposed on him by his official obligations as an important leader in the Cuban government so that he could return to the life of a revolutionary guerrilla fighter and carry out the global struggle against Western imperialism, which he had come to consider his main mission in life. His total commitment to his convictions in this regard and the feeling that time was running out on his ability to fulfill his mission were his reasons for leaving Cuba in 1965.

According to Fidel Castro, he knew Che had wanted to go to fight in South America for many years, since the time Che joined the Cuban revolutionary movement in Mexico. In fact, Che told Castro then that once the Cuban revolution triumphed he wanted to be free to go fight in Argentina. Castro revealed this in his 1987 interview with the Italian journalist Gianni Minà (Deutschmann 1994:116).

> Che very much wanted to go to South America. This was an old idea of his, because when he joined us in Mexico . . . he did ask one thing: "The only thing I want after the victory of the revolution is to go fight in Argentina"—his country—"that you don't keep me from doing so, that no reasons of state will stand in the way." And I promised him that. It was a long way off, after all. Firstly, no one knew if we would win the war or who was going to be alive at the end—and he surely, because of his impetuousness, had little chance of coming out alive. . . . Once in a while, in the Sierra and afterward, he would remind me of this plan and promise. He was certainly farsighted in this.

After the success of the Cuban revolution, Castro said Che "grew more enthusiastic about the idea of making a revolution in South America," and as the years went by he became increasingly impatient to carry out his desire to play an important role in this historic struggle.

CHE'S AFRICAN DIARY

Che realized shortly after arriving in the Congo that the rebels could not win because of their corrupt and weak leaders, their failure to organize support among the local population, their distrust of one another, and their hopeless lack of discipline. In this regard, it is relevant to note the following observation he made in what has become known as his Congo diary (Guevara 2000:235):

> The leaders of the movement pass most of their time outside of the territory. . . . Organizational work is almost null, due to the fact that the mid-level leaders do not work, in fact they do not know how to work, and every one distrusts every one else. . . . Lack of discipline and lack of self-sacrifice are the dominant characteristics of the guerrilla troops. Naturally, with these troops one cannot win a war.

In Tanzania after he was forced to leave the Congo, Che wrote a 153-page manuscript about the failure of his Congo mission. Che wrote this account of his Congo experience during his stay in the Cuban embassy in Dar es Salaam, Tanzania, during the months he lived there in secrecy. This manuscript, *Pasajes de la guerra revolucionaria: Congo*, was kept secret for more than 30 years, until it was edited and first published in 1999 by his wife Aleida March and Richard Gott (the English translation was published in 2000. See Guevara 2000).

This ruthlessly honest document reveals among other things that Che decided he would accompany the contingent of armed Cubans sent to the Congo without first informing and obtaining the consent of the Congolese rebel leaders such as Laurent Kabila. Thus, Che states in this document:

> I hadn't told any of the Congolese about my decision to fight there. In my first conversation with Kabila I had not been able to do so

because nothing had yet been decided, and after the plan was approved [by Fidel Castro] it would have been dangerous for my project to be known before I arrived at my destination; there was a lot of hostile territory to cross. I decided, therefore, to present a fait accompli and act according to however they reacted to my presence. I was not unaware of the fact that a negative would place me in a difficult position, because now I couldn't go back, but I calculated that it would be difficult for them to refuse me. (page 10)

Although the Congolese rebel leaders did not object to Che's presence as the commander of the Cuban contingent, they were concerned about his presence in the Congo. Moreover, he found it difficult to meet with them and soon realized there was little prospect for the rebels to achieve victory since these leaders were ineffective and their forces were incapable of defeating the existing neocolonial regime, which had the backing of the Belgian, British, and U.S. governments.

Che also blamed himself for the failure of the Congo mission. He wrote: "I set off with more faith than ever in the guerrilla struggle, yet we failed. My responsibility is great; I shall not forget the defeat nor its most precious lessons. I learned certain things in the Congo. Some mistakes I will never make again, others perhaps I will—and there will be new ones that I shall commit" (Guevara 2000:235).

Although he said he continued to have faith in his foco theory for creating a popular revolution, he made the following scathing critique of his own actions in the Congo:

> I was at the head of a group of Cubans, no more than one company strong, and my function was to be their real leader who carried them to the victory that would hasten the development of a genuine popular army. My peculiar situation, however, made of me a soldier representing a foreign power, an instructor of Cubans and Congolese, a strategist, and a high flying politician in an unfamiliar setting. . . . Had I been a more authentic soldier, I might have had more influence in the other spheres of my complicated relationships. I have described how I reached the point of safeguarding the cadre (my own precious person) at particularly disastrous

moments in which I found myself, and how I allowed subjective considerations to gain the upper hand in the closing moments.

From this passage in his diary, it is clear that Che was deeply critical of his own behavior and the many limitations he confronted in the Congo. He engaged in this self-critique with a view to avoiding repetition in the future of the errors that he felt he had committed in the Congo.

However, Che's subsequent mission to Bolivia appears to have failed for some of the same reasons as the Congo mission. For example, in Bolivia Che repeated the tactic of inserting himself secretly into another country at the head of a foreign military group and into a situation that lacked both the objective and subjective conditions necessary for a successful revolutionary movement.

THE LEGACY OF CHE'S MISSION IN AFRICA

It is interesting to note that although Che's mission to the Congo was a bitter defeat for him and his Cuban companions, the lessons Cuba's leaders learned from this unsuccessful effort to assist the Congolese rebels helped them to be much more successful in the military and political support they provided to liberation movements and leftist governments throughout Africa during the following decades. Without a doubt, the best example of this success was Cuba's involvement in Angola.

Between April 1965, when Che first promised Antônio Agostinho Neto the leader of the liberation movement fighting the Portuguese colonial rulers of Angola that Cuba would assist the liberation struggle in his country, and May 1991, when the last Cuban combatants left Angola, some 450,000 Cubans (7% of the Cuban population) had served in this worn-torn country (Harris 2009). They helped the liberation movement gain Angola's independence and then helped the new government of President Neto defeat two South African military interventions and a bloody insurgency backed by the U.S. government. They also helped the Angolan government repulse an invasion from Zaire (now the Democratic Republic of the Congo) in the longest and largest military campaign in Africa since World War II.

Cuban support played a key role in Angola's liberation and defense and in the liberation of Guinea-Bissau and Cape Verde from Portuguese

THE SECRET MISSION IN AFRICA

colonial domination, and Cuba also helped defend the newly independent government of the Congo Republic (Brazzaville), formerly a French colony, from neocolonial forces intent on overturning it. They played an important role in the liberation of Mozambique from Portuguese colonial rule, as well as the liberation of the white-settler-controlled former British colony of Rhodesia (Zimbabwe). Moreover, the Cuban military victories against the white South African forces in Angola greatly contributed to the liberation of Namibia and to the ultimate downfall of the white supremacist apartheid regime in South Africa itself. This regime was greatly weakened by the demoralizing defeat the combined Cuban, Angolan, and Namibian forces inflicted on the white South African troops in Angola and Namibia.

Nelson Mandela, the first president of the new Republic of South Africa, established after the downfall of the racist apartheid regime in that country, is among the many African leaders who have praised the Cubans for the assistance they provided in these struggles for independence. He has repeatedly thanked the Cubans for their contribution to the victory of his people over racist domination and imperialism. For example, at the public opening of the Southern Africa–Cuba Solidarity Conference in 1995, President Mandela (1995) said:

> Cubans came to our region as doctors, teachers, soldiers, agricultural experts, but never as colonizers. They have shared the same trenches with us in the struggle against colonialism, underdevelopment, and apartheid. Hundreds of Cubans have given their lives, literally, in a struggle that was, first and foremost, not theirs but ours. As Southern Africans we salute them. We vow never to forget this unparalleled example of selfless internationalism.

At a more individual level, Che's brief presence in the Congo changed dramatically the life of the Congolese teenager who served as his translator during the months he and his companions operated in the Fizi Baraka mountain range near the border between the Congo and Tanzania. Freddy Ilanga, who spoke both Swahili and French, had been a newspaper vendor and was just 16 years old when he was assigned by the rebel leadership to serve as Che's translator during the time he and his Cuban comrades carried out their then secret mission of providing support to the Congolese rebels. Freddy Ilanga's brief encounter with the legendary Che and his Cuban companions placed him on the path of an incredible journey that took him from being a teenage rebel in the eastern Congo to Cuba where he studied medicine, married a Cuban woman, and became a brain surgeon.

As a young African who saw the whites in his country as racist oppressors, he knew nothing about the Cuban Revolution and at first he considered Che to be a sarcastic white man (Doyle 2004). But he soon came to admire Che. He was particularly impressed with how Che treated the Africans around him with respect. In those days in the Congo, this was something Freddy had never seen.

Shortly before Che and his companions pulled out of the Congo, they arranged for Freddy to be sent to Cuba, where he finished his schooling, went to the university to become a doctor, and then specialized in pediatric neurosurgery. Although Freddy never returned to the Congo before he died in Cuba, today in Africa there are hundreds of Cuban doctors and African doctors who were trained in Cuba (Harris 2009).

Ironically, Kabila seized control of the government of the Congo in 1997, at the head of a military force that originated in the same region of the country where Che and his Cuban comrades had established their training base in 1965. Backed by the governments of Rwanda and Uganda, Kabila's forces managed to topple the long-time dictatorial regime of General Mobutu Sese Seko, the U.S.-backed military strongman who had seized power in November 1965, the same month Che and his men were forced to abandon their mission in the Congo. Kabila was assassinated by a member of his own staff in an unsuccessful coup attempt in 2001, and his son replaced him as the Congolese head of state.

CHE'S SECRET RETURN TO CUBA IN 1966

In November 1965, Che left the Congo as secretly as he had entered seven months earlier. After leaving the Congo, he spent a couple of months in secrecy in the Cuban embassy in Dar es Salaam, Tanzania. During this time, Castro gave Che's wife, Aleida, permission to visit him, and she arrived in Tanzania in mid-January 1966 (March 2008:200). For Aleida, this visit was what she had dreamed might happen some day. It enabled them to be completely alone together without their children and the constant circle of subordinates and comrades that had previously surrounded him in Cuba.

During their stay in the Cuban embassy in Dar es Salaam, they slept, ate, read, and conversed in a large dining room that was converted into living quarters for them. During this time, Che went over the notes he had written during his seven months in the Congo and wrote a lengthy manuscript that was primarily intended as a report for Cuba's top leaders on the failure of his mission and what he had learned about the possibilities for assisting liberation movements and leftist governments in Africa.

This manuscript was read by Fidel Castro and a few other key officials of the Cuban government but kept secret for more than 30 years. As in the case of his Bolivian diary, Aleida March played a central role in its publication. It was published in English with the title *The African Dream: The Diaries of the Revolutionary War in the Congo*, with the addition of an introduction written by the well-known British journalist and historian Richard Gott (2000).

In Castro's 1987 interview with the Italian journalist mentioned above, he revealed what happened after Che was forced to withdraw from the Congo (Deutschmann 1994:119). According to Castro:

> Having now spent about six months in Zaire, Che stayed for a while in Tanzania, assessing the experience he had just lived through. His conduct on the mission was, as always, exemplary to the highest degree. His stay in Africa was temporary, awaiting the creation of conditions for traveling to South America.

But as Castro explained in this interview, Che's situation was now greatly complicated by the fact that during his absence his resignation letter had been made public by the Cuban government in response to the growing rumors and outrageous stories circulating about his mysterious disappearance from public view in Cuba. To quote Castro (pages 119–20):

> Once the letter had been made public—politically it had become unavoidable to publish it—Che, with his particular character, felt very awkward about returning to Cuba after having said farewell.

But in the end, I persuaded him to return, because it was the best move given all the practical matters he wanted to take care of. So, he secretly returned to Cuba. He stayed several months, training in a remote mountain region . . . with those who were to accompany him [to Bolivia].

It was a bitter blow for him to return secretly to Cuba after spending seven months in the Congo without having anything to show for his efforts and after having resigned his important positions in the Cuban government. The experience, however, seems to have made Che more determined than ever to undertake a successful revolutionary mission outside of Cuba, but this time in his native South America.

Upon his return to Cuba from the Congo, Che found solace in the fact that one of his grandest dreams had come true; an intercontinental organization representing the underdeveloped countries of the world, with its headquarters in Cuba, had been founded only a few months before his return by Fidel Castro. From January 3 to 15, 1966, the first conference of the Organization of Solidarity of Asian, African, and Latin American Peoples—referred to thereafter as the Tricontinental—was held in Havana, with some 400 delegates from the underdeveloped world attending. As it turned out, Che's revolutionary ideas were the central topic of discussion among the delegates, and this undoubtedly reinforced his determination to carry out the realization of one of his oldest dreams: the liberation of Latin America's oppressed and exploited masses. This dream was bolstered by his belief that Cuba would become truly independent of the Soviet Union only when additional revolutionary governments were established in Latin America that could provide support to Cuba.

Che's return to Cuba was never made public (Deutschmann 1994:119). He remained in hiding during the entire period that he stayed there. Almost immediately after his return, he began to prepare a new mission that he felt would not have the limitations of the abortive undertaking in the Congo. He chose Bolivia as the site for a revolutionary guerrilla foco, which he himself would organize and lead. In October 1966, he once again left Cuba, as secretly as he had entered, to begin this undertaking.

Chapter 9

CHE'S FINAL MISSION IN BOLIVIA

Che's final mission was carried out in Bolivia, in the heart of South America. Bolivia is a starkly beautiful country that combines towering snow-capped mountains and a high-altitude, windswept, treeless dry plateau with deep tropical valleys and a wide expanse of tropical lowlands in the eastern portion of the country that borders Brazil. The country is divided into two distinctive parts by the massive wall of the Andes Mountains, which traverse the country from north to south. The mountains and high plateau in the western portion of the country have such an otherworldly terrain and such unusual colors that they look more like Nepal or the alternate reality of another planet than a country in the heart of the South American continent near the equator. This part of the country contains the *altiplano*, the great high plateau of the South American continent. Here the descendants of the ancient Incan civilization, with their herds of llamas, live an impoverished existence some two and a half miles above sea level. The vastness and barrenness of this windy plateau give it a haunting beauty all its own, and anyone who has been to this part of the world carries away unforgettable memories of magnificent panoramas, azure blue skies filled with white puffy clouds that look close enough to touch, and snow-covered peaks bathed in the soft, multicolored glow of an indescribably beautiful sunset.

On the altiplano are Bolivia's major mining centers and the focal point of national politics, the capital city of La Paz. Situated at 11,900 feet in a deep basin on the altiplano, La Paz is the highest capital city in the world. The approach by land to the city is from the altiplano. Consequently, the first view one receives of La Paz is from some 2,000 feet directly above it. The view of the shiny tin-roofed city in the basin below takes one's breath away. Far below sprawls the glittering city and, in the distance beyond, the snowy peaks of the mystical Mount Illimani (sacred to the Incas) tower to a height of over 21,000 feet.

La Paz is a fascinating blend of the old and new. Together with modern buildings and late-model cars, one sees churches built by the Spaniards over four centuries ago; and in every street, Indian women with their characteristic bowler hats, colorful shawls, and babies carried on their backs. It is a bustling, sunny city, filled with color, lots of hilly streets, Spanish colonial style buildings, and an atmosphere of excitement and activity. It has a breezy, cool, and dry climate, and because it is so high the atmosphere is thin and it is easy to lose one's breath without too much exertion.

Over the mountains from La Paz lies the city of Cochabamba, an important agricultural center in the heart of an 8,400-foot-high valley where the climate is temperate and the soil quite fertile. Farther east, the mountains drop toward the tropical savannas and plains of eastern Bolivia. The most important city in this area is Santa Cruz, located at the foot of the eastern slopes of the Andes. Santa Cruz is known for its colonial Spanish architecture and its beautiful women of Spanish descent, but today it has all the characteristics of a boom city. The growing economy of the area is based on sugar, cotton, rice, oil, and cocaine (it was rumored in the 1980s and 1990s to be the capital of Bolivia's international cocaine trade). Approximately 200 miles south of Santa Cruz lies the town of Camiri, the only other sizable urban center in the eastern part of the country. Camiri is Bolivia's oil and gas center, and although it is not comparable to Santa Cruz in either importance or size, it too has experienced an economic boom.

Despite the eastern portion of Bolivia accounting for approximately 70 percent of the total land area of the country, only about one-fourth of Bolivia's small population lives east of the Andes (the population of Bolivia was approximately 4 million in 1967 when Che and his guerrilla force were there and today it is over 9 million). The real heartland of Bolivia is located on the *altiplano*. It is there the vast majority of the country's population live and there the main loci of economic and political power are to be found. Moreover, most of the important events in Bolivian political history have taken place on the altiplano.

Before choosing Bolivia as the site of his guerrilla operation, Che considered several other countries, particularly Argentina and Peru. There was nothing he would have liked better than to bring the revolution to his native Argentina. This was something he had planned for many years. But it was obvious the situation in Argentina was not favorable for such an undertaking in 1966. In 1964, a Cuban-backed and Guevara-inspired guerrilla force attempted to establish itself in northern Argentina, but the effort ended in total failure a few months later without having realized a single military engagement (Castañeda 1997: 247–50). The leader of this group was the Argentine Jorge Masetti, who was a close friend of Che's in Cuba. Together they had planned the Argentine operation in early 1963. Their objective at the time was to establish a chain of guerrilla focos from northern Argentina to Peru.

However, Masetti's small force was defeated by the harsh environment of northern Argentina, where his group tried to establish a guerrilla foco, their poor organization, and their inability to attract any popular support. In the end, those members of his guerrilla band who did not die from starvation and exposure were either taken prisoner or killed by the Argentine police and armed forces. The death of Masetti and the three Cuban comrades from Guevara's own bodyguard who had gone with Masetti to help establish the guerrilla foco in Argentina was a bitter reminder to Che that Argentina was not the most suitable place for him to establish an armed revolutionary movement in 1966.

As for Peru, the situation there was not any more favorable than in Argentina. In 1966 that country had an elected civilian government with a moderately progressive program (Taibo 1996:612–16). Moreover, the government and the army had effectively suppressed several guerrilla uprisings in isolated parts of the country during the preceding two years. Che also considered Colombia, Venezuela, and Brazil, but never very seriously (Anderson 1997:678). In the end, Bolivia was chosen because it was considered to have the best revolutionary potential and because it afforded the ideal strategic location. It was in the center of the continent and bordered Argentina, Brazil, Chile, Paraguay, and Peru.

Che had been in Bolivia for a short time in 1953, when he had traveled there with his friend Carlos "Calica" Ferrer, and his impression of the country at that time undoubtedly influenced his choice of Bolivia in 1966. As previously mentioned in chapter 3, he was there during a period when the country was literally infected with revolutionary enthusiasm. Less than a year before, thousands of miners, peasants, and deserters from the Bolivian army had revolted and brought down the then existing military regime. When Che arrived in La Paz in 1953, the old army had been disbanded, the largest foreign-owned mines in the country had been nationalized, and the peasants had taken possession of many of the large landed estates following the enactment of the new government's agrarian reform law. The streets were filled with singing and loud demonstrations, and everywhere he saw the armed peasants and workers of the revolutionary militia. He surely must have thought of these armed peasants and workers in 1966 when he chose Bolivia as the place to initiate his revolutionary movement, since he firmly believed the revolution of those days had been subsequently betrayed by opportunistic politicians and army generals corrupted by *Yanqui* dollars, U.S. military advisers, and the CIA.

Most of Che's information on Bolivia appears to have come from several Bolivian Communists, who had helped previously with the Masetti operation, and from Che's aide, José María Martínez Tamayo (Papi) who was sent to Bolivia in March 1966 to make the preliminary preparations for Che's new operation (Castañeda 1997:334). Most of these Bolivian Communists had received military training in Cuba. They assured Papi the country was ripe for a Cuban-type revolution and all that was needed was Cuban support. They informed him there was widespread discontent in Bolivia with the military-backed regime of President Barrientos, and they contended this government could fall at any moment. They also spoke of the country's strong revolutionary tradition, of the visible and often resented U.S.-dominant presence in the country's economic and political affairs, and of how the mining centers were virtual caldrons of rebellion. Finally, they confirmed what Che and the Cuban intelligence service already knew, that the Bolivian security and military forces were perhaps the most ineffective and badly organized in Latin America.

As a result, Che decided Bolivia was the appropriate location for his operation. He minimized the fact that Bolivia's Communists were badly split along pro-Soviet and pro-Chinese lines and the leader of Bolivia's pro-Soviet Communist Party, Mario Monje, had told Castro during the Tricontinental conference in 1966 he was interested himself in establishing a guerrilla foco in Bolivia.

Bolivia had great strategic importance for Che since it is the *corazón* (heart) of South America and borders most of the major countries on the continent. From Bolivia, Che hoped his revolutionary effort would extend in every direction and involve all of South America. The expedition to Bolivia was designed to create a guerrilla *madre*, or mother base, that would provide training and a jumping-off point for a series of

Che Guevara's Zone of Combat in Bolivia, 1967. Adapted from Pepe Robles.

revolutionary guerrilla forces that would engulf the entire continent in a revolutionary struggle for a unified and socialist Latin America (Siles del Valle 1996:29–38).

Once he had decided on Bolivia, Che selected the southeast of the country for his initial guerrilla foco. He chose the southeast because it offered relatively close access to neighboring Argentina, Brazil, Chile, and Paraguay. In addition, he assumed that in this area, because of its isolation and sparse population, his guerrilla force would be able to develop without being discovered before it was ready to begin operations. This region of the country is part of the Gran Chaco region, which stretches into Paraguay. Its climate is semiarid to semi-tropical and has only two seasons: summer and winter. There are rain and hot, humid conditions during the summer months from December through March, but the winter months from April through November consist of dry, hot days and cool nights, when the temperature can drop below freezing. Median temperatures vary from 73 to 83 degrees F (23 to 28 degrees C), but this region can have the hottest days in Bolivia. When the humidity is low the dry heat can reach extreme temperatures, up to 115 degrees F (46 degrees C) during the daytime.

The specific location chosen as the central base of operations for Che's group was the Ñancahuazú River valley. In this semi-tropical, scrub-forested valley, Che planned to train the nucleus of his guerrilla movement, build fortifications, and establish caches of supplies and arms. Once his force was ready for combat, he planned to move north and threaten three of Bolivia's major cities: Cochabamba, Santa Cruz, and Sucre. This would enable the guerrillas to control the railway line that runs from northern Argentina to Santa Cruz, as well as to cut the U.S.-owned Gulf Oil Company pipeline that ran from Santa Cruz to Camiri. Later, Che planned to locate a second guerrilla base farther east, on the slopes of the Andes.

Che planned to begin military operations in May 1967, following six months of preparation. In the opening phase, he planned to divide his force into several small bands and have them strike simultaneously at widely dispersed points north of the Ñancahuazú area. In this way he hoped to force the Bolivian army to disperse its forces over a large area, while his guerrillas made a slow withdrawal toward the Ñancahuazú River valley, where they could rely on previously established caches of supplies and fortifications. Che reasoned that if the inexperienced Bolivian army attempted to follow the guerrillas into the Ñancahuazú River valley, they would be at the mercy of these guerrilla bands. As his guerrillas demonstrated their capacity to win victories against the Bolivian army, Che believed many of the country's peasants and miners would come to the support of the movement.

Che also assumed that once his guerrilla movement was well established and drawing widespread support and public attention, conditions would become more favorable for guerrilla operations in Peru and Argentina (Taibo 1996:615). He planned to have a guerrilla group operating in the Ayacucho region of Peru by the end of 1967 and another force in northern Argentina sometime after that. The Bolivian base of operations was to be a training ground for the nucleus of both the Peruvian and Argentine forces.

Che revealed his overall strategy in the message he sent to the second conference of the Tricontinental in 1967. It was entitled: "Create Two, Three, Many Vietnams." In this message, it is clear he believed a successful guerrilla insurgency in Latin America would force the United States to commit itself directly to the contest, creating a second Vietnam in the heart of South America. His conception of the course of events that would follow the appearance of his guerrilla movement in Bolivia is revealed in the following passage from his message to the conference:

> New outbreaks of war will appear in these and other Latin American countries, as has already occurred in Bolivia. And they will continue to grow, with all the vicissitudes involved in this dangerous occupation of the modern revolutionist. Many will die, victims of their own errors; others will fall in the difficult combat to come; new fighters and new leaders will arise in the heat of the revolutionary struggle. . . . The Yankee agents of repression will increase in number. Today there are advisers in all countries where armed struggle is going on. . . . Little by little the obsolete weapons that are sufficient for the suppression of small armed bands will be converted by the Americans into modern arms, and American advisers will be converted into combatants, until, in a given moment, they will see themselves obligated to send increasing quantities of

> regular troops to assure the relative stability of a power whose puppet national army disintegrates before the attacks of the guerrillas. This is the road of Vietnam. It is the road that other people will follow, and it is the road that Latin America will follow. . . . We must definitely keep in mind that imperialism is a world system, the final stage of capitalism, and that it must be beaten in a great worldwide confrontation. (Deutschmann 1997:322–23)

From this message, it is clear Che was counting on U.S involvement in Bolivia and he saw this as a means of gaining the support of both Bolivian and international public opinion.

As for the ultimate goal of the continental revolutionary movement Che was hoping to start in Bolivia, this too was revealed in his message to the Tricontinental conference. He said:

> We can summarize our hopes for victory as follows: the destruction of imperialism through the elimination of its strongest bulwark: the imperial dominion of the United States of North America. This will be accomplished through the gradual liberation of its subject peoples, either one by one or by groups, drawing the enemy into a difficult struggle outside of its territory; and cutting it off from its bases of support, i.e., its dependent territories.

Thus, for Che, Bolivia was to be the first step in a grand plan to liberate all of Latin America from U.S. influence and convert it into a bastion of socialism and anti-imperialism. Everything, therefore, depended on successfully establishing in Bolivia a guerrilla madre that would develop into a successful revolutionary movement of continental dimensions.

Prophetically, however, the final sentences in his message to the Tricontinental Conference suggested what was to come:

> Wherever death may surprise us, let it be welcome if our battle cry has reached even one receptive ear; if another hand reaches out to take up our arms, and other men come forward to join in our funeral dirge with the rattling of machine guns and with new cries of battle and victory.

Death did surprise Che in Bolivia, and his battle cry has reached many receptive ears over the years since then.

Che could not seek the support of the pro-Chinese Communists in Bolivia because the leaders of the rival pro-Soviet Communists in Bolivia had told Fidel Castro their party planned to set up a guerrilla foco in the country. It appears these leaders purposely misled Castro into believing they were going to do this in order to outflank the more militant, pro-Chinese Communists, who they were afraid were interested in doing this with Cuban help (Anderson:682–87). Che was aware of this political situation, and he distrusted Monje and the other leaders of Bolivia's pro-Soviet Communist Party. Consequently, he relied primarily on a small number of pro-Cuba supporters within Monje's pro-Soviet Communist party to make the preliminary preparations for his guerrilla operation. These were individuals who had previously spent some time training in Cuba, and Che knew many of them personally. He felt they could be trusted to lay the groundwork for his operation without telling even the leadership of their party what they were doing.

The most important of Che's Bolivian contacts were two brothers—Roberto "Coco" and Guido "Inti" Peredo. These two brothers helped convince Che that Bolivia was the ideal base for a guerrilla operation. Because of this and perhaps because Che saw these two brothers as the future Raúl and Fidel Castro of Bolivia, he entrusted them with the most important aspects of the preliminary preparations for his guerrilla foco.

Coco and Inti had participated in the efforts that were made in 1960 to establish guerrilla focos in Salta, Argentina, and Puerto Maldonado, Peru. They had joined the Communist Party's youth wing at an early age and their previous efforts to establish Cuban-style guerrilla focos made them ideal candidates for the guerrilla force Che organized in Bolivia. They also owned and operated a taxi in La Paz. This vocation gave them a perfect cover for their clandestine activities. Sometime during the summer of 1966, they both traveled to the southeast and located themselves in Camiri, Bolivia's petroleum center. There they made friends with some of the local inhabitants and let it be known they were interested in buying land in the area north of Camiri for the purpose of establishing a ranch and cereal farm.

In September they succeeded in buying an abandoned ranch in a largely uninhabited region near the Ñancahuazú River, 50 miles north of Camiri. In addition, they rented some adjacent property from their only neighbor, Ciro Argañaraz, a local landowner and cattle rancher.

While Inti returned to La Paz to take care of their personal affairs, Coco began readying the ranch for the arrival of Che and his Cuban comrades. He contracted two local men to work the ranch and planted several different varieties of cereals. He also bought some cattle, hogs, and poultry. During this period, Coco traveled the winding dirt road from the ranch to Camiri in his new Toyota jeep almost daily. On this road, about 12 miles from the ranch, is the small village of Lagunillas. Coco stopped there on several occasions to buy vegetables and fruit. The large amounts of supplies he transported to the ranch in his jeep aroused the suspicion of many of the local villagers. Many of them, as well as the landowner, Argañaraz, assumed the Peredo brothers were cocaine merchants or cattle thieves.

Meanwhile, in La Paz, Che's other Bolivian collaborators made arrangements for receiving Che's group and their equipment. They obtained a house and a warehouse in the center of the city, where they stored arms and ammunition, which they received hidden in bags of cement mix. These were shipped from Cuba to the port of Arica in northern Chile and from there sent by rail to La Paz.

One of Che's prime contacts in La Paz during this period, and later the only female member of his guerrilla force, was a woman known by the code name of Tania. Her real name was Haydée Tamara Bunke. She was a German Argentine Che had met in Communist East Germany and who had come to Cuba on the invitation of Che. While there, she became a member of the small circle of Argentines who met frequently at Che's house. Tania left Cuba and entered Bolivia in 1964 with a false Argentine passport. In early 1965 she obtained a job working for Gonzalo López, director of information in the presidential palace. In addition to working for López, Tania also successfully passed herself off as a professor of languages. This gave her an opportunity to travel widely throughout the country, ostensibly for the purpose of studying the languages and folk songs of the indigenous (Indian) population. In her spare time she worked her way into some of the capital's artistic, cultural, and diplomatic circles. Her contacts provided Che with valuable information and assistance. Through her direct access to documents and forms in the Information Office of the Presidency she was later able to provide Che and some of his Cuban companions with very impressive credentials that allowed them to travel quite freely within the country.

Che arrived in Bolivia, around November 1, 1966, on a plane from São Paolo, Brazil. He entered Bolivia as a clean-shaven, bald man wearing glasses. He had two false Uruguayan passports, and it is not clear which of the two he actually used to enter Bolivia. The passports were issued under the names of Ramón Benitez and Adolfo Mena. The fingerprints on both passports are exactly the same as those that were later identified by various governments as belonging to Che. The photographs on both passports are also the same. On close examination they reveal a clean-shaven, bald Che Guevara wearing glasses. Both passports have the same dates of entry and departure from Madrid airport.

Che was accompanied by one of his longtime Cuban comrades: Alberto Fernández (whose code name was Pacho). Upon arrival they contacted Tania, and she gave Che a truly extraordinary document: it accredited Che (Adolfo Mena in this case) as a special envoy of the Organization of American States. According to this document, he was in Bolivia to conduct research on the social and economic relations prevailing in the rural areas of Bolivia.

With Che carrying this document, Che and Pacho traveled to the Ñancahuazú ranch in two separate jeeps, arriving there the night of November 6. Che brought to Bolivia a contingent of 12 Cubans. Most of the members of this handpicked group were veterans of Che's guerrilla

Che Guevara in his guerrilla camp in Nancahuazu, 1967. Richard L. Harris.

column in the Sierra Maestra. Some held the rank of comandante in the Cuban army. Many of them had served in important posts in the Cuban government and armed forces, and several were members of the Central Committee of the Cuban Communist Party. All of these individuals were tied to Che by unquestioning personal loyalty. Some had been with him in the Congo. They were willing to follow him to hell if he asked them to do so, and in the end only three of them returned home to Cuba alive.

The Bolivian members of the guerrilla force were largely recruited by Coco and two other Bolivian agents, known by the code names of Rodolfo and Sánchez. The latter two men also served as liaisons between Che's group and the support network in the urban areas during the period before Che's guerrilla force was discovered. The entry in Che's diary at the end of November 1966 reveals he hoped to increase the number of Bolivians in his force to at least 20 before beginning military operations.

In December at the Ñancahuazú ranch he met with Mario Monje, the leader of the pro-Soviet Bolivian Communist Party, to discuss the possibility of receiving men and assistance from his party. However, Monje refused to support the guerrilla operation and send men unless he was in charge of it. He made it clear his party could not officially support the guerrilla operation. However, he offered to resign from the party, obtain at least its neutrality, and bring several cadres of men to join those already in training, provided Che agreed to give him both the political and military command of the entire operation and a free hand to seek the support of the Communist parties in the other South American countries where Che planned to extend his guerrilla movement.

Monje's conditions for supporting the guerrilla movement were totally unacceptable to Che. He told Monje he could accept no conditions concerning his leadership of the military operations. He knew, in the kind of revolutionary struggle he was planning, the military leadership of the struggle would have to come from the guerrilla force itself, not from a politician or group of politicians hundreds of miles from the scene of battle. Nor was he about to turn over the command of a movement that, in its final phase, would engulf all of Latin America to someone he considered lacked both the proper revolutionary vision as well as the necessary military experience. As for Monje's resigning from his position as leader of the party, Che said he considered this a tremendous error, since it would accommodate those in his party who should be publicly condemned for their hypocrisy.

Che's experience in the Congo also led him to reject Monje's conditions. The poor leadership of the Congolese rebels provided by their leaders such as Laurent Kabila was certainly on his mind and his experience in the Congo made him all the more determined to keep control over both the political and military direction of the guerrilla force in Bolivia rather than relinquish it to weak and untrustworthy local political leaders such as Monje (Guevara 2000:x–xi).

Monje met with the Bolivians in Che's group and told them they could stay with Che and be expelled from the party, or they could support the party and return with him to La Paz. Much to Monje's surprise, all the Bolivians present said they preferred to stay with Che. The next morning, Monje announced he was leaving for La Paz. Che realized Monje had disagreed with him over who should command the movement as a pretext to escape any responsibility for cooperating with Che's group. Che appears to have seen through Monje's subterfuge at the time; he noted in his diary that Monje had discovered from Coco that he (Che) would not compromise on the crucial question of who was to lead the movement. Che realized Monje had disagreed with him over who should command the movement so that he would have an excuse to not support Che's group.

If Monje had accepted the political leadership of the movement (while deferring to Che's military leadership) and had sent members of his party to fight with Che's nuclear group, then the guerrilla operation might not have suffered later from the stigma of being directed and organized by foreigners. After Che's guerrilla force was discovered and it became known it was led by Che and a group of Cubans, the Bolivian government was able to argue convincingly that the guerrillas were foreigners intervening in the domestic affairs of the country.

By the end of March 1967, Che had succeeded in recruiting approximately 20 Bolivians. Some had trained like Coco and Inti in Cuba specifically for fighting in the guerrilla operation. The remainder were dissident members of the youth wing of Monje's party and unemployed miners from the tin-mining areas on Bolivia's high plateau.

The unemployed miners were recruited by Moisés Guevara (no relation to Che), an important union leader among the leftist tin miners in

Oruro. Moisés had broken away from the pro-Chinese Communist Party in Bolivia and had traveled several times to Cuba, where he had met Che. Although Monje was opposed to involving Moisés in the guerrilla force, Che's Bolivian contacts invited Moisés to join the force with some of his miners. Moisés agreed and brought eight men with him to the Ñancahuazú camp in February 1967.

In addition to the Cubans and the Bolivians, Che's guerrilla force included among its members three Peruvians known by the code names of El Chino, Negro, and Eustaquio, respectively. El Chino (Juan Pablo Chang, who was a Peruvian of Chinese descent) was supposed to establish Che's planned guerrilla foco in Peru. He brought Eustaquio, a radio operator, and Negro, a physician, to Che's camp during the latter part of February. They were to be joined later by an additional number of Peruvians who were to train with Che's force and then return to their country to start another guerrilla foco there.

The total number of combatants in the guerrilla force stood at 39 when the first encounter between the army and Che's group took place on March 23, 1967. Most of the leadership positions were held by Cubans. Che appointed his old comrade in arms from the Sierra Maestra Comandante Juan Vitalio Acuña (code name Joaquín) as his second in command of the guerrilla force and also leader of the rearguard. He also appointed Cubans to the posts of leader of the vanguard, chief of operations, chief of services, and chief of supplies. Inti and Coco were the only two Bolivians entrusted with any leadership responsibilities. Inti was placed in charge of finances and appointed political commissar to the Bolivians. Coco, who was initially placed in charge of urban contacts and recruitment, was later incorporated into the guerrilla force and assigned various responsibilities.

No additions to the guerrilla force took place after the outbreak of hostilities in late March. Instead, the size of Che's force was steadily reduced as each encounter with the army took its toll. Che had hoped to recruit peasants from the local area once his force began operations, but he failed to recruit even a single peasant after the fighting began.

Che's original plan was to begin military operations north of the Rio Grande and then slowly withdraw southward across a terrain carefully prepared with caches of arms and ammunition, food supplies, and fortified bases. He needed perhaps another month before this plan would have been ready to be put into operation. But he had to discard it when the army discovered his main base after receiving credible reports about the presence of guerrillas in the Ñancahuazú area during the first few weeks of March.

On the morning of March 11, two of Moisés Guevara's new recruits left the main camp, ostensibly to go hunting. They took the path leading down to the river, but instead of going to the east, where the best hunting area was, they disappeared in the direction of Camiri. A few days later, they were arrested and brought to the headquarters of the Fourth Army Division in Camiri. There they gave their captors a detailed report concerning all they knew about the guerrilla operation. They gave the army detailed information about the location of the guerrillas' camp, the number of people there, and most of the guerrilla force being away at the time on a training and reconnaissance march to the north. They said they had been told Che Guevara was the leader of the operation and he was with the others in the north.

The information these two deserters and several local people gave the Bolivian authorities led to the discovery and subsequent annihilation of Che's guerrilla force. This information enabled the army to locate Che's main base before he and his men were ready to begin military operations. It also gave the army the initiative from the beginning of the conflict until its tragic termination some six months later. Timing was a crucial factor in Che's strategy, and the premature initiation of hostilities threw his whole operation off balance. His small force of men was never really able to recover from the shock of having their central base discovered before they were ready to begin fighting. All of Che's subsequent efforts were little more than futile, though valiant, attempts to put up a good fight in the face of overwhelming odds. He and his men seem to have deluded themselves during the first few months of fighting into believing their operation still could succeed, but in reality their fate was sealed from the beginning. It was just a matter of time before they were caught or killed.

Che had written of the extreme danger a guerrilla force faces during its preparatory stage in "Guerrilla Warfare: A Method." He pointed out that the future of a revolutionary movement depends on how the nuclear guerrilla force handles itself when the enemy first moves against it. According to Che, unless the guerrillas are able to develop their

Bolivian soldiers occupying Che's camp after he and his men had abandoned it, 1967. Richard L. Harris.

capacity to attack the enemy during the early stage of the struggle, they have little prospect of surviving (in Guevara 1963).

As a result of the army's discovery of their main base, Che and his men were forced to withdraw into a relatively confined area. He had originally planned to have his force operate across a zone carefully prepared with caches of supplies and fortified bases, but the army's discovery of their main base forced Che and his men to move into an area about which they knew very little and where they had difficulty finding food and places to hide.

Only Che's will to succeed and his refusal to accept defeat can explain his optimism about the future of his guerrilla operation after the discovery of his force at the end of March. Anyone else undoubtedly would have concluded under the circumstances there was no choice but to abandon the entire venture and escape while it was still possible to do so. But not Che; until the end he continued to believe his effort would succeed. Perhaps he kept thinking of how high the odds had been against the success of Castro's operation after the *Granma* disaster, when only 12 members of the original 80-man invasion force survived the landing on Cuban soil and made their way to the Sierra Maestra.

Chapter 10

THE TRAGIC DEATH OF A REVOLUTIONARY

Between March 23, 1967, when Che's guerrilla force was first discovered by the Bolivian authorities and October 8 when Che was captured, his small guerrilla force was able to carry out a series of hit and run attacks on the Bolivian army. (The information in this chapter relies heavily upon the author's original research; see Harris 2007:143–67.) However, they suffered steady losses and Che grew increasingly ill since he had no medicine to treat his frequent severe asthma attacks. At the end of August, the guerrilla column under Joaquín (Che's Cuban comrade Comandante Juan Vitalio Acuña Nuñez) was ambushed and all but one member of the column were killed by the army. Among the losses was the guerrilla force's only female member, Tania (Tamara Bunke). By the middle of September, the remaining column under Che's command was being encircled by an increasing number of troops, and the news of the army's successful encounters in late September with his column near La Higuera, a small hamlet of about 100 inhabitants 90 miles Southwest of the city of Santa Cruz, was received by the military high command and the government of President Barrientos as a clear sign victory was almost within their grasp. In Vallegrande, the main town in this area, the new Second Manchego Ranger Regiment had just arrived after finishing 19 weeks of special counterinsurgency training from U.S. Army Special Forces personnel. By dawn on September 27, the first units of this new regiment had moved into the region around La Higuera. A unit of these U.S.-trained Rangers captured one of the Bolivian members of Che's guerrillas force who was code-named Camba (his real name was Orlando Jiménez Bazán) and was able to interrogate another Bolivian member of Che's column named León (Antonio Rodríguez Flores), who had deserted the guerrilla force and turned himself over to the army following a particularly bloody engagement in which several members of Che's force were killed.

In his diary, Che acknowledged his losses were very great in the La Higuera area, particularly the death of three of his best comrades. He considered the loss of his Bolivian lieutenant Coco (Roberto Peredo Leigue, who had been trained in Cuba and Vietnam) the most grievous loss. In addition, he noted in his diary that his Cuban comrade Miguel (Manuel Hernández, who had been with him since 1958) and the Bolivian doctor with the code name Julio (Mario Gutierrez Ardaya) had been magnificent fighters and the human value of all three was inexpressible. His diary also reveals that the last days of September were extremely tense ones for him and his men. They were forced to move by night and hide during the day, and on more than one occasion they were nearly discovered by the soldiers who were searching for them.

By the end of the month, it was clear to everyone in Che's small force they were in a desperate position. A circle of troops was closing in around them, and their every move was being reported to the army by the local population. Their tragic plight was summed up cryptically by Che in his diary: "Our conditions are the same as last month, except now the army is demonstrating increasing effectiveness in its actions and the campesinos are giving us no support and have turned into informers."

Nevertheless, Che still believed they could continue their mission. Thus, he noted in his diary: "The most important task is to escape and look for more propitious zones; and then afterwards our contacts, in spite of the fact that the whole apparatus is disrupted in La Paz where they have given us severe blows." In view of the circumstances, however, Che and his comrades had little chance "to escape and look for more propitious zones." They were completely surrounded by thousands of troops and unable to move rapidly across the difficult terrain owing to their wounds and fatigue.

Throughout the first few days of October, Che and his group, now reduced to 16, spent most of the daylight hours on the crests of the ridges north of La Higuera and the nights in the hollows at the bases of these ridges. On the evening of October 3, Che heard a news broadcast concerning Camba and León, and he made the following entry in his diary: "Both gave abundant information about Fernando [Che's own code name], his illness and everything else." Che added sarcastically: "Thus ends the story of two heroic guerrillas." On October 4, Che wrote that he had heard a commentary on the radio whose conclusion had been that if he was captured by troops of the Fourth Army Division, he would be tried in Camiri, but if by the Eighth Division, he would be tried in Santa Cruz.

On Saturday, October 7, the last day Che made an entry in his diary, he and his men camped in one of the many ravines near La Higuera. There they encountered an old woman herding goats and attempted to question her about the presence of soldiers in the area, but they were unable to obtain any reliable information. Afterward, fearing that the old woman would report them, Che ordered two of his men to go to her house and pay her 50 pesos to keep quiet. He noted in his diary, however, that he had little hope that she would do as instructed. He began this last entry in his diary with a notation that it had been exactly 11 months since the inauguration of his guerrilla movement.

Apparently, the old woman or someone else who had seen Che and his group pass through the area reported their presence to the army in La Higuera. By the morning of Sunday, October 8, several companies of Rangers were deployed in the zone through which Che's small force was moving. Early that morning Captain Gary Prado and his company of Rangers, all recent graduates of the U.S. Army Special Forces training camp near Santa Cruz, took up positions on the heights of the Quebrada de Yuro, one of the most rugged ravines in the area. Che and his men, after marching the night before, had stopped to rest in this ravine until they could resume marching under cover of darkness.

About noon, a small probing unit from Prado's company made contact with the guerrillas. In this initial encounter, two soldiers were killed and several others wounded. The lieutenant in charge of the unit radioed Captain Prado for assistance. The subsequent series of events reads like a scenario out of a U.S. Army counterinsurgency manual. Captain Prado immediately deployed the rest of his troops in a circle around the guerrillas. Meanwhile, Che divided his small force into two groups in an effort to confuse the Rangers and escape. The group led by Che moved toward the closest exit from the ravine. However, the hill commanding this exit was occupied by a sizable number of troops and had been chosen by Captain Prado as the site of his command post. As Che and his group came within shooting range of Prado's men, they found themselves caught in a rain of automatic weapons fire.

Captain Prado watched the guerrillas disperse and run for cover through his field glasses and ordered Sergeant Bernardino Huanca and his men to descend in pursuit. A few minutes later, Sergeant Huanca fired a burst from his submachine gun at a guerrilla moving through a thicket of thorn bushes. One bullet sent the guerrilla's black beret flying off his head, while two others tore into his leg and forced him to the ground. The fallen guerrilla was Che. As he lay helpless the Rangers began to concentrate their fire on the area where he had fallen. But Willy (Simón Cuba, one of Moisés Guevara's recruits whom Che had begun to regard as a potential deserter) rushed to his side and helped him out of the line of fire and up one side of the ravine. As the two scrambled upward, they ran into four Rangers who were positioning a mortar. The Rangers ordered them to surrender, but Che, supporting himself against a tree, fired his carbine in answer. The soldiers returned the fire. A few seconds later, a bullet hit the barrel of Che's carbine, rendering it useless and wounding him in the right forearm. At this point, Che reportedly raised his hands and shouted: "Don't shoot! I'm Che Guevara, and I'm worth more to you alive than dead." A few yards away, Willy threw down his rifle and also surrendered.

It was approximately 4:00 in the afternoon when Che and Willy were brought before Captain Prado. The latter immediately ordered his radio operator to signal the divisional headquarters in Vallegrande and tell them that they had captured Che Guevara. When the radio operator established contact with Vallegrande he shouted: "Hello, Saturno, we have Papa!" ("Saturno" was the code name for Colonel Joaquín Zenteno, commandant of the Eighth Bolivian Army Division, and "Papa"

THE TRAGIC DEATH OF A REVOLUTIONARY   165

was the code name they used for Che). In disbelief, Colonel Zenteno asked Captain Prado to confirm the message. Following the confirmation, there was general euphoria among Colonel Zenteno's divisional headquarters staff. When the back patting subsided, Colonel Zenteno radioed Prado to immediately bring Che and any other prisoners to La Higuera.

Since the Rangers had come into the Quebrada de Yuro on foot, Che had to be transported the seven kilometers to La Higuera stretched out in a blanket carried by four soldiers. Willy was forced to walk behind with his hands tied against his back. They arrived in La Higuera shortly after dark. The prisoners were placed in the little town's two-room schoolhouse, Che in one room and Willy in the other. Later the Rangers brought in a third guerrilla, a Bolivian named Aniceto (Aniceto Reinaga), who had been taken prisoner near where Che and Willy were captured. He was placed in the classroom with Willy. The bodies of four other guerrillas were also brought to La Higuera that night.

Che Guevara and CIA agent Felix Rodriguez, left, after Che was captured on October 8, 1967. Richard L. Harris.

The remaining group of guerrillas, led by Inti Peredo, had gone to the opposite end of the Quebrada when Che ordered the column to separate. They were able to hide until nightfall and then slip out of the ravine. In subsequent weeks, half the members of this second group were killed by the army. Of those who survived, the three remaining Cubans fled the country via Chile, and the three surviving Bolivians who included Inti went into hiding.

During the night of October 8, and the next morning, Che was interrogated by various army officers, including Major Miguel Ayoroa, Colonel Andrés Selich, Captain Prado, and Colonel Zenteno. He was also questioned by the CIA agent who called himself Félix Ramos (Félix Rodríguez), one of the Cuban exiles sent by the CIA to participate in the counterinsurgency campaign against the guerrillas. Che refused to answer any of their questions, but he did exchange a few words with some of the officers and soldiers around him. At one point, one of the younger officers asked Che what he was thinking about. At first, Che ignored him, but when he overheard the officer say sarcastically to another officer that he (Che) was probably thinking about the immortality of the burro, Che answered: "No, I'm thinking about the immortality of the revolution." On another occasion, one of the junior officers, who had drunk too much in celebration of Che's capture, tried to harass him. Che responded by punching the officer in the face. Although Che's wounds were painful, they were not serious, and he remained conscious during this entire period.

In La Paz, President Barrientos and the high command of the Bolivian Armed Forces held an emergency meeting to decide what to do with Che. They ruled out any prospect of prosecuting him through judicial proceedings, because they reasoned a trial would focus world attention on him and present the Communists with a propaganda field day. Moreover, since Bolivia did not have the death penalty, they feared that if Che remained alive as their prisoner, sympathizers from all over the world would converge on Bolivia in an effort to save him or carry on his fight. They decided, therefore, that Che had to be executed immediately. Moreover, they decided that they would announce he had died from wounds received in battle.

Early on the morning of Monday, October 9, the top-ranking officers in La Higuera received the order from La Paz to execute Che. They in turn instructed the noncommissioned officers present to carry out the order. Since none of the latter were anxious to do so, they chose lots to determine who would execute Che. Several hours before, these noncommissioned officers, as well as the officers and the soldiers on guard around the schoolhouse where Che was being held prisoner, had divided among themselves the money and personal effects taken from Che after his capture. His watches, carbine, compass, Parker fountain pen, two berets (including the one with a bullet hole through it), belt, stainless steel dagger, two pipes, and cigarette holder were the most important pieces of booty distributed among those who had had the honor of participating in the capture of the famous guerrilla leader.

Shortly before noon on Monday, October 9, 1967, some 24 hours after Che and his men had been discovered in the Quebrada de Yuro, Sergeant Mario Terán walked to the little schoolhouse in La Higuera to carry out the order sent down from the Bolivian government's top leaders in La Paz. He had drawn the shortest straw. When he entered the classroom where his victim was waiting, he found him propped up against one of the walls. Che guessed the nature of Sergeant Terán's mission and calmly asked him to wait a moment until he stood up. Terán was so frightened by the prospect of what he had to do that he began to tremble. He turned and ran from the schoolhouse. But both Colonel Selich and Colonel Zenteno ordered him to go back and shoot Che without further delay. Still trembling, Terán returned to the classroom, and without looking at his victim's face, he fired a burst from his carbine. The bullets slammed into Che's chest and side, passed through his body, and made large holes in the soft adobe wall of the classroom. The sergeant had been told not to inflict any wounds in Che's head or heart so that the army could later claim that he had died from wounds received in combat. However, while Terán's carbine was still smoking, several soldiers pushed past him into the classroom. They said that they too wanted to shoot Che so that they could boast that they had shot the famous Che Guevara. Sergeant Terán weakly nodded his approval and they began firing.

When the shooting was over, there were nine bullet wounds in Che's body, two of which were obviously instantaneously fatal. Moments later, Willy and Aniceto were executed by another sergeant in Captain Prado's company. The shooting resounded through the streets of the village, startling the townspeople and causing them to crowd around the little schoolhouse. In a short time, the entire town knew what had taken place there.

Soon after Che and his comrades were shot, the senior army officers and the CIA agent, Félix Rodríguez, left La Higuera by helicopter for the army headquarters in Vallegrande. Che's body was wrapped in canvas and strapped to the runner of a helicopter bound for Vallegrande. At the Vallegrande airstrip, nearly half the population of the town awaited the arrival of Che's body. Colonel Zenteno had announced several hours earlier that Che was dead and would soon be brought to Vallegrande.

When the helicopter arrived in Vallegrande, it landed on the side of the airstrip away from the waiting crowd of townspeople, reporters, and soldiers. Before the rotor of the helicopter had stopped, Che's body was loaded into the back of a white Chevrolet panel truck (the type used at the time as ambulances throughout most of Latin America) and transported at high speed through Vallegrande's narrow streets to the Señor de Malta Hospital.

The body was placed in an adobe laundry shack apart from the main hospital building. In this shack several officials washed the blood from

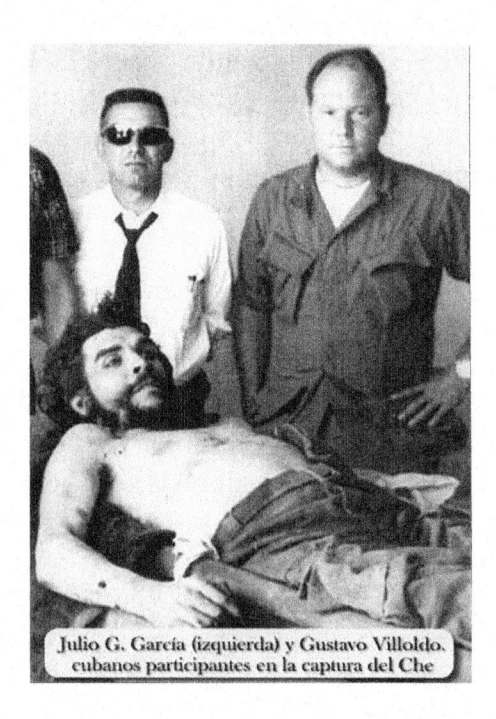

Two CIA agents, Julio Garcia and Gustavo Villoldo, who were present at Che Guevara's autopsy on October 9, 1967. Richard L. Harris.

THE TRAGIC DEATH OF A REVOLUTIONARY   169

Che's body, made an incision in his neck for embalming fluid, and took his fingerprints. According to two British journalists who arrived on the scene early, the entire process appeared to be under the supervision of a CIA agent who called himself Dr. Eduardo González (Gustavo Villoldo). He refused to let the two journalists photograph Che, and when they asked him in English where he was from, he answered sarcastically: "From nowhere!"

Soon General Alfredo Ovando, head of the Bolivian Armed Forces, and a number of other top military figures came to see the body of the famous guerrilla. By this time, a large crowd had excitedly collected around the shack. They probably would have broken through the cordon of soldiers trying to hold them back had it not been for the quick intervention of General Ovando. The general explained that they all had a right to see Che but that they would have to wait until the doctors and other officials had finished preparing and identifying the body.

Once the doctors and the officials had finished their work, the soldiers allowed the waiting newsmen to enter the shack and take pictures. Afterward, they let townspeople file past to view the corpse. Throughout the night a silent file of staring townspeople, peasants from the surrounding area, and soldiers passed by the body. Che's body was on a stretcher that had been placed across the length of a concrete laundry sink. He was nude from the waist up—the officials had removed his jacket during the preceding investigation and preparation. The bullet wounds in his chest and sides were almost inconspicuous. He looked amazingly alive. Not only were his eyes open and brilliant but there was a haunting smile on his lips. Pictures of this vibrant and serene expression were conveyed around the world by the news media.

Che's body was exhibited in the hospital at Vallegrande for approximately 24 hours. What happened to it afterward was a mystery to the world until almost 30 years later. On October 11, 1967, General Ovando first stated that the body had been buried in the Vallegrande area. The next day, however, General Ovando's office officially announced that the body had been cremated, and President Barrientos said a few days afterward that Che's ashes had been buried in a hidden place somewhere in the Vallegrande region. Almost nine months later, an article in the Peruvian paper *La Prensa* claimed that members of President Barrientos's personal guard had told a high functionary in the Peruvian police, when the Bolivian president visited Lima in July, that Che's body had been taken to the United States by the CIA in order to prevent it from falling into the hands of Marxists intent on sanctifying his remains. But a few days later, President Barrientos's personal guard publicly denied that any of its members had said anything to anyone about Che's body during the president's visit to Peru.

In any case, the rapid disposal of the body was probably motivated by the impending arrival in La Paz of Che's brother, Roberto Guevara, who was intent on claiming the body and taking it back to Argentina. When Roberto, a lawyer, arrived in Bolivia on October 12, he was told that it was impossible for him to see his brother's body since it had been cremated the day before. Not wanting to believe that his brother had been killed, Roberto asked to see the hands that the Bolivian officials claimed that they had cut from the body as proof that it was really Che Guevara that they had killed. But he was denied even this request and was forced to return to Argentina without having seen any evidence that his brother died in Bolivia. However, a few days later, a team of Argentine police experts arrived in La Paz in response to an invitation by President Barrientos sent to General Onganía, the military dictator ruling Argentina at the time. The Argentine police experts were allowed to examine Che's hands and compare his fingerprints with those in the files of the Argentine Federal Police. On their departure, they issued an official statement to the effect that the fingerprints were identical and belonged to Ernesto "Che" Guevara.

The contradictions in the official statements given by the Bolivian authorities with regard to the disposition of Che's body were minor compared to those that appeared in statements concerning how and when Che died. On October 13, Dr. José Martínez Casso, one of the two doctors at the Señor de Malta Hospital who had been asked by the military to conduct an autopsy on Che's body, reported to the press that Che had received two mortal wounds, one in the lungs and the other in the heart. He also stated that, on examining the body shortly after it had been brought to the hospital in Vallegrande, he had estimated that Che had died not more than five or six hours earlier. The doctor's statements obviously indicated that Che had died from wounds he received shortly before being brought to Vallegrande, not during the battle in the Quebrada de Yuro on the previous Sunday.

THE TRAGIC DEATH OF A REVOLUTIONARY

Yet on the same day that Dr. Martínez Casso made his statement, Colonel Zenteno stated before a press conference that although he was not able to say precisely when Che had died, it was "almost immediately after he was wounded in combat." This was contradicted on the same day by General Ovando, who stated that Che had died early Monday morning (October 9) as a consequence of wounds received the previous afternoon in combat. Although Che could not have lived overnight with a fatal bullet wound in both his heart and lungs, General Ovando denied emphatically and indignantly the suggestion that Che had been shot to death after he was taken prisoner.

The seemingly endless capacity of the Bolivian officials to contradict themselves not only made it clear that Che had been executed but also demonstrated that the government and military were incapable of discussing the matter without creating confusion and making embarrassing errors. The government's bungled efforts to sell Che's campaign diary (obtained along with other important items when he was captured in the Quebrada de Yuro), and the incredible circumstances surrounding the clandestine delivery of the diary for free to Cuba by none other than one of the top officials in President Barrientos's cabinet, were further evidence of the weaknesses, both moral and otherwise, in the Bolivian regime. Indeed, the entire episode involving the release of his diary had the appearance of a nightmarish comedy of errors. This tragic comedy occurred when I arrived on the scene in Bolivia some eight months after Che's death.

The success of any guerrilla movement depends on the degree of support it receives from the civilian population in its area of operations. Che knew this truth well and mentioned it frequently in his writings on guerrilla warfare. For example, he wrote:

> It is important to emphasize that the guerrilla struggle is a mass struggle, it is the struggle of a people.... The guerrilla fighter therefore relies on the complete support of the people of the area. This is absolutely indispensable. (Guevara 1960)

However, the complete absence of popular support for his guerrilla operation in Bolivia was one of the main reasons, if not the prime reason, that his mission there failed.

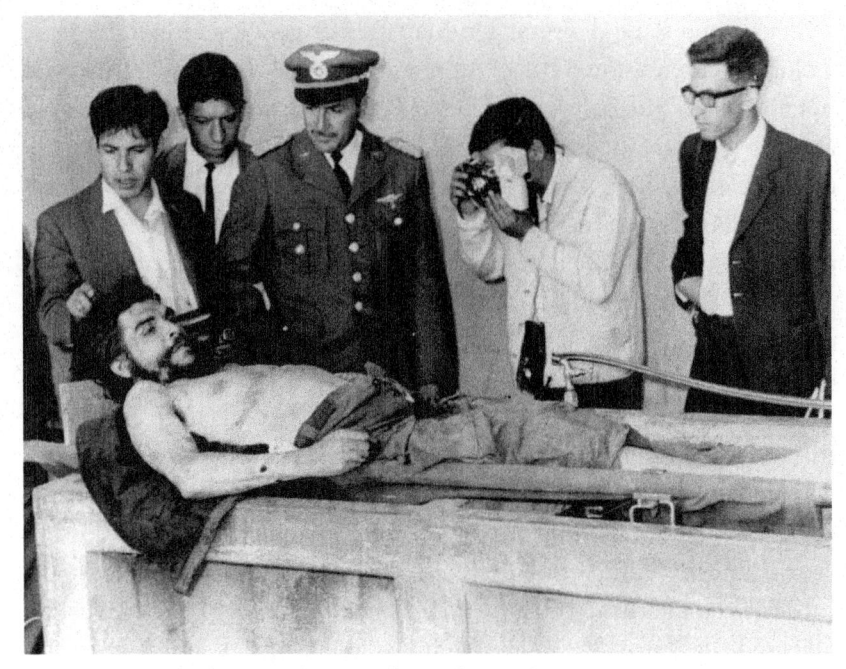

Che Guevara's body on display in Vallegrande. AP Images.

Revolutionary guerrilla warfare depends on, and is a struggle for, the loyalties of the civilian population. Close guerrilla-civilian cooperation enables guerrillas to develop a superior system of intelligence, have extreme mobility, cache an inexhaustible source of supplies, and surprise the enemy's forces when they are off guard. Without close ties to the civilian population, guerrillas cannot develop even the minimal level of capabilities necessary for successful guerrilla warfare.

REASONS FOR THE LACK OF POPULAR SUPPORT FOR CHE'S GUERRILLA MOVEMENT

One of the reasons Che's guerrilla movement failed to obtain any popular support in Bolivia is the majority of Bolivians at that time believed their country had already undergone its revolution of national liberation. Although Che visited Bolivia shortly after the revolution of 1952, he failed to perceive then or later how much importance the Bolivians attached to this event. In fact, for many Bolivians, the revolution of 1952 was regarded in much the same way as the Cubans regard their revolution. Because Che did not understand this fact, and because his Bolivian sources of information did not convey it to him, he believed his guerrilla movement would be able to capitalize on the hostility and discontent he assumed the Bolivian people felt toward their political rulers.

What Che failed to understand is the revolution of 1952 gave the Bolivian masses, for the first time in Bolivian history, what they perceived as a real stake in the social order as well as a sense of involvement in the political system and cultural community of their country. Despite the military coup of 1964 and the consequent fall from power of the National Revolutionary Movement (the group that spearheaded the revolution of 1952 and governed the country until the military coup), the changes set in motion by the revolution had continuing relevance for most of the Bolivian population in the mid-1960s when Che and his comrades arrived on the scene. These developments had a profound impact on the character of Bolivian politics and contributed greatly to the development of a sense of national consciousness among Bolivia's rural masses.

Che failed to appreciate the importance of this national consciousness and believed the Bolivian peasantry and the workers would provide a popular base for his revolutionary guerrilla movement in Bolivia and subsequently in neighboring countries. However, conditions for creating a successful revolutionary foco were obviously not present in Bolivia in the mid-1960s. In the first place, the guerrillas could not hope to win the support of the rural masses by offering to give them land. Since 1952 Bolivia's peasants had controlled the land and the entire countryside. Moreover, they had seen some improvement in their political, social, and economic status and they had hopes of greater improvement.

This is not to say that they were well off, for their situation was, and still is, one of the worst in Latin America. Nevertheless, they were much better off in the mid-1960s than they had been in the past. Furthermore, the peasants were not isolated from the centers of national political power. Through their local syndicates they had a significant voice in the country's political affairs, and certain groups, such as the campesinos in the Cochabamba area, even had direct access to President Barrientos. Consequently, the leaders of the peasant syndicates and many of their members did not regard the political authorities as enemies of the people.

In view of the peasantry's increased involvement in national affairs, they perceived Che's guerrilla movement in totally different terms than he expected. Instead of supporting Che's guerrilla movement, they opposed it. For example, at the end of June 1967, the National Congress of Farm Workers issued a public declaration in which they denounced the guerrillas as an "anti-national force, financed from abroad and destined to create nothing but confusion and disruption." This group further stated that they were ready to cooperate with the armed forces "in totally liquidating this foreign aggression that is attempting to undermine in a systematic manner the economic and social development of our people."

That the Bolivian public perceived the guerrillas as foreigners seriously handicapped the guerrilla movement. Saddled with this stigma, it was impossible for them to win widespread popular support among the general population. In fact, certain Bolivian observers referred to the foreign character of Che's guerrilla movement as its "original sin." Since the guerrilla operation was neither organized nor led by Bolivians, it aroused a nationalistic reaction among nearly every segment of Bolivian society. The foreign character of the guerrilla operation also made it possible for President Barrientos and the Bolivian military to wrap themselves in the Bolivian flag and play the role of defenders of the Bolivian nation.

Even if Che's group had not been marked with the stigma of "foreign intruders," it seems highly unlikely they would have been able to establish a base of popular support among the peasantry in the southeast of Bolivia. The peasantry would not have been receptive to any type of armed uprising. The fact that Che and his group were considered foreigners, of course, made it impossible for them to develop an armed uprising among the rural population, and so they found themselves isolated and surrounded on all sides by informers and government sympathizers.

U.S. INVOLVEMENT IN THE DEFEAT OF CHE'S GUERRILLA FORCE

Sensationalist claims that the U.S. Central Intelligence Agency (CIA) brought down Che have no factual foundation at all. To be sure, the

THE TRAGIC DEATH OF A REVOLUTIONARY 175

CIA was ever present during the entire episode; they certainly were determined to see that Che was defeated and, if possible, captured. However, they were not responsible for the failure of Che's guerrilla operation or his execution. In fact, the U.S. government and the CIA appear to have opposed the idea of executing Che. Purely for professional reasons, the CIA wanted to keep him alive. This appears to have been the position of the U.S. government from the highest levels down to the two CIA agents on the scene. Thus, in his (now declassified) memorandum to President Lyndon Johnson confirming the death of Che Guevara, Walt Rostow (who was the president's special assistant for National Security Affairs) told the president the following:

> CIA tells us that the latest information is Guevara was taken alive. After a short interrogation to establish his identity, General Ovando—Chief of the Bolivian Armed Forces—ordered him shot. I regard this as stupid, but it is understandable from a Bolivian standpoint given the problems which the sparing of French Communist and Castro courier Regis Debray has caused them.

Rostow also provides in this memorandum his analysis of the "significant implications" of Che's death. He wrote:

- It marks the passing of another of the aggressive, romantic revolutionaries like Sukarno, Nkrumah, Ben Bella . . . and reinforces this trend.
- In the Latin American context, it will have a strong impact in discouraging would-be guerrillas.
- It shows the soundness of our "preventive medicine" assistance to countries facing incipient insurgency—it was the Bolivian 2nd Ranger Battalion, trained by our Green Berets from June–September of this year that cornered and got him.

Rostow closed the memorandum with the comment that he had "put these points across to several newsmen" (Rostow 1967).

Gustavo Villoldo, one of the two CIA agents on the scene at Che's capture, claims: "At no time did I or the CIA have a say in executing

Che . . . that was a Bolivian decision" (Tamayo 1997). The other CIA agent present was Félix Rodríguez, who later became the president of the militant Cuban-exile organization Brigade 2506. He has claimed repeatedly he was under CIA instructions to "do everything possible to keep him alive," but Rodríguez has also admitted he transmitted the order to execute Guevara that came by radio from the Bolivian high command to the soldiers at La Higuera. And he also claims he directed them not to shoot Guevara in the face so that his wounds would appear to be combat related (*Miami's Cuban Connection* 2006).

Rodríguez contends he personally informed Che that he would be killed. He told *Miami's Cuban Connection* in a 2006 interview: "I walked in and gave the order to untie him. Che had asked if we could untie him and let him sit down. Later, the order came from the Bolivian government to shoot him. I tried in all my power to stop them because of my instructions to take him to Panama for the CIA. . . . At the end, I asked him if he wanted me to do something for his family. He said 'Tell my wife to marry again and try to be happy.' We shook hands, hugged. I left the room and someone came in and shot him." Later in this interview he said it was Sergeant Mario Terán who shot Che. After Che was executed, Rodríguez claims he took Che's Rolex watch, which he has proudly shown reporters over the years.

If the CIA agents advised the Bolivians to keep Che alive, this advice was clearly rejected by the Bolivian government's top leaders, who felt they could not afford to allow the famous revolutionary to live. Bolivia had no death penalty, so they were afraid an imprisoned Che would become a cause célèbre that would attract leftists to the country from around the world. Moreover, if they turned him over to the CIA, they would give the world and the Bolivian people the impression the U.S. government was running things in Bolivia. They felt they had no other choice politically but to execute Che. They also decided to cover this up by claiming he died after capture from wounds received in battle.

Exaggerated claims about U.S. involvement in the defeat of Che's guerrilla force have also been made with regard to the use of infrared aerial cameras by U.S. planes to detect and locate the guerrillas. One journalist in particular asserted the mud ovens used by the guerrillas made it possible for the U.S. Air Force to pinpoint their location at all times by using new, highly sensitive heat-detecting cameras in an around-

THE TRAGIC DEATH OF A REVOLUTIONARY 177

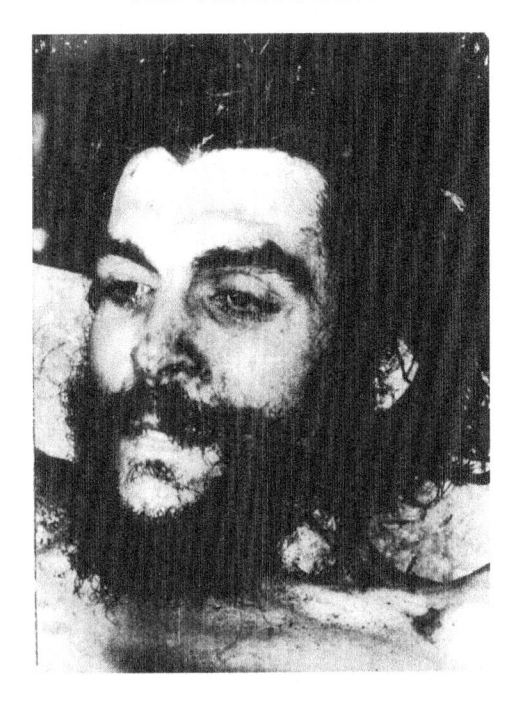

Bolivian Army photo of Che Guevara's face shortly after his death, 1967. Richard L. Harris.

the-clock aerial surveillance of the combat zone. However, after leaving their main camp in the Ñancahuazú area, where they did have a mud oven, the guerrillas never stayed anywhere long enough to build another one. In fact, they rarely even built fires.

Furthermore, the Bolivian authorities knew at least the general location of the guerrillas throughout the entire period from their initial discovery to their elimination in October. They did not have to rely on such sophisticated American gimmickry as heat-sensing infrared cameras. For one thing, during the first four months of operations, Che's column clashed with the army fairly frequently, and it was possible to ascertain simply from these encounters their general location. Moreover, the army constantly received information about them from the local peasantry. In fact, the irony of the situation is that the Bolivian military knew far more about the guerrillas than the latter knew about the army—the exact reversal of the usual situation in guerrilla warfare.

In sum, the U.S. involvement in Bolivian affairs was extensive, but the U.S. contribution to the military defeat of Che's guerrilla operation was minimal and then only at the end. To be sure, the U.S. trained the

Rangers of the Second Manchego Rangers Regiment who were responsible for capturing Che and almost completely eliminating his small force in October 1967. However, Che's guerrilla operation was already defeated prior to the arrival on the scene of the U.S.-trained Rangers. His force had lost over half of its original members and had failed to win any popular support. Moreover, the hostility of the pro-Soviet Communist Party leaders and the indifference of the other leftist groups in Bolivia, together with the capture of the guerrillas' urban contacts in La Paz, had left Che and the tattered remnants of his original force completely and hopelessly isolated by the time the Rangers entered into combat against them.

Chapter 11
CHE'S DIARY AND HIDDEN REMAINS

Following Che's capture and execution, the Barrientos government decided to sell Che's diary to the publisher willing to pay the highest price (the information in this chapter is based on the author's original research; see Harris 2007:227–56). However, while the Bolivians were negotiating the sale of the diary, the Cuban government mysteriously obtained a copy and released it through publishing houses in Latin America, Europe, and the United States. By publishing the diary before the Bolivians could sell it, the Cuban government was able to score a significant propaganda victory and greatly embarrass the Barrientos regime. Moreover, the questions about how the Cubans got a copy of the diary gave rise to serious doubts in Bolivia about the integrity of the government and the armed forces. Clearly, someone in the civilian side of the government or the military had placed a copy of this top-secret document in the hands of the Cuban government.

Che's diary was made public in Havana on July 1, 1968, shortly after I had arrived in La Paz, and within a few days it was distributed by leftist publishers in Chile, Mexico, France, Italy, West Germany, and the United States. A few weeks later, on July 17, Antonio Arguedas, Minister of the Interior and a close friend of President Barrientos, fled to Chile and was denounced by General Ovando as the traitor who had provided the Cuban government with photographic copies of Che's diary. The Bolivian public was stunned by the news, and most of the population regarded Arguedas's actions as a national disgrace.

Since Arguedas had been President Barrientos's right-hand man, the whole affair seriously undermined the public's confidence in the Barrientos regime and within 24 hours plunged the country into a grave political crisis that broke apart the coalition of political parties that had previously supported Barrientos. At the same time, the three main opposition parties (the rightwing Socialist Falange, the centrist National Revolutionary Movement, and the Trotskyist Revolutionary Party of the Nationalist Left) issued a manifesto calling on the Barrientos government to resign. They also called a mass demonstration in the capital on July 20, which resulted in a violent clash with the police and the death of a captain of the Civil Guard.

The leaders of the demonstration were arrested, and Barrientos declared a nationwide state of emergency. He also called on the peasant syndicates in the Cochabamba area to come to his assistance, and 5,000 armed campesinos from the Cochabamba Valley were mobilized and moved to the outskirts of La Paz. This appears to have been the turning point in the crisis. Soon thereafter Barrientos received expressions of public support from the various military garrisons throughout the country, as well as several important political groups. Ironically, the crisis arising from the publication of Che's diary, and particularly Arguedas's part in the whole affair, almost toppled the Barrientos regime—something Che's guerrilla operation never came close to achieving while he was alive.

But the Arguedas affair did not end there. Much to everyone's surprise, approximately a month after his flight from the country, Antonio Arguedas voluntarily returned to Bolivia to stand trial for his actions. In Chile Arguedas had publicly declared that he wanted to return to Bolivia to clear his name. However, most Bolivians assumed he had received a large sum of money from the Cubans in return for Che's diary, so no one took seriously his announced intention to return home. This made it all the more surprising when he did return to Bolivia, following a month-long odyssey that took him to Buenos Aires, Madrid, London, New York, and Lima, before arriving back in La Paz.

When he arrived in Bolivia, Arguedas told the press that he had returned in order to clear his conscience and face the consequences of his past actions. His exact words to the Bolivian press were the following:

> I am not looking for publicity. I only want to tell the truth about everything that occurred in my career as a subsecretary and minister of government, and alert not only the present government of Bolivia, but all the governments of Latin America, as to how North American imperialism undermines their intelligence services in order to introduce errors, to distort, to present a completely different picture of reality, to obstruct their economic relations with other states, and finally to keep them under its control.

He said he had returned in order to regain his personal dignity by telling the truth at the moment when it was most appropriate to do so. In this regard, he reminded the reporters he had been the favorite of both the Americans and the most reactionary political elements in Bolivia prior to his sending Che's diary to Fidel Castro, and that he had given up a promising political career because of his disgust over the undermining of Bolivia's national sovereignty by U.S. political and economic interests.

At the press conference following his return to Bolivia, Arguedas refuted the suggestion that he had given a copy of Che's diary to Fidel Castro because he was a Castroite or because he was a Communist. He denied being either a Castroite or a Communist and stated that he was a nationalist first and a Marxist second. With regard to the accusation that he had received a large sum of money for the diary, Arguedas angrily retorted that this was another of the CIA's insidious attempts to discredit him by slander. He argued that if it had been money he was after, it would have been unnecessary for him to sell Che's diary to the Cubans. Arguedas pointed out that as minister of internal affairs he could have made a fortune in bribes from the Americans if he had wanted to do so. He said he had documents hidden outside the country that, among other things, proved that a U.S. engineering firm (which he named) had offered him a bribe of $1.5 million to see that they were awarded a government contract for the construction of two new highways. In other words, he argued that he had rejected bribes of much greater amounts than the $500,000 it was rumored he had received from the Cubans for the diary.

The Arguedas affair is one consequence of Che's guerrilla operation that Che himself could never have foreseen. Arguedas's actions shook the Barrientos regime to the core, whereas Che's guerrilla activities, at least before the Arguedas affair, had the effect of strengthening the Barrientos regime and the Bolivian military. By calling into question the integrity of the government and the armed forces, Arguedas's actions weakened the Barrientos regime and the public's confidence in the existing political system. Moreover, Arguedas's return to Bolivia and his revelations about the nature of the CIA's interference in Bolivian affairs called into question the role of the United States government and companies in that country. In fact, the Arguedas affair provides shocking evidence about the nature of the U.S. government's involvement in the domestic affairs of Latin American countries.

Following his press conference in the Ministry of the Interior the day of his return to Bolivia, Arguedas was placed in strict confinement and not allowed to make any further statements to the press. However, within a few months he was released from prison as a result of the Bolivian high court's decision that it did not have the authority to try him. According to the high court, the Bolivian legislature was the only body competent to try a former minister of state for acts of treason committed while in office. Because of the court's decision, Arguedas was released from prison pending action by the legislature.

He kept a low profile after his release, but within a short time several attempts were made on his life. Twice bombs were thrown at him, and on June 6, 1969, he and a Spanish journalist accompanying him were machine-gunned while walking on the street in La Paz. Both Arguedas and the journalist escaped with minor wounds. However, Arguedas was hospitalized for almost a month, and immediately following his release from the hospital, he sought asylum in the Mexican embassy.

In a statement he gave to the press at the time, he explained that his intentions were to leave Bolivia and go to Mexico. He said that he had decided to leave Bolivia because of the increasing political instability in the country following the death of President Barrientos (who was killed when his personal helicopter crashed in mysterious circumstances) and because of the recent attempts on his life. He gave as an additional reason the failure of the government to take any action whatsoever against the agents of U.S. imperialism who were at work undermining Bolivia's national sovereignty.

During this time, Arguedas was the author of yet another incredible episode. He secretly arranged for Che's hands, in a glass container of formaldehyde, and a plaster mask of his face (made in Vallegrande) to be sent to Cuba in much the same manner as he had arranged for the copies of Che's diary to be sent there. However, in this case, the existence and transfer of these items to Cuba were not discovered until many years later. In fact, to this day, the story of Che's hands and his death mask is not widely known.

CHE'S HANDS AND DEATH MASK

The odyssey of these two items is more complex and more difficult to follow than the story of Che's diary. The man who cut off Che's hands and made his death mask out of plaster was Roberto "Toto" Quintanilla, an official in Arguedas's ministry. Like many of the other figures associated with Che's death, he was killed under unusual circumstances in November 1970. An unknown woman gunned him down with an automatic weapon in his office in Hamburg, Germany, where he was serving as the Bolivian consul. Nothing more is known about him than this. According to Arguedas, Che's hands and his death mask were given to him by General Ovando after they had been inspected by the team of Argentine criminal investigators sent to Bolivia to verify Che's fingerprints.

General Ovando instructed Arguedas to dispose of both items immediately and to leave no traces of them. However, Arguedas chose to ignore Ovando's orders and gave them for safekeeping to a close friend named Jorge Suarez, a Bolivian writer and the editor of the daily newspaper *Jornada*. In a little known interview that Suarez gave Argentine journalist Uki Goñi in 1995, Suarez claimed Arguedas asked him to come to his office seven or eight days after Che's death. Arguedas told him he wanted to discuss something very personal and urgent. When Suarez went to his office, Arguedas produced a glass container and a translucent bag, the contents of both Suarez could not at first see clearly. After

Arguedas motioned for him to come closer and examine the two objects, Suarez saw two hands floating in the glass container and he saw a white plaster mask in the bag. As he studied the mask closely he saw that it was an extraordinarily good replica of Che's face with his eyes open. He could even see the details of his beard. It did not appear to be the face of someone dead, rather of someone very much alive. Suarez told Goñi he would never forget that face (Goñi 1995).

Arguedas explained to Suarez that General Ovando had given him strict instructions to incinerate the hands and the mask and then scatter the ashes in a river, but that he had decided not to follow these orders. He asked Suarez to take the items with him and hide them in his home. Although he was shocked and frightened, Suarez agreed to do what his friend asked him. According to Suarez, Arguedas said he was an admirer of Che and that the top levels of the Bolivian military and the U.S. embassy as well as certain other influential people did not trust him. In fact, he said the U.S. embassy suspected him of being a revolutionary and a possible contact for the guerrillas. By not destroying the death mask and Che's hands Arguedas said that he was risking his life.

Suarez made a sort of sarcophagus, or stone coffin, for the items under the floor of his bedroom and hid them there. Although his house was searched several times by the Bolivian secret police while Arguedas was in prison, Che's hands and death mask were not discovered. They stayed under the floor in his bedroom until Suarez left Bolivia in 1969 as the new ambassador to Mexico, appointed by the military government of none other than General Ovando. Suarez told Goñi (1995) that the Bolivian intelligence services and the CIA concluded afterward that he had probably carried Che's hands and death mask out of the country in his diplomatic pouch, so they discontinued looking for them. However, he had left them hidden under the floor of his bedroom.

Meanwhile, following his release from prison, Arguedas sought refuge in the Mexican embassy while his request for political exile to Mexico was under consideration. When he learned that Suarez was leaving the country for Mexico, he made arrangements to have Che's hands and death mask taken to Cuba in much the same way he had arranged for Che's diary to be taken. In July 1969, he asked his journalist friend Víctor Zannier to arrange for the two items to be sent to Cuba. Zannier in turn delegated the mission to Jorge Sattori and Juan Coronel. Although they were members of the pro-Soviet Bolivian Communist Party, Zannier felt they could be trusted, and he figured they could use the party's international connections to get out of the country and travel to Cuba. Juan Coronel kept the glass container with Che's hands and the bag with his death mask wrapped up in old newspapers under his bed for five months while he and Sattori made their arrangements to go to Cuba by way of Europe and the Soviet Union.

Coronel was struck by how much the death mask revealed Che's features, and he described the glass container as cylindrical, about 10 inches high and 7 inches wide, and sealed with red wax. Inside were two hands floating in a brownish liquid. They appeared to have belonged to someone who had been quite strong. He said they were covered in a beautiful film (most likely the ink used to record Che's fingerprints), and they appeared to have been amputated with an inadequate instrument that left an irregular cut just before the wrists. Coronel's description of the way the hands were amputated matches the image in the shocking photographs of Che's hands that were taken by the Argentine criminal investigators who were sent to Bolivia to prove that the Bolivian military had indeed captured and killed the famous Che Guevara. Their story and the photos they took were not released until many years later (De Carlos 2006). In their photographs, Che's hands are seen palm up on a newspaper page with the curled fingers covered in ink and the ink bottle and pad next to them.

ARGUEDAS'S ODYSSEY

The Mexican embassy arranged for Arguedas to leave Bolivia and go to Mexico in 1969, where I met him briefly at a conference in Cuernavaca. He appeared to be quite happy in Mexico. However, he subsequently left Mexico for Cuba, where he was celebrated for his actions (Anderson 1997:745) and lived for nine years. While he was living in Havana, he was visited several times by Antonio Peredo (Estellano 2000), the oldest brother of Coco and Inti. Peredo is a well-known Bolivian journalist, political activist, and university professor. According to Peredo, Arguedas lived a very disciplined and studious existence while he was in Cuba, and he regularly spent his days doing research in the libraries.

In 1979 Arguedas returned to Bolivia and disappeared from public view. In the mid-1980s, his name appeared again in the press because he was accused of being involved in an armed group that kidnapped a wealthy businessman. Although his involvement in this affair was never proved conclusively, he was arrested and remained in prison from 1986 to 1989. After his release, he dropped out of sight again and did not surface until 1997, the year the search for Che's remains in Bolivia reached a crescendo and became a highly publicized international effort. During this period, the media and some of the people involved in the search for Che's remains tried to locate Arguedas to see if he could tell them where Che's body had been buried. However, the police found Arguedas first and arrested him for supposedly leading a gang that was planning to kidnap businessmen in order to extract ransom money from their families and business associates. He was released by the police while awaiting trial, and he immediately went into hiding. Subsequently, he was declared a fugitive from justice when he failed to appear in court on the date of his trial.

During this time, he told Antonio Peredo that he had in his possession the names of everyone involved in the drug trade in Bolivia, and that many people knew this. For this reason, he told Peredo: "I'm a dangerous man" (Estellano 2000). By this time, the Bolivian police were trying to link him to a series of bombings in La Paz. They arrested three men who they said belonged to a terrorist group that was led by Arguedas, but they were unable to present any serious proof that he was involved in this group.

Between November 20 and December 16, 1999, there were six bombings in random locations around La Paz that made no sense and that were never explained by the police. The police accused Antonio Arguedas of being responsible for the bombings and for the deaths of several people who were killed by the bombings. He did not turn himself into the authorities and remained in hiding.

In February 2000, the police reported that he was killed in La Paz when a bomb he was carrying exploded. The police said he belonged to a right-wing group called C-4, which had declared war against Castroism, drugs, and corruption in Bolivia. But Arguedas's family members and local political observers expressed serious doubts about the police account of his death (Estellano 2000). It remains unclear whether his death was accidental or intentional. One newspaper account suggested that the police explanation of Arguedas's death provided an ironic metaphor for his zigzagging political life. According to this account, instead of moving the timer on the bomb to the right to start its timing sequence, he moved it to the contact point on the left, and it instantly blew up in his hands (*Clarín.com* 2000). Of course, it is more likely he was killed by the police. The true story of his death may never be known.

CHE'S BODY

As for Che's body, after it was displayed in Vallegrande it disappeared from public view and became a state secret. Since the Bolivian military refused to give any information to the public about this subject, there was considerable speculation about what happened to it. Some people believed the CIA had taken Che's body back to the United States, others that his body had been cremated and his ashes spread over the jungle by air, and some thought he was buried in a secret location. It now appears that the CIA agent Gustavo Villoldo was responsible for burying Che's body in an unmarked grave near the Vallegrande airport along with six of Che's former companions in arms. At least this is where his bones were ultimately uncovered.

Thirty years after his death and following an almost 2-year search, in July 1997 a team of Cuban and Argentine experts found his remains with those of six of his comrades in an unmarked grave at the edge of the Vallegrande airport. The Cuban-Argentine team conclusively identified one of the skeletons as being Che's remains on the basis of its facial bone structure, teeth, and absence of hands (Rother 1997). It also was found with a jacket and was not wearing socks, consistent with the last photographs taken of Che after he was killed, which show him lying on a jacket and without socks.

The search for and discovery of Che's remains in Bolivia adds yet another page to the remarkable story of his life and death and reveals that his legacy continues to take on new dimensions as time passes. On November 26, 1995, the *New York Times* published an article containing statements of retired Bolivian army general Mario Vargas Salinas to the effect that Che's body had been buried under the landing strip at the

Vallegrande airport (Castañeda 1997:404–5). In fact, the widow of Colonel Andrés Selich told the journalist Jon Lee Anderson, who was collecting information for his biographical book on Che Guevara, that her husband and a couple of other Bolivian army officers (including Vargas) had buried Che's body and the bodies of six of his comrades in two unmarked graves dug by a bulldozer near the Vallegrande airport (Anderson 1997:742). When Anderson questioned Vargas (who wrote a book in 1988 about Che's Bolivian operation), he told Anderson that all the bodies had been buried in one unmarked grave near the edge of the airport. The reporting of these details of Che's death, especially in the *New York Times* by Thomas Lipscomb (November 26, 1995:3), caused a political uproar in Bolivia. It also stirred a great deal of interest in the international media and gave rise to a flood of new information about Che's death and his fatal Bolivian mission.

Under pressure from the national and the international press, the president of Bolivia ordered the army to recover the bodies of Che and his comrades. What followed was a rather bizarre and highly publicized search for their bodies by an odd assortment of Bolivians, Cubans, and Argentines, which attracted many onlookers and reporters (Anderson 1997:xv). The whole affair turned out to be a source of considerable embarrassment for the Bolivian government and military since it resurrected a controversial chapter in Bolivia's political history. For his part in the whole affair, Vargas was placed under house arrest for revealing state secrets.

The little town of Vallegrande, with a population of approximately 8,000 people, was in the news again, but this time because of the presence of Cuban forensic anthropologists and geologists. At first, they located the remains of only 5 of the guerrillas, a fraction of the 32 guerrillas who were killed in the area and buried in unmarked graves. But for 16 months there was no sign of Che's body.

Meanwhile, Vallegrande's municipal government leaders declared Che's remains were a "national patrimony" and imposed a moratorium on the search until mid-June 1997. Someone in the town also started promoting a $70 per day walking tour of the route taken by Che and his comrades before they were caught and killed, and there was talk of creating a museum. Loyola Guzman, who had been the treasurer of the clandestine urban network that supported Che's guerrilla force before she and the others were arrested and imprisoned by the Bolivian authorities, stated publicly that Che's remains should rightfully remain in Bolivian soil. She argued that "his life was an example of heroic internationalism that no single country should monopolize." Following her release from prison, Guzman returned to leftist activism and was very much involved in the campaign for the defense of human rights in Bolivia. In 2006 she was elected to the Constituent Assembly in Bolivia as one of the representatives of the Movimiento al Socialismo (MAS, or Movement toward Socialism). In Che's diary, he noted that "Loyola made a very good impression on me. She is very young and sweet, but one notes a strong determination."

THE DISCOVERY OF CHE'S BODY

The Cuban team met until 4 A.M. on June 28, 1997, before they decided where to focus their day of digging, according to Alejandro Inchaurregui, one of a team of Argentine forensic anthropologists who were called in to help the Cubans (Tamayo 1997). Ground radar surveys made by the Cuban-Argentine search team earlier in 1997 had discovered a dozen spots of disturbed earth that they thought could be grave sites. Three of these sites appeared to be human made, and they decided to concentrate on these sites using a bulldozer—not the preferred tool of forensic specialists. However, time was running out for the Cuban-Argentine team of experts because of changing political circumstances in Bolivia.

They set the blade of the bulldozer to remove four inches of dirt with each pass of the blade. They found nothing at the first site, but at the second site after 18 passes the bulldozer blade uncovered the remains of a human skeleton. As they continued to dig they found the remains of a total of seven bodies in two groups, separated by two and a half feet. The bodies were buried in a pit between the edge of Vallegrande's old dirt airstrip and a nearby cemetery. The searchers were overcome with emotion when they examined the remains of the second body that was in the middle of the first group of three skeletons. The skeleton had no hands. Since they knew Che's hands had been amputated after his death, they were almost certain they had finally found his remains. The American author Jon Lee Anderson was present during the digging on this day, and according to Anderson: "Just seeing the genuine excitement, the genuine euphoria on the face of the Cubans there [made] me certain this was Che's remains . . . they were simply overcome, crying and hugging each other" (Tamayo 1997).

However, they still had to prove to the Bolivian government that the remains were those of Che and obtain permission to send them to Cuba. According to the Argentine forensic anthropologist Inchaurregui, the Bolivian Ministry of Interior officials had warned them they needed to move fast, since the inauguration of Bolivia's newly elected right-wing president and former military dictator, Hugo Banzer, was rapidly approaching and they assumed he would likely block the removal of Che's remains. Thus, on the night of July 5, 1997, a convoy of vehicles with the remains of the guerrillas made the 150-mile trip at full speed along the dangerous mountain roads between Vallegrande and the provincial capital of Santa Cruz.

In Santa Cruz, Che's remains were quickly identified. The team of examiners was composed of experts from the Institute of Forensic Medicine in Havana, the director of Che's personal archive María del Carmen Ariet and the Argentine forensic anthropologists. They matched the evidence of bullet wounds in the bones of Skeleton 2 with the historical facts of Che's death. The excavated teeth of Skeleton 2 matched a plaster mold of Che's teeth made in Cuba before he left for the Congo. The mold had been made in the event he died in combat and his body had to be identified. Moreover, there was other evidence to support the conclusion that the remains were indeed those of Che Guevara.

For example, retired Bolivian Air Force General Jaime Nino de Guzman, the helicopter pilot who flew Che's body and the bodies of the other guerrillas killed in or near La Higuera to Vallegrande, spoke with Che in La Higuera shortly before he was killed. He recalled that Che was shot in his right calf, his hair was matted and dirty, his clothes were shredded, and his feet were shod in rough handmade sandals. According to General Nino de Guzman, Che kept his head high, looked everyone in the eye, and asked only for something to smoke. The general told a reporter: "I took pity since he looked so terrible, and gave him my small bag of imported tobacco for his pipe. He smiled and thanked me" (Tamayo 1997). When the Argentine anthropologist Inchaurregui inspected the jacket dug up next to Che's remains, he found a small bag of pipe tobacco in the inside pocket that had apparently been missed by the soldiers who searched Che's body after he was killed in La Higuera. General Nino de Guzman acknowledged that this was irrefutable evidence the remains were indeed Che's. He told a reporter: "I must tell you I had serious doubts at the beginning. I thought the Cubans would just find any old bones and call it Che. . . . But after hearing about the tobacco pouch, I have no doubts" (Tamayo 1997).

The Bolivian government gave the Cubans permission to take Che's remains to Cuba along with those of all the other guerrillas who were found buried in unmarked graves in Bolivia, including the bones of Tania (Haydée Tamara Bunke, the only woman in Che's guerrilla force) and Joaquín (Comandante Juan Vitalio Acuña Nuñez, Che's Cuban comrade and the second in command of the guerrilla force). Thus, on October 11, 1997, almost exactly 30 years after Che's death, his remains and those of the other six fallen comrades found buried with him were placed on display in flag-draped caskets inside the monument to José Martí in Havana (*Los Angeles Times*, October 12, 1997:A1). With a huge 50-foot mural of Che overlooking the Plaza de la Revolución, hundreds of thousands of Cubans waited in line to pay their respects. After seven days of official mourning and national homage to Che's life and ideals, the caskets were taken to the city of Santa Clara, where Che had led the guerrilla column that scored a decisive victory in the Cuban Revolution. In Santa Clara, Che's coffin was placed in a newly constructed mausoleum at the base of a large statue of him holding a rifle in his hand.

At the quasi-religious ceremony held in Santa Clara, and in the presence of Che's widow, Aleida March, their two daughters and their two sons, Fidel Castro praised Che's qualities as the ideal revolutionary. He closed his homage to Che before the assembled crowd with the following words: "Thank you, Che, for your history, your life and your example. Thank you for coming to reinforce us in the difficult struggle in which we are engaged today to preserve the ideas for which you fought so hard" (Rother 1997).

In the midst of this massive public veneration of Che, his daughter Aleida Guevara, who is a doctor like her father, told a press conference that her father always shunned public adulation when he was an important public figure in Cuba and that he probably would have been embarrassed by all the celebrations in his honor. She also said that it hurt to see the image of her father marketed for commercial purposes on ashtrays, beer, and jeans, but that she hoped some young people would see beyond this commercialism and search for the ideals that her father stood for, especially in a globalized society that is losing all its values (Fineman 1997). Like his older sister, Che's son Camilo Guevara, a lawyer in the Cuban Ministry of Fisheries, is protective of his father's memory and image. He also has criticized what he characterizes as "the bad intentions" of some of the authors of the books published about his father.

Interestingly, in many of the articles published by U.S. newspapers on the return of Che's remains to Cuba and the celebrations that were held in his honor, the reporters used the opportunity to criticize Cuba's socialist system and Che Guevara's ideas on revolution. They characterized them as anachronistic and no longer relevant in the contemporary period. However, the defeat of Che's guerrilla operation in Bolivia does not indicate that an armed revolution is impossible in Latin America. As long as the existing political and economic elites in the region continue to postpone badly needed social and economic reforms and the gap between the rich and the poor continues to increase, popular insurrection will remain on the agenda in Latin America and in other parts of the world with similar conditions. Moreover, the use of repressive and undemocratic measures by those in power to block peaceful and legal efforts to bring about basic economic, political, and social reforms invariably provokes the use of nonpeaceful and extralegal means by those who see they have no other options if they want to create a more just social order.

Chapter 12
CHE'S ENDURING LEGACY

Che left an enduring legacy that has grown rather than diminished over the years since his death in 1967. At the public tribute to Che held in the Plaza de la Revolución in Havana following his death in 1967, Fidel Castro (1967) heralded Che's legacy when he said:

> If we want a model of a person that does not belong to our time but to the future, I say from the depths of my heart that such a model, without a single stain on his conduct, on his actions, or his behavior, is Che!

Castro anticipated in his speech what has over the years become true: in Cuba and for his many admirers around the world Che has become a heroic model of the totally committed revolutionary, the selfless human being who dedicates his life for the common good to bring about a better future for humanity. In socialist Cuba, he is held up as the most outstanding example of the kind of human being Cuba's socialist society is preparing for the 21st century and the socialist future just over the horizon.

Moreover, in the more than four decades that have passed since his death, Che has become an international revolutionary icon, a famous symbol of resistance to social injustice around the world. His romantic image and the revolutionary example he has left behind as his legacy have taken on a transcendent quality that appeals to people in diverse cultures and circumstances. An examination of the reasons for this phenomenon is of considerable importance, since it reveals a great deal about the nature and global significance of Che's enduring legacy.

CHE HAS BECOME A REVOLUTIONARY ICON

Since his death, posters displaying Che's portrait have appeared in almost every major city in the world. The Che on these posters and placards is a heroic figure, with the unmistakable beard, beret, and piercing eyes that have come to be associated with this legendary revolutionary. In many of these mass-produced portraits of Che, the heroic face that peers out from them somehow seems to combine in one human countenance all the races of mankind. His eyes and mustache appear Asiatic,

Che Guevara's iconic poster image. Fitzpatrick.

while the darkness of his complexion seems African, and the shape of his nose and cheeks are distinctively European. Perhaps this partially explains why he has become an icon for radical political activists, guerrillas, rebels, leftist students, and intellectuals on every continent, and why, for example, his face is often the only white one to appear alongside those of nonwhite revolutionary heroes in Africa, Asia, and Latin America.

Following his death, in the late 1960s and throughout the 1970s leftist students, radical intellectuals, and revolutionary movements around the world constantly quoted Che's famous dictum "The duty of every revolutionary is to make the revolution." They believed, as did Che, revolutions are made by people who are willing to act, not by those who are waiting for the appropriate objective conditions or for orders from the official Communist Party or the leaders of the Soviet Union or China. It is interesting in this regard to note the official Communist press in the Soviet Union, Eastern Europe, and the People's Republic of China during the 1970s and 1980s often referred to the young leftists in these radical student and political movements as "Guevarist hippies" and "left-wing adventurers." However, such attacks were a matter of little importance to these movements, since they regarded Guevara's activist revolutionary ideas as an alternative to the overly dogmatic and bureaucratic party lines of the more orthodox Communists who were in power in the Soviet Union and China and to the tepid reformism of the moderate socialist and social democratic parties in Western Europe and elsewhere.

Because of his undaunted and fiercely independent revolutionary idealism, Che became the idol of the New Left during the late 1960s and 1970s in the United States and Great Britain, the bulwarks of capitalism and bourgeois democracy. For a time, students at the London School of Economics and Political Science, one of the most hallowed of Britain's institutions of higher education, greeted each other with the salutation "Che." In the United States, buttons, shirts, placards, and posters with Che's face were present at nearly every antiwar demonstration during the Vietnam War years. Significantly, they have appeared again in the protests against the wars in Iraq and Afghanistan.

In Latin America, where Che gave his life fighting for ideals, his name became a battle cry among leftist students, intellectuals, and workers during the 1970s and 1980s. His death at the hands of the

Che Guevara's image on Cuban three-peso note. Richard L. Harris.

Bolivian army made him an instant martyr for all those who were opposed to the ruling elites and the glaring social injustices that plague this troubled region of the world.

Today, many Latin Americans remember and admire him for his uncompromising revolutionary idealism, his sensitivity to the plight of Latin America's impoverished masses, the rapid worldwide fame he acquired as one of the top leaders of the Cuban government during the heady days following the Cuban Revolution, and his willingness to die fighting for the realization of his ideals of social justice, anti-imperialism, and socialism. Che truly belongs in the pantheon of the region's most famous revolutionary leaders—José Martí, Augusto César Sandino, Emiliano Zapata, Pancho Villa, Camilo Torres, and Fidel Castro.

CHE'S LEGACY IN CUBA

In Cuba, Che holds one of the highest positions in Cuba's pantheon of revolutionary heroes and martyrs. Less than a week after Fidel Castro acknowledged Che had indeed been killed by the Bolivian military, hundreds of thousands of Cubans silently filled Havana's Plaza de la Revolución to listen tearfully to Castro as he told dozens of anecdotes about Che and praised Che's outstanding intellectual, political, and military virtues. Backed by a huge portrait of Che and flanked by Cuban flags, Castro gave notice of the importance the Cuban regime would give in the future to Che's revolutionary example. Near the end of his tribute to his fallen comrade, Castro said:

CHE'S ENDURING LEGACY

> If we ask ourselves how we want our revolutionary fighters, our militants, and our people to be, then we must answer without any hesitation: let them be like Che! If we wish to express how we want the people of future generations to be, we must say: let them be like Che! If we ask how we desire to educate our children, we should say without hesitation: we want our children to be educated in the spirit of Che! (Deutschmann 1994:78)

Today, the Cuban regime continues to educate the youth of the country about Che. His picture is in every Cuban school, and Cuba's schoolchildren learn by heart quotations from his writings and his letters. All know the stirring hymn "Seremos como el Che" (We will be like Che), which is sung on many occasions.

Several generations of Cubans also know this famous paragraph from Che's farewell letter to his children:

> Remember that the revolution is what is most important and that each one of us, alone, is worth nothing. Above all, always remain

Che Guevara's image on the present-day Ministry of the Interior in Havana, Cuba. Mark Scott Johnson.

capable of feeling deeply whatever injustice is committed against anyone in any part of the world. This is the finest quality of a revolutionary. (Deutschmann 1997:349)

Part of his legacy is his children. With his first wife, Hilda Gadea, he had a daughter, Hilda Beatriz Guevara Gadea, born February 15, 1956, in Mexico City (she died of cancer August 21, 1995, in Havana, Cuba, at the age of 39). With his second wife, Aleida March, he had four children: Aleida Guevara March, born November 24, 1960, in Havana; Camilo Guevara March, born May 20, 1962, in Havana; Celia Guevara March, born June 14, 1963, in Havana; and Ernesto Guevara March, born February 24, 1965, in Havana.

His daughter Aleida is a medical doctor and an important Cuban political figure in her own right. She represents the family at most public functions. His sons Camilo and Ernesto are lawyers, and his daughter Celia is a veterinarian and marine biologist who works with dolphins and sea lions. Among them they have eight children, Che's grandchildren. It is also rumored Che had another child from an alleged extramarital relationship with Lilia Rosa López, and this child is supposedly Omar Pérez, born in Havana March 19, 1964 (Castañeda 1998:264–65).

For a regime that wishes to instill a revolutionary socialist and internationalist consciousness in its young, there is no better example than Che. His revolutionary ideals and personal example have become part of the social consciousness of several generations of Cubans. And he remains the Cuban model for the 21st-century socialist—"the new human being who is to be glimpsed on the horizon," which he wrote about in his now famous essay "Socialism and Man" (1965).

Elsewhere, Che has also become a pop hero. In the United States, western Europe, and Latin America his image has become commercialized through the marketing of shirts, handkerchiefs, music albums, CD covers, posters, beer, ash trays, jeans, watches, and even towels imprinted with his picture or name. As a pop or commercialized hero figure, Che is often depicted in a sardonic or satirical manner. In this commercialized iconic image he is not the heroic revolutionary figure the Cuban leaders and his contemporary admirers hold up as the model of the 21st-century human being; rather, he is a humorous or satirical caricature. For his family and friends as well as those who admire Che as a heroic revolutionary, the use of his famous image to market products in the capitalist marketplace is just as denigrating as the image of Che held by his avowed enemies, who regard him as a fanatical killer, a psychopath, or a sinister Communist renegade.

The phenomenon of hero worship and the process by which individuals become popular heroes have always been something of a mystery. In all times and places there appears to be a need for heroes. However, in times of great change, this need seems greatest. Today, people around the globe see their societies and humanity in general undergoing far-reaching changes. Many find their lives adversely affected by these changes and are frightened about the future that these changes may bring, while others hope for significant improvements in society and the quality of their own lives through radical changes in the existing order. Both groups appear to need the assurance that human beings can control their fate and shape the future according to their desires. They sometimes find this assurance in the words and deeds of an exceptional individual, whose courage and individual efforts to shape the future according to his or her ideals, even if seemingly unsuccessful, give them inspiration. This appears to be one of the reasons Che continues to be such a popular hero.

Che had the courage to act in accordance with his ideals. He gave his life fighting for a brave new world that he believed he could help bring into being. It is little wonder he is admired for this. As a Latin American Catholic priest I met in Bolivia said shortly after Che's death: "To pass one's life in the jungle, ill clothed and starving, with a price on his head, confronting the military power of imperialism, and on top of that, sick with asthma, exposing himself to death by suffocation if the bullets did not cut him down first, a man, who could have lived regally, with money, amusements, friends, women, and vices in any of the great cities of sin; this is heroism, true heroism, no matter how confused or wrong his ideas might have been. Not to recognize this is not only reactionary, but stupid."

Che's exceptional devotion to the realization of his ideals was truly heroic, and indeed it would be foolish not to recognize this. Those who recognize the heroism in his character and actions cannot help admiring Che, regardless of whether they agree with his revolutionary politics and utopian ideals. Che continues to be a hero for all those who admire and are inspired by his idealism and his exceptional human courage.

EL HOMBRE NUEVO—THE NEW HUMAN BEING

Che's vision of the new human being (*el hombre nuevo*) inspired not only him and his comrades but also the young Bolivian revolutionaries who followed in his footsteps a few years after his death. After escaping the Bolivian military's efforts to hunt down the last survivors of Che's guerrilla force, Inti Peredo and Darío (a Bolivian whose real name was David Adriazola) went into hiding in the jungles of northern Bolivia. There they organized another guerrilla force to continue the struggle initiated by Che (Siles del Valle 1996:38–40). However, this guerrilla force was short lived and in 1969 both Inti and Darío were caught and killed in the Bolivian capital city of La Paz. Thus, they too sacrificed their lives fighting, like Che and their former comrades, for a new society and a new kind of human being.

During this period, Che's concept of *el hombre nuevo* and many of his other revolutionary ideals found sympathy among many of the adherents of an unorthodox Christian body of theory and practice know as Liberation Theology (Boff and Boff 1988). In the 1960s and 1970s, this body of socially concerned and unorthodox religious views gained significant support among the more progressive elements of the Catholic Church in Latin America. Many of its adherents established close links with the revolutionary movements in the region. And in some cases the most progressive sectors of the Church, influenced by the ideals of Liberation Theology, joined radical Marxist and neo-Marxist political movements in Bolivia and in other countries such as Chile, Peru, Brazil, Nicaragua, El Salvador, and Guatemala.

After the deaths of Inti Peredo and Darío, this convergence of views resulted in the participation of some of the younger members of Bolivia's Christian Democratic Party in a revolutionary guerrilla movement that called itself the Ejército de Liberación Nacional (National Liberation Army), the same name used by Che's group. This movement was led by none other than Osvaldo "Chato" Peredo, the younger brother of Inti and Coco Peredo (Siles del Valle 1996:40–43). In 1970 this movement attempted to establish a guerrilla foco near the mining town of Teoponte, north of the capital of La Paz. They were quickly surrounded and defeated by the Bolivian army, and in a totally unnecessary act of brutality many of them were massacred by the army after they offered to surrender. Only a few survived, largely as a result of the intervention of the local leaders of the Catholic Church. Chato Peredo, who is now a psychotherapist in La Paz, was one of the few survivors who were imprisoned and later released (Anderson 1997:745).

After the massacre by the Bolivian army of most of the young participants in the Teoponte guerrilla foco, an important change began to take place in Bolivian popular culture and politics. Although the idea of guerrilla warfare was rejected as a viable form of resistance to the military regime, important elements within Bolivian society began to idealize and even venerate Che and the other fallen guerrillas as martyrs (Siles del Valle 1996:44–45). Che's death, his concept of the new human being, the ideals of Liberation Theology, the deaths of so many idealistic young Bolivians in the revolutionary movements inspired by Che and his comrades—all these elements combined to exert a major influence on Bolivian popular culture, literature, and politics that has continued to this day. It is even possible to speak today of the sanctification of the guerrillas in the minds of many people in Bolivia.

SIGNIFICANCE AND EFFECTS OF CHE'S FAILED BOLIVIAN MISSION

Indeed, the death of Che Guevara and the failure of his guerrilla operation in Bolivia have not stopped attempts to bring about meaningful change in the region through armed revolution. In fact, Che's failure helped to clarify what is needed to organize a successful armed insurrection against an unjust and oppressive regime. Subsequent revolutionary movements have appeared in Latin America and in other parts of the world since Che's death, and in most cases they have taken into account the importance of mobilizing mass political support for their movements in urban as well as rural areas.

The revolutionary movements that occurred in Central America during the late 1970s and 1980s were founded on this approach. Since the 1990s the Zapatista revolutionary movement in southern Mexico, described in chapter 6, and the Bolivarian revolution in Venezuela (led by that country's leftist president Hugo Chávez Frías) have been based on mass political support organized in both urban and rural areas. Significantly, they frequently give homage to Che's revolutionary legacy.

Che's failed mission in Bolivia proved, among other things, that a well-trained and committed revolutionary guerrilla force is not sufficient to detonate a successful revolution. Che's Bolivian operation demonstrated that unless an armed movement mobilizes popular support among the middle and working classes in urban areas as well as poorer sectors of the rural population it will be isolated and wiped out by government troops using what are now commonly understood counterinsurgency tactics. In other words, the creation of a popular-based, multiclass revolutionary movement is widely regarded today as the basic prerequisite for a successful popular revolution. It is, of course, far more difficult to create than a guerrilla foco in a relatively isolated rural area, but it is not outside the realm of possibility in the present global order. In fact, this type of popular-based revolutionary movement has emerged in recent years in various parts of the world (in Latin America, the Middle East, Africa, and Asia) and will surely emerge again in the near future.

As the preceding discussion seeks to make clear, Che's death and the failure of his guerrilla operation in Bolivia have enriched the international pool of revolutionary theory and practice. The lessons learned from the failure of his movement have led many revolutionary or rebellious political and social groups around the world to develop more successful strategies for gaining power. Moreover, as a result of Che's willingness to die for his revolutionary ideals and his martyrdom in the pursuit of these ideals, he has become a universal model of revolutionary courage and commitment, and his example continues to inspire new generations of revolutionaries and leftist political activists around the world.

More than four decades have passed since Che Guevara was killed in the little village of La Higuera in Bolivia. However, the social injustices against which this famous revolutionary fought—first in the Cuban revolution, then in the Congo, and finally in Bolivia—are very much in existence today. For this reason, Che's revolutionary life and death continue to inspire those who struggle against these injustices, particularly in Latin America.

Che's revolutionary legacy can be found in the words and deeds of workers, poor peasants, middle-class university students, intellectuals, shantytown dwellers, the leaders of indigenous communities, and the landless and the homeless—from the tip of Argentina to Mexico's border with the United States, from the Andean valleys of Peru and Bolivia to the cities and vast Amazonian region of Brazil, and of course everywhere in Cuba. Che is the focus of hundreds of books and articles, as well as films, paintings, sculptures, and murals, in Europe, North America, South America, Africa, and Asia. Today his face and name are known throughout the world, and his revolutionary legacy has acquired an enduring global significance. In particular, the shift to the left in contemporary Latin American politics has created renewed interest in Che's revolutionary ideals, his struggle against social injustice and his dedication to the revolutionary unification of Latin America.

As his first wife, Hilda Gadea (2008:21–22), wrote in her book about Che, for many people around the world he is the "exemplary revolutionary" and "a man of principle whose true understanding is essential to the struggle for justice in Latin America and other parts of the world." They see him as an "example for the young generation of the Americas and the world" to follow because of "his faith in mankind, his love for the dispossessed, and his total commitment to the struggle against exploitation and poverty."

Chapter 13

¡CHE VIVE!—CHE'S CONTINUING INFLUENCE IN LATIN AMERICA

In Latin America, Che is as politically important today as he was when he died in Bolivia over four decades ago. In some ways he is even more important now. In recent years there has been a dramatic shift to the left in the politics of most Latin American countries. This shift in the political orientation of this important region of the world has given rise to renewed interest in Che Guevara's ideals of Pan-American unity, anti-imperialism, and humanist socialism.

This rather remarkable change of direction in the region's politics is largely in response to the failure of the neoliberal agenda of free-market and free-trade capitalism pursued by the U.S. government, the International Monetary Fund, the World Bank, the Inter-American Development Bank, and most of the governments of the region since the 1980s. The neoliberal economic and social policies promoted by these Washington-based institutions (often referred to as the Washington Consensus) have widened the gap between the rich and the poor, while they have denationalized the economies and privatized the governments of most of the countries in the region. The tidal wave of popular opposition to these neoliberal policies and to the adverse effects of the accompanying globalization of these societies (i.e., the denationalization of their economies so that they can be more effectively integrated into the expanding global capitalist system) has generated new political movements and new populist leaders who openly identify with Che Guevara's ideals and his revolutionary struggle.

CHE AND CONTEMPORARY BOLIVIAN POLITICS

There is no better example of Che's influence than Bolivia. After suffering for decades under U.S.-backed right-wing governments, which imposed neoliberal policies that adversely affected the majority of the population, the country's largely indigenous population has risen up in opposition and found its political voice. The political mobilization of the poor majority of the country led to the election in the fall of 2005 of Bolivia's leftist president Juan "Evo" Morales, who won the election with some 54 percent of the votes. Popularly known as Evo, he is of indigenous descent (Aymará) and is the leader of the Movimiento al Socialismo (MAS, or Movement toward Socialism). As previously mentioned in chapter 11, Antonio Peredo—the oldest brother of Coco, Inti, and Chato Peredo—and Loyola Guzman, who was a member of the urban support network for Che's guerrilla force in Bolivia, are prominent members of MAS, as are many other leftist intellectuals, workers, and peasants in Bolivia.

Morales is the first person from Bolivia's indigenous majority to lead the country since the Spanish conquest subjugated the indigenous population 500 years ago. He and the other leaders of MAS are outspoken admirers of Che Guevara. They have placed photos of Che in the national parliament building and a portrait of Che made from local coca leaves in the presidential offices. The MAS-led government has initiated a constitutional revision of the country's governmental system, an agrarian reform program, and nationalization of the country's mining and natural gas industries. Thus, the Morales government is reversing the direction of Bolivia's economic, social, and political development. Instead of privatization of public services and denationalization of the economy, the country's new leadership is committed to regaining national control over the country's mining and natural gas industries and using the revenues from these industries to finance a people-centered, equitable, and environmentally sustainable program of social and economic development.

Before his official inauguration as president of Bolivia on January 22, 2006, Morales went to the archaeological site and spiritual center of Tiwanaku, the capital of one of the most ancient cultures in the world, where he was crowned the honorary supreme leader of the Aymará and was given gifts from representatives of indigenous peoples from all over the Americas. In the speech that he gave at the La Puerta del Sol, or the Door of the Sun, which is the gateway into the ancient temple of Kalasasaya, Morales said that "the struggle that Che Guevara left uncompleted, we shall complete" (Granma January 23, 2006). Afterward, in the speech he gave at his inauguration, he included Che among the fallen heroes in the 500-year struggle of his people for their freedom.

Even more significant is that Morales went to La Higuera, where Che was killed, to celebrate Che's 78th birthday on June 14, 2006. He is the first Bolivian head of state to have ever visited the village and he chose this date to pay tribute to Che, to officially open the medical center the government of Cuba donated to the village, and to congratulate the local graduates of the literacy program Yes I Can, which has been advised and equipped by the Cuban government. Che's son Camilo Guevara was present as well as the Cuban ambassador to Bolivia and a number of Cuban doctors in their white coats. Morales pledged Bolivia's solidarity with Cuba and Venezuela and said he would be willing to take up arms to defend them if they are attacked by the United States (Delacour 2006). Hugo Moldiz, a journalist who is the coordinator of the political front of some 30 different popular organizations that support Morales's government, told the press that the medical clinic and the literacy program demonstrated the relevance of Che's revolutionary struggle, since one of the reasons he gave his life fighting in Bolivia was to ensure that the Bolivian people had access to adequate health care and education (Mayoral and González 2006).

Accompanied by Bolivian government officials and the Cuban ambassador, President Morales also went to inaugurate the installation of modern medical equipment at the Vallegrande hospital—the same hospital where Che was last seen before his body was secretly buried near the airstrip in Vallegrande. Today, the laundry building where Che's body was laid out for examination and where the last photos were taken of

Che Guevara statue in La Higuera, the site of his death in Bolivia. Cony Jaro.

him has become a shrine in his memory. Morales's visit to La Higuera and Vallegrande as the Bolivian head of state is the first time that any high government official in Bolivia has paid tribute to Che Guevara and his guerrilla mission in Bolivia. Moldiz, who has close ties to Cuba, told the press that Morales's tribute to Che was consistent with the path of Morales's own struggle and with the identification of his government with the ideals of Che.

CHE AND CONTEMPORARY POLITICS IN VENEZUELA AND ECUADOR

Che's ideas about the need to create new human beings guided by socialist morality and his critique of bureaucratism have found particular resonance in Venezuela today (Munckton 2007). The regime of Hugo Chávez has widely distributed copies of the critical essay Che wrote on bureaucratism while he was a minister in the Cuban government. But even though Chávez has pointed to Cuba as an important source of inspiration, he has emphasized that Venezuela will have to create its own form of socialism to fit its particular history and conditions. The emphasis on direct democracy in Venezuela is consistent with this perspective,

¡CHE VIVE!   209

and Chávez contends that the only way to overcome poverty is to give power to the poor. Thus, he and his supporters contend that the Bolivarian revolution will create a democratic, humanist socialism rather than the bureaucratic, authoritarian style of so-called socialism that existed in the Soviet Union. It is in this context that Che's revolutionary legacy has found the most fertile soil in Venezuela and Bolivia today. His writings, his deeds in the Cuban Revolution and his personal sacrifice in the struggle for human liberation and social justice are a source of great inspiration and guidance to the Venezuelans and the Bolivians who are struggling for these same ideals today.

In Ecuador, Che is also held in high esteem. Much like Chávez and Morales, the country's new leftist president Rafael Correa Delgado laced his acceptance speech on January 15, 2007, with references to Simón Bolívar and Che Guevara. He said his country needs to build a 21st-century socialism to overcome the poverty, inequality, and political instability that have plagued the Ecuadorian people. Both Chávez and Morales were special guests at Correa's inauguration. With them at his side, Correa said: "Latin America isn't living an era of changes"; rather, "it's living a change of eras" and "the long night of neoliberalism is coming to an end" (Fertl 2007). Che would have been happy indeed to hear what Correa said afterward. He said: "A sovereign, dignified, just and socialist Latin America is beginning to rise." Exactly the kind of language Che used four decades earlier.

CHE'S CONTEMPORARY POPULARITY OUTSIDE LATIN AMERICA

Critical observers of Che's contemporary popularity in North America, Europe, and other regions outside Latin America are quick to point out that his iconic image has become a global brand, often devoid of any ideological or political significance when it is used to market certain products. They dismiss his continuing appeal to youth as merely a case of "adolescent revolutionary romanticism" and radical chic (O'Hagan 2004). However, while it is true Che's image has become quite profitable and is used to market a wide variety of goods to young people in the United States and elsewhere, his image still has political significance. Consequently, his image was removed from a CD carrying case recently in the United States after it sparked significant criticism in the media, in which Che was compared with Osama bin Laden and Adolf Hitler (Reyes 2006). Target Corporation, the large retail company that distributed the product in question, felt compelled to withdraw it from sale and issue a public apology for selling the item. This incident is proof that Che's supposedly apolitical iconic image still has too much political significance for many shoppers in the global capitalist shopping mall.

Moreover, even in the United States, the center of global capitalism, Che still finds political admirers. When asked several years ago why his father is perceived as a devil by American corporations and believers in the free market, Che's son Camilo accurately pointed out that "he is a devil for the U.S. government and American multinationals" but that "many North Americans admire and respect El Che" and "they fight injustice in American society under his banner" (HUMO 1998). Thus, one sees Che Guevara images along the U.S.-Mexico border as manifestations of activism. Although Che Guevara was not Mexican, his image has been appropriated by activists in the Mexican community within the United States who seek more access to education and civil rights, and the use of his image can be seen as a critique of current U.S. immigration policy. Camilo also correctly noted that there are people in the United

Fidel Castro and Hugo Chavez at Che Guevara House Museum, 2006. AP Images.

States who declare their solidarity with Cuba and seek to lift the U.S. economic blockade against his country.

Prominent public intellectuals such as Régis Debray in France, Jorge Castañeda in Mexico, Alvaro Vargas Llosa in Peru (son of the famous novelist Mario Vargas Llosa), Pacho O'Donnell in Argentina, and others have done their best to demystify and dismiss the significance of the enduring popularity of Che, particularly among young people. One of the most representative members of this group of critics is the British-born liberal savant Christopher Hitchens, who supported the Cuban revolution in the 1960s but has since called himself a recovering Marxist. In a 1997 review article of Jon Lee Anderson's biography of Che and Che's posthumously published *The Motorcycle Diaries* Hitchens argued that Che's enduring popularity is a contemporary case of classic romantic idolatry. In what has become a familiar argument among intellectuals in the United States and Europe for dismissing Che's iconic popularity, Hitchens asserts that "Che's iconic status was assured because he failed. His story was one of defeat and isolation, and that's why it is so seductive. Had he lived, the myth of Che would have long since died" (Hitchens 1997).

Thus, Hitchens and other intellectuals who share his perspective claim Che "belongs more to the romantic tradition than the revolutionary one," since "to endure as a romantic icon, one must not just die young, but die hopelessly" and, according to Hitchens, "Che fulfils both criteria." However, there is a fundamental factual inaccuracy and a false premise in this thesis. Che did not die young. Someone who dies at 39 is hardly young (except to those over 50). His death was untimely to be sure, but he was not young when he died. Furthermore, Hitchens and the other intellectual demystifiers of Che's iconic popularity fail to comprehend the continuing political and ideological significance of his iconic legacy.

The waving banners, the graffiti on the walls, the posters, the T-shirts, the videos, the films, the books, the pamphlets, the photos, the songs, the tattoos, and the cries of "¡Che Vive!" on the lips of people around the world provide overwhelming evidence that Che Guevara represents a powerful symbol of one of the most outstanding examples in modern history of resistance to injustice, inequality, exploitation, and political domination. And this is true for people literally around the world. Che continues to be a popular hero for many people—of all ages—for the same reason that Bolivia's President Evo Morales, in his late 40s, says he admires Che: "I admire Che because he fought for equality and for justice," and "he did not just care for ordinary people, he made their struggle his own" (Rieff 2005).

As art historian Trisha Ziff has astutely noted: "Che's iconic image mysteriously reappears whenever there's a conflict over injustice [and] there isn't anything else in history that serves in this way" (Lotz 2006). More than anything else, as Ziff acknowledges, Che is a symbol of opposition to imperialism and "in the end, you cannot take this meaning out of the image." Ziff is correct in asserting that the meaning of Che's image is that of the *guerrillero heroico*—the heroic guerrilla fighter against imperialism, and particularly U.S. imperialism.

CHE'S INFLUENCE ON CONTEMPORARY LATIN AMERICAN POLITICS

But in contemporary Latin America, Che is more than a powerful symbol of resistance to U.S. imperialism; his values and many of his ideas continue to be extremely relevant to the current political reality and the shift to the left in Latin American politics. His views and revolutionary life are finding increasing resonance among the new political leaders, new political movements, and rank-and-file political activists in the region. They find Che's vision of a socialist future and his ideas about how to get there to be directly relevant to their efforts to end the region's tragic pathology of distorted, neocolonial, and unequal development. Che's ideals and vision of a united, free, and socialist Latin America are a source of inspiration for their pursuit of emancipatory, equitable, and sustainable alternatives to the disempowering, inequitable, and unsustainable structures and values of 21st-century global capitalism. Che is much more than a popular symbol of uncompromising defiance to injustice and imperial domination; his revolutionary vision of the future and ideas about how to wage the struggle to get there are relevant to the contemporary efforts being made to bring about a revolutionary transformation of the basic economic, political, and social structures in Latin America and the Caribbean.

As a sign of how times have changed in the region, a little more than a month after President Evo Morales paid a historic tribute to Che Guevara in La Higuera and Vallegrande, a similar unprecedented event took place in nearby Argentina. It will most likely become a legend of its own. Following an important meeting in Córdoba, Argentina, of the MERCOSUR (Southern Common Market) to which Cuba was invited and Venezuela was accepted as a new member, Hugo Chávez and Fidel Castro made a historic pilgrimage to Alta Gracia to tour Che's boyhood home (*Adn mundo.com* 2006).

Since 2001 the middle-class house, now called Villa Nydia, where Che lived as a boy has served as a museum dedicated to his memory. On July 22, 2006, almost four decades after Che's death, two of the most important heads of state in Latin America paid a highly publicized visit to Che's boyhood home. When they arrived, the waiting crowd of several thousand people responded with a chorus of chants: "Fidel, Fidel, Hugo, Hugo" and "¡Se siente! ¡Se siente! ¡Guevara está presente!"—"One feels it! One feels it! Guevara is present!" (Rey 2006).

As they emerged from their vehicles, the two heads of state waved to the crowd and stopped at the entrance to the house in front of a bronze statue of Che modeled after a photograph taken when he was eight years old. They admired the statue and then went inside for an emotional encounter with the memorabilia of Che's boyhood and family life. Castro was surprised to learn that Che's parents rented the house, and he asked how much rent they had paid (*Adnmundo.com* 2006). When the director of the museum said she really didn't know, Castro jokingly reproached her for not knowing this important fact. At one point, Castro broke down and cried in front of a large picture of Che's mother Celia with her young children around her, including the young Che. Then, Castro and Chávez met with some of Che's childhood friends who were waiting in the house, including Calica Ferrer, who accompanied Che on his trip to Bolivia and Peru in 1953. Castro and Chávez viewed Che's birth certificate, handwritten letters, and a motorbike like the one he rode around Argentina. Ariel Vidoza, a childhood friend of Che, answered some of Castro's questions about Che's childhood. Among the answers she gave, she said: "Ernesto didn't like the rich much. He preferred to play with us, the poor ones" (Rey 2006).

As they left the house they posed for photographs with Che's boyhood friends in front of the statue of the young Ernesto. To the reporters waiting outside, Chávez said with a great deal of emotion in his voice: "I came to feed my soul. I am leaving with the batteries of my soul charged for 80 more years of revolutionary struggle and battles" (Venezolana de Televisión 2006). With tears in his eyes, Castro told the reporters and the crowd that he was sorry he and Chávez could not stay longer and waved to the onlookers, who were clapping and cheering.

No one could possibly have imagined such an event 40 years ago, even 10 years ago. It was a historic scene: Che's comrade in arms, the famous 20th-century revolutionary leader Fidel Castro (80 years old at the time), and Hugo Chávez, one of Latin America's new 21st-century revolutionary leaders, standing shoulder to shoulder in front of Che's boyhood home, which is now a museum of the revolutionary life of the legendary Che Guevara. There they stood in Alta Gracia (High Grace), Argentina, surrounded by a cheering crowd of thousands in Che's homeland, where not too many years earlier a bloody military dictatorship had ruthlessly disappeared anyone thought to be sympathizers of Guevara and Castro.

As the caravan of cars carrying Fidel Castro and Hugo Chávez left Alta Gracia for Córdoba, they passed a building in Che's hometown where

Laundry building in Vallegdrande, Bolivia, 2006, where Che's body was exhibited in October 1967. Rafael Rodriguez.

someone had written on the wall in bold red letters: "¡Che Vive!" (Che Lives!) There are similar Che Vive slogans on the walls of the laundry building in Vallegrande, Bolivia, where Che's half-nude body was displayed after he was killed over 40 years ago (O'Hagan 2004). What the visit of Fidel Castro and Hugo Chávez to Che's boyhood home in Alta Gracia, Ecuadorian President Correa's televised comments, and the Che Vive slogans on walls in many parts of Latin America and the world reflect is what his wife, Aleida March, wrote in her foreword to Che's Congo diary (Guevara, March, and Gott 2000:1): "Men do not die when their life and example can serve as a guide to others, and when those others succeed in continuing their work."

BIBLIOGRAPHY

Adnmundo.com. 2006. "Fidel Castro y Chávez Visitan Casa de Infancia del Che Guevara." July 22, http://www.adnmundo.com/contenidos/politica/castro_chavez_hogar_che_guevara_22_07_06_pi.html.
Anderson, Jon Lee. 1997. *Che Guevara: A Revolutionary Life* (New York: Grove Press).
BBC News. 2001. "Che Guevara Photographer Dies." May 26, http://news.bbc.co.uk/2/hi/americas/1352650.stm.
Boccanera, Jorge. 2000. "Antonio Arguedas: Un Destino Latinoamericano." *Clarin.com*. March 12, http://www.clarin.com/suplementos/zona/2000/03/12/i-00801e.htm.
Bockman, Larry. 1984. "The Spirit of Moncada: Fidel Castro's Rise to Power, 1953–1959." Marine Corps Command and Staff College, http://www.globalsecurity.org/military/library/report/1984/BLJ.htm.
Boff, Leonardo, and Clodovis Boff. 1988. *Cómo Hacer Teología de La Liberación* (Madrid: Paulinas).
Bonachea, Ramón, and Marta San Martín. 1974. *The Cuban Insurrection, 1952–1959* (Chicago: Transaction Publishers).
Caligiuri, Francisco, and Augusto Piccon. 2007. *Ernesto "Che" Guevara de la Serna: Su Infancia Mas Alla del Mito* (Alta Gracia, Argentina: Coleccion Raices).

Castañeda, Jorge. 1998. *Compañero: The Life and Death of Che Guevara* (New York: Alfred Knopf).
Castro, Fidel. 1994. *Che: A Memoir* (Melbourne, Australia: Ocean).
Castro, Fidel. 2000. "A Necessary Introduction." In *Bolivian Diary*, Ernesto Guevara, xx–xxxviii (London: Pimlico).
Castro, Fidel. 2001. "Speech at the Ceremony Commemorating the 45th Anniversary of the Landing of the *Granma* Expedition and the Birth of the Revolutionary Armed Forces, Santiago de Cuba, December 2, 2001." http://www.cuba.cu/gobierno/discursos/2001/ing/f021201i.html.
Clarin.com. 2000. See Boccanera, Jorge. 2000.
Cooper, Marc. 2003. "Remembering Allende." *Nation*. September 29, http://www.thenation.com/article/remembering-allende.
Daily Motion. 2008. "Ecuador, Rafael Correa Habla de Ernesto Che Guevara." TV interview with President Correa. July 15, http://www.dailymotion.com/video/x64pgf_ecuador-rafael-correa-habla-de-erne_news.
Debray, Régis. 1967. *Revolution in the Revolution?* (New York: Grove Press).
Debray, Régis. 1975. *La Guerrilla de Che* (Mexico City: Siglo XXI).
De Carlos, Carmen. 2006. "La Historia Oculta de las Manos del Che." April 16, http://www.vulcanusweb.de/dialogando/manos-del-Che.htm.
Delacour, Justin. 2006. "Bolivia's President Pays Homage to Che Guevara." *Latin America News Review*. June 14, http://lanr.blogspot.com/2006/06/bolivias-president-pays-homage-to-che.html.
Deutschmann, David, ed. 1994. *Che: A Memoir by Fidel Castro* (Melbourne, Australia: Ocean Press).
Deutschmann, David, ed. 1997. *Che Guevara Reader* (New York: Ocean Press).
Doyle, Mark. 2004. "Retracing Che Guevara's Congo Footsteps." BBC World News Online. November 25, http://news.bbc.co.uk/2/hi/africa/4036605.stm.
Estellano. 2000. *Punto Final*. March 24, http://www.puntofinal.cl/000324/nactxt2.html.
Evita Peron Historical Research Foundation (EPHRF). 1997. *To Be Evita*. http://www.evitaperon.org/Principal.htm.
Fertl, Duroyan. 2007. "Ecuador's Correa Calls for Socialist Latin America." *Green Left Weekly*, no. 695. January 24, http://www.greenleft.org.au/2007/695/36103.
Fineman, Mark. 1997. "30 Years After His Death, Cuba Honors Its Che," *Los Angeles Times*. October 12, http://articles.latimes.com/1997/oct/12/news/mn-42107.
Gadea, Hilda. 2008. *My Life with Che* (New York: Palgrave Macmillan).

Gambini, Hugo. 1968. *El Che Guevara* (Buenos Aires: Paidos).
García Bernal, Gael. 2004. "Star of 'Motorcycle Diaries' Lashes Out Against U.S. Distribution Policies." *Studio Briefing—Film News*. September 27, http://www.imdb.com/name/nm0305558/news?year=2004.
Gerassi, John, ed. 1968. *Venceremos: The Speeches and Writings of Ernesto Che Guevara* (New York: Simon and Schuster).
Goñi, Uki. 1995. "Las Manos del Che." *Buenos Aires*. December 1, http://geo citi.es/CapitolHill/Lobby/4766/che16.html.
Granma. January 23, 2006. See Mayoral, Maria Julia and Jorge Luis Gonzalez. 2006.
Guevara, Che. 1960. "The Essence of Guerrilla Struggle." In *The Che Reader: Writings on Politics and Revolution*, editor and translator unknown, introduction to the second edition (2005) by David Deutschmann (New York: Che Guevara Studies Center and Ocean Press).
Guevara, Che. 1961. *La Guerra de Guerrillas*. Note that this book was first published in 1961 in Havana by Talleres de INRA, but has been republished several times since then, most recently in 2006 by Ocean Press (New York). There is an English translation titled *Guerrilla Warfare* with an introduction by Marc Becker, which was published in 1998 by Bison Books (Winnipeg, Canada).
Guevara, Che. 1963. "Guerrilla Warfare: A Method." *SoJust.com*. http://www.sojust.net/essays/che_guerrilla_warfare.html.
Guevara, Che. 1965. "Socialism and Man." Note this essay was first published on March 12, 1965, but it has been republished in *The Che Reader: Writings on Politics and Revolution* (New York: Che Guevara Studies Center and Ocean Press, 2005).
Guevara, Che. 1968a. *Diario del Che en Bolivia* (Santiago: Punto Final).
Guevara, Che. 1968b. "Guerrilla Warfare: A Method." In *Venceremos: The Speeches and Writings of Ernesto Che Guevara*, ed. John Gerassi, 266–79 (New York: Simon and Schuster).
Guevara, Che. 1968c. *Reminiscences of the Cuban Revolutionary War*. See Guevara, Che. 1996.
Guevara, Che. 1985. *Che Guevara: Guerrilla Warfare*. Introduction and Case Studies by Brian Loveman and Thomas M. Davies Jr (Lincoln: University of Nebraska Press).
Guevara, Che. 1996a. *The Motorcycle Diaries: A Journey around South America*. Translated by Ann Wright (New York: Verso Books).
Guevara, Che. 1996b. *Episodes of the Revolutionary War, 1956–1958*. Edited by Mary-Alice Waters (New York: Pathfinder Press). Note that this book

was first translated into English in 1968 as *Reminiscences of the Revolutionary War*, and retranslated in 1996 as *Episodes of the Cuban Revolutionary War, 1956–1958*, and then published again in 2005 as *Reminiscences of the Cuban Revolutionary War: Authorized Edition (Che Guevara Publishing Project)* (New York: Ocean Press).

Guevara, Che. 1999. *Pasajas de la Guerra Revolucionaria: Congo* (Milan: Sperling and Kupfer Editori).

Guevara, Che. 2000. *Bolivian Diary* (London: Pimlico).

Guevara, Che. 2001. *The African Dream: The Diaries of the Revolutionary War in the Congo*. Translated from the Spanish by Patrick Camiller; with an introduction by Richard Gott and a foreword by Aleida Guevara March (New York: Grove Press).

Guevara, Che. 2002. *Back on the Road: A Journey Through Latin America*. Translated by Patrick Camiller with an introduction by Richard Gott and a foreword by Alberto Granado (New York: Grove Press).

Harris, Richard. 2000. "The Effects of Globalization and Neoliberalism on Latin America." *Journal of Developing Societies*, Special issue, Spring, 1–28.

Harris, Richard. 2007. *Death of a Revolutionary: Che Guevara's Last Mission* (New York: W.W. Norton).

Harris, Richard. 2008. "Dependency, Underdevelopment and Neoliberalism." In *Capital, Power and Inequality in Latin America and the Caribbean*, eds. Richard Harris and Jorge Nef, 49–95 (Lanham, MD: Rowman and Littlefield).

Harris, Richard. 2009. "Cuban Internationalism, Che Guevara, and the Survival of Cuba's Socialist Regime." *Latin American Perspectives* 36 (3): 27–42.

Harris, Richard, and Jorge Nef, eds. 2008. *Capital, Power and Inequality in Latin America and the Caribbean* (Lanham, MD: Rowman and Littlefield).

Harris, Richard, and Carlos Vilas, eds. 1995. *Nicaragua: Revolution under Siege* (London: Zed Press).

Hearman, Vannessa. 2003. "CUBA: Aleida Guevara—The Left Should Not Abandon Its Core Principles." *Green Left Weekly*, no. 546 (July 23), http://www.greenleft.org.au/2003/546/29908.

Hitchens, Christopher. 1997. "Goodbye to All That." *New York Review of Books*. July 17, http://www.nybooks.com/articles/archives/1997/jul/17/goodbye-to-all-that/.

HUMO. 1998. "An Interview with Camilo Guevara, Son of El Che, in Belgium," no. 43/3032 (October 16). English translation of Belgian magazine article at http://www.thechestore.com/Che-Guevara-interview-Camilo.php.

Klein, Herbert. 1984. *Historia General de Bolivia* (La Paz, Bolivia: Juventud).
Kornbluh, Peter. 2007. "The Death of Che Guevara: Declassified." *National Security Archive Electronic Briefing Book No. 5*. March 5, http://www.gwu.edu/~nsarchiv/NSAEBB/NSAEBB5/index.html.
Lotz, Corrina. 2006 "Che as Revolutionary and Icon." March 22, http://www.aworldtowin.net/reviews/Che.html.
Malloy, James. 1989. *Bolivia: La Revolución Inconclusa* (La Paz, Bolivia: Ceres).
Mandela, Nelson. 1995. "'Internationalism Contributed to Victory': South African President Nelson Mandela Addresses Cuba Solidarity Conference." *Militant* 59 (39) (October 23), http://www.hartford-hwp.com/archives/43b/122.html.
March, Aleida. 2008. *Evocación: Mi Vida al Lado del Che* (Bogotá, Colombia: Espasa).
Matthews, Herbert. 1961. *The Cuban Story* (New York: George Braziller).
Mayoral, Maria Julia and Jorge Luis Gonzalez. 2006. "We Are Following in the Path of Comandante Guevara." *Granma International/Online Edition*. June 15, http://www.granma.cu/ingles/2006/junio/juev15/26seguimos.html.
Miami's Cuban Connection. 2006. "Che Guevara's Capturer Hugged Che before He Was Executed." Posted by ocorral@miamiherald.com, April 21, in Spy vs. Sly, http://blogs.herald.com/cuban_connection/spy_vs_sly/index.html.
Moore, Don. 1993. "Revolution! Clandestine Radio and the Rise of Fidel Castro." April, http://donmoore.tripod.com/central/cuba/rebel1.html.
Munckton, Stuart. 2007. "Marxism and the Venezuelan Revolution." *Green Left Weekly*, no. 700 (February 28), http://www.greenleft.org.au/node/37067.
North American Congress on Latin America (NACLA). 2010. "Media Accuracy on Latin America," https://nacla.org/mala.
O'Hagan, Sean. 2004. "Just a Pretty Face?" *Observer* (London), July 11, http://observer.guardian.co.uk/review/story/0,6903,1258340,00.html.
Osborne, Lawrence. 2003. "Che Trippers." *New York Observer*. June 15, http://www.observer.com/node/47682.
Prado, Gary. 1990. *The Defeat of Che Guevara: Military Response to Guerrilla Challenge in Bolivia* (New York: Praeger).
Redford, Robert. 2004. Interview by Tavis Smiley. *Tavis Smiley*. November 8, http://www.pbs.org/kcet/tavissmiley/archive/200411/20041108_redford.html.
Rey, Debra. 2006. "Hugo, Fidel and Che United." *Guardian* (Manchester). July 24, http://www.guardian.co.uk/world/2006/jul/24/cuba.mainsection.

Reyes, Robert Paul. 2006. "Viva Che Guevara; Shame On Target Corp!" *American Chronicle*. December 22, http://www.americanchronicle.com/articles/view/18309.

Rieff, David. 2005. "Che's Second Coming." *New York Times*. November 20, http://www.nytimes.com/2005/11/20/magazine/20bolivia.html.

Rodríguez, Félix (Félix Ramos). 1989. *Shadow Warrior* (New York: Simon and Schuster).

Rojo, Ricardo. 1968. *My Friend Che* (New York: Dial Press).

Rostow, Walt. 1967. "White House Memorandum to the President on Death of Che Guevara." quoted in Kornbluh, Peter. "The Death of Che Guevara: Declassified." *National Security Archive Electronic Briefing Book No. 5*. October 11, http://www.gwu.edu/~nsarchiv/NSAEBB/NSAEBB5/index.html.

Rother, Larry. 1997. "Cuba Buries Che, the Man, but Keeps the Myth Alive." *New York Times*. October 18, http://www.nytimes.com/1997/10/18/world/cuba-buries-che-the-man-but-keeps-the-myth-alive.html?ref=ernesto_guevara.

Schlesinger, Stephen, and Stephen Kinzer. 1982. *Bitter Fruit: The Untold Story of the American Coup in Guatemala* (New York: Anchor/Doubleday).

Siles del Valle, Juan Ignacío. 1996. *La Guerrilla del Che y La Narrative Boliviana* (La Paz, Bolivia: Plural Editores).

Taibo, Paco Ignacío. 1996. *Ernesto Guevara, También Conocido como EL CHE* (Mexico City: Editorial Joaquín Mortiz).

Tamayo, Juan. 1997. "The Man Who Buried Che." *Miami Herald*. September 19, http://www.fiu.edu/~fcf/cheremains111897.html.

Vilas, Carlos. 1996. "Fancy Footwork: Regis Debray on Che Guevara." *NACLA Report on the Americas* 30 (3) (November/December): 9–13.

FURTHER READING: PRINT AND ELECTRONIC SOURCES

Even though I am considered an expert on Che Guevara and have tried to stay on top of the expanding body of literature, it is not possible to keep track of everything published or produced in every informational format. The following selected list of print and electronic sources on Che Guevara is targeted primarily at secondary school and undergraduate students and secondarily at a broader audience of people who know very little about Che Guevara but are interested in knowing more.

There are three major biographies of Che Guevara, all three written during the late 1990s. They are as follows:

- *Che Guevara: A Revolutionary Life* by Jon Lee Anderson (New York: Grove Press, 1997, new edition 2010), 814 pages.
- *Compañero: The Life and Death of Che Guevara* by Jorge G. Castañeda (New York: Alfred A. Knopf, 1997), 456 pages.
- *Ernesto Guevara, Also Known as Che* by Paco Ignacio Taibo II, 2nd ed. (New York: St. Martin's Griffin, 1999), 704 pages.

These three biographies are now somewhat out of date because of new information about the discovery of Che's hidden remains in Bolivia, their transfer to Cuba in 1997, and recent political developments in Latin America that have given a new significance to Che's revolutionary example, ideals, and political legacy.

There is also an interesting book on Che by Fidel Castro with a preface by Jesús Montané and an introduction by David Deutschmann: *Che: A Memoir by Fidel Castro*. It was first published in 1994 and republished in 2000 by Ocean Press (New York). This short book of 168 pages provides a great deal of insight into the relationship that existed between Fidel Castro and Che Guevara from the early days of the Cuban revolutionary struggle in the 1950s to Che's final missions in Africa and Bolivia in the middle and late 1960s. However, it is essentially a collection of the various speeches given by Fidel about Che over the years since Che's death and it is not a biography per se.

An early biography of Che written in Spanish, *El Che Guevara* by Hugo Gambini (Buenos Aires: Paidos, 1968), I relied on in writing the first edition (1970) of my book on Che Guevara, *Death of a Revolutionary: Che Guevara's Last Mission* (New York: W. W. Norton, 2007). This biography by Gambini has been republished several times in Spanish and has been a best seller. The last reprint was in 2007 by Planeta (Mexico City). Another biography written about the same time by Che's erstwhile friend Ricardo Rojo *My Friend Che* was translated and published in English in 1969 (New York: Grove Press, 1968). Both biographies are now outdated because a great deal of information has been made public over the last few decades about the lesser known aspects of Che's life, and this information was not available to the authors of these two books. Nevertheless, they are important sources of information on Che Guevara's life.

There is Che's autobiographical publication, *The Motorcycle Diaries: A Journey around South America* (London: Verso, 1995), which provided the basis for Robert Redford's very successful film, *The Motorcycle Diaries*, with Gael García Bernal playing the lead role of Che. This film was released in 2007 and is now available in CD and DVD format. However, *The Motorcycle Diaries* is not a truly comprehensive autobiography of Che Guevara. These lucid and brief narrations and reflections written while he was traveling around South America in his early 20s bring us into intimate contact with him at an important and formative period in his life and they allow us to travel back in time to meet the man before he became a revolutionary. They do not, however, touch on the rest of his life.

The two books written about Che Guevara by his first and second wives are of great importance. They reveal aspects of his character and his personal life that are not to be found in the other biographies mentioned above. Hilda Gadea's *My Life with Che* was first published in English in 1972, but was republished by Palgrave Macmillan in 2008 with a foreword written about her by her brother Ricardo Gadea. More recently, Che's second wife, Aleida March, published her account of her life with Che under the title of *Evocación: Mi Vida al Lado del Che* (Bogotá: Espasa, 2008). This memoir has not yet been published in English. Both of these books are fascinating and reveal as much about their remarkable authors as they do about Che.

ONLINE BIOGRAPHIES AND BIOGRAPHICAL DOCUMENTARIES

Other biographies and biographical documentaries on Che are accessible on the Internet or in CD/DVD format. They vary in quality and detail and provide a general account of Che's life, death, writings, and speeches. The following are some of the best examples:

CHE: Rise and Fall (Che Guevara: The Documentary). This video documentary stars Alberto Granados and Alberto Castellanos and is directed by Eduardo Montes-Bradley. It was released in July 2006 in DVD format.

"Che Guevara" by Ariel Dorfman, a brief biography at The Time 100 (most important people of the century) Web site, http://www.time.com/time/magazine/article/0,9171,991268,00.html.

"Ernesto 'Che' Guevara (1928–1967)—Guerrilla Warrior and National Hero of Cuba," a brief biography on Che that is part of The Biography Project, an Independent Reference Resource at Popsubculture. Com, http://www.popsubculture.com/pop/bio_project/ernesto_che_guevara.html.

Companero Che.Com is a website that contains a biography of Che Guevara along with videos and songs on Che as well as his speeches, both in audio and written format, Che's letters and quotations, exclusive CIA, U.S. State Department and Pentagon declassified intelligence reports on Che, and a photo gallery capturing him in important events of his life—the Cuban Revolution, the Congo, Bolivia, Argentina, Mexico,

Guatemala, childhood, adulthood, and his death, http://www.companeroche.com/index.php?id=6.

The *Che Guevara Internet Archive* contains a brief biography and a good selection of his writings, speeches, etc., http://www.marxists.org/archive/guevara/index.htm.

Comandante Che Guevara: Hasta la Victoria Siempre is a recent six-part documentary film in English on the life and death of Che Guevara directed by Ferruccio Valerio, which can be viewed at YouTube.com, http://uk.youtube.com/watch?v=gBnCfToCvUY.

El Che—Investigating a Legend (1998). This video documentary is available in DVD format. It is excellent for those who don't know much about Che Guevara since it provides an engaging and thorough synopsis of his entire career, with an explanation of his political thought.

MAJOR WORKS

The following is a list of Che Guevara's major published works that have been translated into English (and many other languages) and important publications that contain selections of his most important writings and speeches. Anyone interested in learning more about Che Guevara should read these publications.

- *The African Dream: The Diaries of the Revolutionary War in the Congo* by Ernesto Che Guevara; translated by Patrick Camiller, with an Introduction by Richard Gott, and a Foreword by Aleida Guevara March (New York: Grove Press, 2000).
- *The Bolivian Diary of Ernesto Che Guevara* edited by Mary-Alice Waters (New York: Pathfinder Press, 1994).
- *Che Guevara Reader: Writings on Guerrilla Strategy, Politics & Revolution* by Ernesto Che Guevara; edited by David Deutschmann (New York: Ocean Press, 1997).
- *Che Guevara Speaks: Selected Speeches & Writings* by Ernesto Che Guevara (New York: Pathfinder Press, 2nd ed., 2000).
- *Episodes of the Cuban Revolutionary War, 1956–58* by Ernesto Che Guevara; edited by Mary-Alice Waters (New York: Pathfinder Press, 2005).
- *Guerrilla Warfare* by Ernesto Che Guevara. Compiled by Beta Nu Publishing, 2007. This edition of Che's classic work on guer-

rilla warfare contains the text of his book, as well as two later essays entitled *Guerrilla Warfare: A Method* and his *Message to the Tricontinental*. It also contains a detailed introduction by Brian Loveman and Thomas M. Davies Jr., which examines Guevara's text, life, and political impact.
- *The Motorcycle Diaries: A Journey around South America* by Ernesto Che Guevara, translated by Ann Wright (London: Verso, 1996).
- *Reminiscences of the Cuban Revolutionary War: Authorized Edition*, edited by the Che Guevara Publishing Project (New York: Ocean Press, 2005).
- *Socialism and Man in Cuba* by Che Guevara (New York: Pathfinder Press, 2009).
- *The Marxism of Che Guevara: Philosophy, Economics and Revolutionary Warfare* by Michael Lowy (Lanham, MD: Rowman & Littlefield; 2nd reprint ed., 2007).
- *To Speak the Truth: Why Washington's "Cold War" Against Cuba Doesn't End with Fidel Castro* (New York: Pathfinder Press, 1991). A collection of historic speeches before the United Nations and other of its bodies by Guevara and Castro.

INDEX

Africa: Che's African diary, 138–40, 220; Che's mission to, 97, 126, 195. *See* chapter 8 especially; Che's travels to, 62, 121–23; United States involvement in, 98
agrarian reform, 94–95, 148, 206
Alegría de Pío, Cuba, 71
Algeria, 95, 121, 123
Alta Gracia, 2–4, 7, 213–15
altiplano (high plateau of Bolivia and Peru), 29, 145–47
Anderson, Jon (biographer of Che), 124, 223
Aniceto (member of Che's guerrilla force in Bolivia), 165, 167
Anti-imperialism, 152, 196
APRA (American Popular Revolutionary Alliance), Peruvian political party, 30, 43, 49
Aprista (member of the APRA), 49–50
Arbenz, Jacobo (former President of Guatemala), 51–57, 79

Arévalo, Juan José (former President of Guatemala), 52
Argañaraz, Ciro, 153–54
Argentina: about, 1, 8, 20, 57; Alta Gracia (Che's home town), 2–7, 213–15, 217; Argentine police, 147, 170; Che's birthplace (Rosario), 1; Che's interest in establishing guerrilla force in, 72, 102, 122, 126, 132, 137, 147, 150–51; Che's travels in, 19, 23; Museum of House of Che Guevara (in Alta Gracia), 5 (photo), 213–14; politics of, 6–7, 13–14, 20, 39, 153
Argentine Communist Party, 13
Arguedas, Antonio (former Bolivian Minister of Internal Affairs), 181–87
Aymará (indigenous people of Bolivia), 206–7

Barrientos, René (air force general and former president of Bolivia), 149, 161, 166, 169–70, 174, 179–80, 182

INDEX

Batista, Fulgencio (former Cuban dictator), 59, 61, 65, 75, 80–84, 87–89, 91–93, 96, 115, 126
Battle of Las Mercedes (important battle in Cuban Revolution), 81–82
Bay of Pigs invasion of Cuba, April 1961, by U.S.-backed Cuban exiles, 135
Bayo, Alberto (former colonel in Spanish Republican Army), 61, 63, 72
Ben Bella, Ahmed (former president of Algeria), 95, 121, 123, 175
Betancourt, Rómulo (former Venezuelan political leader), 41
Bolívar, Simón, 60, 209
Bolivarian revolution in Venezuela, 202, 209
Bolivia: about, 145–49; army and armed forces of, 167; Barrientos government, 149, 161, 166, 169, 174, 179–80, 182; Che's burial and remains in, 186–92; Che's capture and death in, 183–85, 202–3; Che's guerrilla mission in, 110, 126–27, 136, 140, 144–45, 202. See chapter 9; Che's revolutionary legacy, 209, 215; Che's travels to, 38–41, 44, 148; Communist parties in, 149, 153, 158, 178; government of President Evo Morales, 206–8; map of, 149; Movimiento al Socialismo (MAS, or Movement toward Socialism), 189, 206; political crisis created by publication of Che's diary, 179–82; and revolutionary reforms, 172; U.S. government's involvement in, 40, 52, 176, 182
Bolivia's pro-Chinese Communist Party, 158
Bolivia's pro-Soviet Communist Party, "the party," 149, 153, 156, 178, 185
Bosch, Juan (revolutionary nationalist leader of the Dominican Republic), 41
Brigade 2506, Cuban-exile organization, 176
Bunke, Haydée Tamara. See Tania
Bureaucratism, 208
Burlatsky, Feder (former advisor to Soviet Premier Nikita Khrushchev), 124

Camiri (Bolivia), 146, 149 (map), 150, 153–54, 159
campesino (English translation is peasant), 108
Cárdenas, Lázaro (former president of Mexico), 65
Castillo Armas, Carlos (led U.S. backed overthrow of President Arbenz in Guatemala), 50, 52–53, 55
Castro, Fidel, 38, 44, 57, 69, 70–83, 87–100, 105, 115, 119, 122–26, 130–39, 142–44, 149, 153, 181, 186, 191, 193, 196, 213–21, 224, 227
Castro, Raúl, 58, 59, 60, 71–73, 82, 94
Castroite, 181
Catholic Church, "the Church," 4, 200–201
Central Intelligence Agency (CIA), U.S., 50, 52, 53, 65, 79, 136, 148, 165–66, 168–70, 174–76, 181–82, 184, 187, 225
Chávez, Hugo (president of Venezuela), 202, 208–9, 213–15, 217
Chichina. See Ferreyra, María del Carmen
Chile, 22–23, 25–29, 148, 150, 154, 166, 179–80, 200
Chilean Communist Party, 29
China: Che's travel to and ideas about, 54, 61, 95, 121; Chinese Revolution, 63; Cuba's relations with, 121–24; international conflict with Soviet Union, 121–24, 149, 153
Christian Democratic Party, 200–201
Cienfuegos, Camilo, 77, 82–84, 88–89
Cold war between the United States and the Soviet Union, 97, 116, 133
Colombia, 23, 33, 41, 52, 56, 147

INDEX

Congo (later called Zaire and Democratic Republic of the Congo): Che's mission to, 102, 123, 126, 131–43, 156, 215, 218, 220, 225–26; Congolese rebels, 122, 133–34, 138, 140, 142; Cuban involvement in, 123, 126, 131, 133–35, 140–42, 156; U.S. involvement in, 98, 133–34

Correa Delgado, Rafael (president of Ecuador), 209, 215, 218

Cuba: Central Bank of, 97, 120; Che's legacy in Cuba, 193, 196–99; Che's participation in Cuban Revolution, 44–45, 58–64, and chapters 4 and 5; Cuban exiles (since Cuban Revolution), 92, 165–66, 168–69, 176; Cuban Revolution, 44–45, 59, 114–15, 119–25, 192, 196–99. *See also* chapters 4 and 5; Cuba's relations with Africa, 134, 140–42; Cuba's relations with rest of Latin America, 115–16, 207–8; Cuba's relations with the Soviet Union and Socialist Bloc, 97, 101, 123–25, 133; Cuba's relations with the Third World, 95, 97–99; Cuba and United States, 59–60, 63, 65, 89, 94, 97, 124, 133; 26th of July Movement, 57–58, 69, 74–75, 78–79, 82, 84, 91

Cuban Communist Party, 119, 123–24, 156

Cuban Missile Crisis of October 1962, 98

Cuban Revolution. *See* Cuba

Dar es Salaam, Tanzania, 122, 138, 142

Darío (David Adriazola, Bolivian member of Che's guerrilla force in Bolivia), 200

Debray, Régis, 177, 211, 218, 222

Dominican Republic, 41, 56, 119, 136

Door of the Sun (gateway into ancient temple of Kalasasaya in Bolivia), 207

Dreke, Víctor Emilio (Che's second in command in the Congo), 132

Dulles, John Foster (former U.S. Secretary of State), 50, 52–53

Eastern European socialist countries (Czechoslovakia, Hungary, Poland, Romania and East Germany), 119–20, 195

Ecuador, 38–41, 149, 208–9, 215, 218

Ejército de Liberación Nacional (National Liberation Army, name of Che's guerrilla force in Bolivia), 200

El Chino (Juan Carlos Chang, Peruvian member of Che's guerrilla force in Bolivia), 158

El Cubano Libre, 79

el hombre nuevo. *See* Guevara, Ernesto Che's ideas about

Escalante, Anibal (former leader of pro-Soviet Communists in Cuba), 102

Escambray Mountains in Cuba, 83–84, 86

FBI (Federal Bureau of Investigation), 42, 59, 65

Ferrer, Carlos "Calica" (Argentine friend and traveling companion of Che), 9, 38, 148

Ferrer, José Figueres (former president of Costa Rica), 42

Ferreyra, María del Carmen ("Chichina"), 20–25, 44

First World (United States and other advanced capitalist countries), 97

Fizi Baraka mountain range between the Congo and Tanzania, 141

foco (focal point or center of guerrilla operations), 105–6, 108, 110, 114, 116, 122, 139, 144, 147, 150, 153, 158, 173, 202

freedom fighters, 115

Gadea, Hilda (Che Guevara's first wife), 8, 43–45, 47–48, 54, 56, 58–65, 67–68, 72–73, 93, 128, 198, 203, 225

232 INDEX

Gambini, Hugo (biographer of Che), 6, 19, 219, 224
García, Eduardo "Gualo," 41–43, 47
García Bernal, Gael (Mexican film actor), 35, 224
General Assembly of the United Nations, 95, 98, 102, 133
Goñi, Uki (Argentine journalist), 183–84
Gott, Richard (British journalist and historian of Latin American affairs), 38, 40, 138, 143, 226
Gran Chaco (arid region of Bolivia), 150
Granado, Tomás and Alberto (Argentine brothers who were Che's friends), 7, 11, 21–22, 24, 35, 37, 44, 104, 225
Granma (name of boat used to take Castro's guerrilla force from Mexico to Cuba), 68–69, 70, 73–74, 80, 95, 160
Guatemala: about, 43, 48, 52; Che's stay in, 38, 41–54, 60; government of President Jacobo Arbenz, 52–54; United Fruit Company and, 41–42, 50–54; U.S. involvement in overthrow of Arbenz, 52–54
Guatemalan Communist Party, 48, 50, 52, 50, 57
guerrilla foco. See *foco*
guerrilla warfare, 61, 63, 171–72, 201, 220, 226. See also chapter 6
Guevara de la Serna, Ernesto "Che": asthmatic condition, 2–4, 6, 8–13, 43, 48–49, 102, 161, 199; biographies of, 6, 223, 224–25; birth and early childhood, 2–5; "Che" nickname, 64; children of, 63, 66–67, 72, 73, 93, 127, 191, 197–98; as cultural icon, 194, 198, 209, 211–12; death of, 161–72, 185, 194, 202; dream of liberating Latin America, 62–63, 101, 103, 114, 144, 152; education and schooling, 3, 7, 9, 12, 15, 17, 37; family life of, 3–4, 10; farewell letters, 102–3, 119, 143; father, 1–2, 6, 10, 14, 19, 24, 35, 73, 93; favorite aunt, Beatriz Guevara, 14–16, 63; fingerprints of, 169–70, 185; friends, 3, 7, 9, 15–16, 19; graduation from medical school, 37; hands amputated, 183–85, 189; ideas about guerrilla warfare, 105–17, 160, 171, 201, 219, 226; ideas about *el hombre nuevo* (the new human being), 128–30, 198–201, 208; ideas about imperialism (including U.S. imperialism), 63, 67, 98–100, 117, 122–23, 126, 132, 134–36, 196, 205, 212; ideas about social injustice, 23, 28, 34, 67, 103, 194, 196, 203, 212; ideas about socialism, 23, 34, 117, 121–22, 129–30, 152, 195; ideas about Third World struggles for national liberation, 99, 121, 123, 136–37, 140, 152; literature on, 203, 211, 223–26; medical training and experience, 12, 16–17, 19–22, 38; mission to Africa (Congo mission), 220. See chapter 8; mission to Bolivia, 147–60, 161–78, 202, 208; mother, 2–7, 10, 14, 33, 44, 49, 50–51, 54, 66, 99, 214; *The Motorcycle Diaries*, 211, 220, 224, 227. See chapter 2; museum in childhood home in Alta Gracia, 3, 5, 213–14; personality, 6–7, 9, 59, 76, 89, 103, 108; poems and poetry, 6, 8, 11, 48, 57, 59, 67, 127; political legacy, 116, 140, 209, 211. See chapter 12; relationship with Aunt Beatriz, 14–16; relationship with Fidel Castro, 59, 65–66, 71, 75, 77, 123, 133, 191, 218, 224; as revolutionary hero, 189, 193–94, 196, 198–200, 212, 225. See chapter 4; revolutionary ideas, 105–6, 117, 120, 128–29, 144, 149, 194–95, 213, 224; sexual experience, 8–9, 15; travels, 19. See chapters 2 and 3; trip to Miami, 34; wives, 8, 35, 43, 54, 56,

60–63, 66–67, 84, 93–94, 126–28, 142, 147, 197, 203, 218, 225; writings, 219–20, 226–27
Guevara, Moisés (Bolivian member of Che's guerrilla force; no relation to Che), 158–59, 164
Guzman, Loyola (member of clandestine urban network that supported Che's guerrilla force in Bolivia), 188–89, 206

Harris, Richard, 5, 155, 160, 165, 168, 177, 201, 220, 221
Holst, Helena de, (Honduran political exile in Guatemala who Che befriended), 49
Huanca, Bernardino (sergeant in charge of Bolivian army unit that captured Che), 164

Ilanga, Freddy (served as Che's translator in the Congo), 141–42
Indians (indigenous people), 20, 29–30, 203, 206–7
Infante, Berta Gilda ("Tita"), 15–16

Joaquin (Juan Vitalio Acuña Nuñez, Cuban member of Che's guerrilla force in Bolivia), 159, 161, 164, 191
Johnson, Lyndon (former president of the United States), 175

Kabila, Laurent (Congolese rebel leader and president), 122, 138, 157
Khrushchev, Nikita (Premier of the Soviet Union), 122
Kwame Nkrumah (former president of Ghana), 121

La Cabaña fortress (in Havana, Cuba), 88, 91–92
La Higuera (Bolivia), 161–63, 165–68, 176, 190–91, 203, 208, 213

La Poderosa ("the Powerful One"; name of motorcycle), 21–22, 26–27
Las Villas Province (Cuba), 82–88
latifundia (big estates), 95
Latin America: about, 205; Che's dream of liberating, 63, 101, 144, 151–52; Che's influence in. *See* chapter 13; colonialism, 29, 68, 79, 206; economic and social problems of, 205–6; media coverage of, 35; politics and history of, 104, 115–16, 151, 203, 205–6; social injustice in, 27–28, 34, 103, 196, 203, 212; U.S. involvement in and relations with, 40, 46, 57, 63, 151–52, 181–82
leftist (adj.) and left-wing (adj.) political parties, movements and leaders, 124, 131, 133–34, 140, 178, 189, 195, 202–3, 206, 209
Liberation Theology, 200–201
López, Antonio "Ñico" (Cuban exile Che befriended in Guatemala), 44–45, 49, 57–59, 73

Malcolm X, 98
Mandela, Nelson (president of the Republic of South Africa from 1994–1999), 141, 223
Mao Tse-tung (led the People's Republic of China (PRC) from its establishment in 1949 until his death in 1976), 94, 122
Maoism, 124
March, Aleida (Che's second wife), 35, 46, 84, 86, 88, 92, 94, 96, 126–28, 130, 132, 138, 142–43, 191, 197, 215, 220–21, 225–26
Mariátegui, José Carlos (Peruvian Marxist philosopher), 31
Martí, José (famous leader of Cuba's struggle for independence from Spain), 45, 68, 191, 197

Martínez Casso, José (physician who performed autopsy on Che), 170–71
Martínez Tamayo, José María (code name "Papi," Cuban member of Che's guerrilla force in Bolivia), 148
Masetti, Jorge (Argentine friend of Che who led unsuccessful guerrilla *foco* in northern Argentina), 122, 147–48
Maté (popular herbal tea in Argentina and surrounding countries), 1, 15, 49, 50
media, 92–93, 169, 172, 186, 188, 210, 221
MERCOSUR (Southern Common Market, which is a regional trade association between Argentina, Brazil, Paraguay and Uruguay), 213
mestizos (rom.) (half-bloods), 30, 39
Metutsov, Nikolai (Soviet official responsible for political relations between the Soviet Union and socialist states such as Cuba and Vietnam), 124–25
Minà, Gianni (Italian journalist), 131, 137
MNR. *See* National Revolutionary Movement
Moldiz, Hugo (Bolivian journalist who coordinators political front that supports President Morales's government), 207–8
Moncada military barracks in Cuba, 1, 44
Monje, Mario (leader of Bolivia's pro-Soviet Communist Party in 1966–1968), 149, 156
Morales, Juan "Evo" (president of Bolivia), 206–7, 209, 212–13
Motorcycle Diaries, The (written by Guevara and made into a film), 19, 22–23, 34–35, 143, 219–20, 224–27
Movimiento al Socialismo (MAS, or Movement toward Socialism in Bolivia), 189, 206

NACLA (North American Congress on Latin America), 221–22
Ñancahuazú River valley, 150–51
Nasser, Abdel (former President of Egypt), 94, 121
National Congress of Farm Workers in Bolivia, 174
National Institute of Agrarian Reform (its acronym in Spanish was INRA), 95, 219
National Liberation Army (Ejército de Liberación Nacional, ELN), 200–201
National Revolutionary Movement (MNR—the Bolivian political party that spearheaded the revolution of 1952 and governed until 1964), 173, 180
Nehru, Jawaharlal (former Prime Minister of India), 94
neocolonial (adj.) and neocolonialism, 95, 98, 120, 123, 131, 134, 139, 141, 212
neoliberal (adj.) and neoliberalism, 205–6, 209, 220
Neto, Antônio Agostinho (leader of national liberation movement and first president of Angola), 140
New Left, 195
New Man. *See* Guevara, Che ideas about *el hombre nuevo*
Nicaragua, 51–53, 116, 200, 221
Nyerere, Julius (leader of national liberation movement and first president of Tanzania), 121

Odría, Manuel (Colombian general and dictator from 1948–1956), 31, 43
Onganía, Juan Carlos (general and de facto president of Argentina from 1966–1970), 170
Organization of Afro-Asian Solidarity, 123
Organization of American States (OAS), 53

INDEX

Organization of Solidarity of Asian, African, and Latin American Peoples—referred to as the Tricontinental, 144, 149, 151–52, 227
Oriente Province (Cuba), 69, 73, 82, 85
Ovando, Alfredo (general and de facto president of Bolivia, 1969–1970), 169, 171, 175, 180, 183–84

País, Frank, 74, 77–78
peasant and peasantry, 38–39, 52, 54, 73–75, 77–78, 83, 86, 93, 95–96, 107–8, 111, 114–15, 148, 151, 159, 169, 173–74, 177, 180, 203, 206
People's Republic of China, 94, 121, 124, 194
Peredo, Antonio (Bolivian journalist and oldest brother of Coco, Inti, and Chato Peredo), 185–86, 206
Peredo, Guido (code name "Inti," Bolivian member of Che's guerrilla force in Bolivia), 153–54, 158, 166, 185, 200–201, 206
Peredo, Osvaldo (nickname "Chato," Bolivian political activist and younger brother of Antonio, Inti and Coco Peredo), 201, 206
Peredo, Roberto (code name "Coco," Bolivian member of Che's guerrilla force in Bolivia), 153–54, 156–58, 162, 185, 201, 206
Perón, Eva (Evita), 13–14
Perón, Juan (general and former president of Argentina), 6–7, 13–14, 39
Peronism, 7, 13
Peru, 23, 27, 29–33, 39–40, 43, 51, 56, 73, 147–49, 151, 153, 158, 170, 200, 203, 211, 214
Peruvian Communist Party, 31
Pesce, Hugo (Peruvian doctor and professor who specialized in Leprology), 31, 40
Peurifoy, John (U.S. Ambassador to Guatemala during the U.S.-backed coup that overthrew the democratic government of Jacobo Arbenz in 1954), 53
Pinar del Rio (Cuba), 53
Pisani, Salvador (director of clinic in Buenos Aires where Che worked as a student), 12–13, 20
Poverty, 28, 39, 44, 115, 203, 209
Prado, Gary (officer in charge of Bolivian Ranger unit which captured Che), 163–66, 222
Pro-Chinese Communist Party of Bolivia, 149, 153, 158
Pro-Soviet Communist Party of Bolivia, 149, 153, 156, 178, 185
Pro-Soviet (orthodox) Communists, 100–101, 125, 156, 194–95

Quebrada de Yuro (rugged ravine in Bolivia where Che was captured), 163, 165, 167, 170–71
Quintanilla, Roberto (colonel in the Bolivian intelligence service who ordered Che's hands to be cut off for fingerprints and a death mask made of his face), 183

Radio Rebelde (rebel radio station established by Che during Cuban Revolution), 79, 88
Ranger Regiment Manchego No. 2 (Bolivian army regiment trained by US advisors to fight Che's guerrilla force in Bolivia), 161–65, 175, 178
Rebel Army (Cuban revolutionary guerrilla force led by Fidel Castro), 72–82, 88, 92–93, 96
Redford, Robert (famous U.S. film actor, producer and director), 35, 222, 224
Redondo, Ciro (Cuban revolutionary who fought alongside Che in the Sierra Madre mountains and was killed in action), 77
right-wing (adj.), 186, 190, 206

INDEX

Rivalta, Pablo (former Cuban ambassador in Tanzania), 132
Rodriguez, Felix (Cuban American CIA agent involved in Che's capture and execution), 165–66, 168, 176, 222
Rojo, Ricardo (Argentine lawyer who traveled with Che to Guatemala and later wrote a book about Che entitled *Mi Amigo el Che*), 39, 47, 222, 224
Rosario (city in Argentina where Che was born), 1
Rostow, Walt (Special Assistant for National Security Affairs under U.S. President Lyndon Johnson), 175, 222

Sánchez, Celia (one of the leaders of the 26th of July Movement and subsequently the Central Committee of the Communist Party of Cuba), 69, 74, 77
Sandinista Front for National Liberation (Frente Sandinista de Liberación Nacional, or FSLN), 116
Sandino, Augusto César (famous Nicaraguan revolutionary leader), 196
Santa Clara (Cuba), 84–88, 93, 191
Santo Domingo (Dominican Republic), 136
Selich, Andrés (Bolivian army officer who buried Che's body as well as other members of his guerrilla force), 166–67, 198
Sierra Maestra (Cuba's largest mountain range), 71, 74–82, 85, 89, 91, 93, 96, 105, 135–36, 156, 158, 160
social inequality, 209, 212
Socialism, 34, 99, 117, 122, 126, 128–29, 152, 189, 196, 198, 205, 209, 219, 227
Socialism and Man in Cuba (written by Che), 129, 219
Socialist Bloc (bloc of countries led by the Soviet Union which had self-styled socialist regimes), 96, 99, 120, 122
Somoza dictatorship (Nicaragua), 53, 116
Soumaliot, Gaston (rebel leader in the Congo), 122
Southern Africa–Cuba Solidarity Conference (1995), 141
Soviet bloc of socialist countries. *See* Socialist Bloc
Soviet Communist Party, 125
Soviet Union, 46, 49, 58, 96–97, 101, 119–25, 133, 144, 185, 194–95, 209
Spain, 45, 67
Spanish Civil War, 6, 61
State Department, U.S., 42, 53

Tania (Haydée Tamara Bunke, only female member of Che's guerrilla force in Bolivia), 154–55, 161, 191
Target Corporation, 210, 222
Terán, Mario (Bolivian sergeant who killed Che), 167, 176
Third World, 97, 99, 101, 107, 121–23, 126, 137
Tita Infante (friend and classmate of Che in medical school), 40, 115
Torres, Camilo, 196
transnational corporations, 107, 194, 210
Tricontinental conferences (of Organization of Solidarity of Asian, African and Latin American People), 144, 149, 151–52
Tshombe, Moise (prime minister of pro-Western regime in Congo), 133–34
Twenty-first century man. *See* Guevara, Che ideas about *el hombre nuevo*

Underdevelopment and underdeveloped countries, 120, 141, 144, 220
United Fruit Company, American-owned, 41–42, 50–54
United Nations, 51, 94, 97, 103, 181

United States (n.); U.S. (adj.): blockade/embargo of Cuba, 120, 228; Che has been idol and pop hero of youth in, 195, 198, 210; imperialism, 58, 98–99, 122, 125, 133, 151–52, 181, 183; involvement in Africa, 97–98, 103, 133; involvement in Bolivia, 40, 148, 151–52, 163, 166, 168–69, 174–78, 182, 184, 187; involvement in capture, execution and burial of Che, 166, 168–70, 174–78, 187; involvement in overthrow of Arbenz government in Guatemala, 50–53; involvement in and relations with Cuba, 89, 93–94, 97, 211; role in Latin America, 42. *See also* Central Intelligence Agency

U.S. Army Special Forces in Bolivia, 162–63, 175

Valdes, Ramiro (Cuban political leader and one of the founders of the 26th of July Movement), 77

Vallegrande (Bolivia), 161, 164, 168–70, 172, 183, 187–89, 190, 207–8, 213, 215

Vargas Salinas, Mario (Officer in the Bolivian army who knew where Che's body was buried after he was executed), 187, 188

Venezuela, 23, 31, 33, 56, 147, 202, 207–9, 213, 221

Vietnam, 98–99, 103, 124, 132, 151–52, 162, 195

Villa Nydia (house in Alta Gracia, Argentina where Che lived as a boy, which is now a museum dedicated to him), 3, 213

Villoldo, Gustavo (Cuban exile who worked for CIA in Bolivia and claims he buried Che's body), 168, 175, 187

Washington Consensus, 205

Western imperialism/domination, 97, 122, 126, 133–34, 137

White supremacist apartheid regime in South Africa, 98, 132, 141

White, Harold (North American professor who befriended Che in Guatemala), 45–49

Willy (Simón Cuba, Bolivian member of Che's guerrilla force in Bolivia), 164–65, 167

World Bank, 205

World War II, 7, 42, 63, 140

Zaire (now the Democratic Republic of the Congo), 131–32, 140, 143. *See also* Congo

Zapata, Emiliano, 196

Zapatista liberation movement in Mexico, 116, 202

Zenteno, Joaquin (colonel in command of the Eighth Bolivian Army Division which surrounded and defeated Che's guerrilla force in Bolivia), 164–68, 171

About the Author

DR. RICHARD L. HARRIS is Professor Emeritus of Global Studies at California State University, Monterey Bay. He has a PhD in Political Science and a Masters of Public Administration from the University of California, Los Angeles. He is a lecturer, researcher, consultant, writer, and editor. He has taught, carried out research, and directed programs at various universities in the United States and overseas, including the University of California, Harvard University, Suffolk University, California State University, the University of San Francisco, La Trobe University in Australia, the University of the Americas in Mexico, the Universidad Autónoma Metropolitana in Mexico City, the Universidad de Chile (Santiago), the Universidad Nacional de Santiago del Estero in Argentina, the University of Zambia, and the University of Ibadan in Nigeria.

Richard Harris is currently the managing editor of the international *Journal of Developing Societies* and one of the coordinating editors of the well-known periodical *Latin American Perspectives*. He carried out field research on Che Guevara in Bolivia and Argentina shortly after Guevara's death in 1967, and he has continued to research and write about Che Guevara since then. He has published books, monographs, and journal articles on a wide range of topics, including Che Guevara, Latin American history and politics, international affairs, globalization, African politics, socialism, democracy, revolutionary change, and public administration. He lives on the Big Island of Hawai'i and travels extensively.

CPSIA information can be obtained
at www.ICGtesting.com
Printed in the USA
LVOW13*0604180717
541290LV00010B/218/P

9 780313 359163